Mary C. Mitoray

Lyn Gillum

Barbara Patrick

Mercedes Bjornson

Michele Jackson

Christa Graham

Cleo Mason

Vivian Ash

Verlon J Ash

Douglass Stakeli

Marjorie Stakeli

Val Toland & Di

Dean A Peterson

Karen Peterson

LeRoy & Eileen Bird

Eldon & Nina Zilles

Dale & Mary Lou Larsen

Doug & Irene Lane

Leonard & Roberta Cagle

Art Trypp

Norma Humphrey

THE THREE INFINITIES

STERLING W. SILL

THE THREE INFINITIES

— To Know —
— To Do —
— To Be —

STERLING W. SILL

BOOKCRAFT INC.
SALT LAKE CITY, UTAH
1969

LITHOGRAPHED IN U.S.A. BY

PUBLISHERS PRESS
SALT LAKE CITY, UTAH

KNOWLEDGE

I   And this is life eternal, that they might know thee the only true God, and Jesus Christ, whom thou hast sent. (John 17:3.)

ACTIVITY

II   Be ye doers of the word, and not hearers only.... (James 1:22.)

Christianity is not just a word. It is a set of activities.

CHARACTER

III   ... What manner of persons ought ye to be? (2 Peter 3:11.) Verily I say unto you, even as I am. (3 Nephi 27:27.)

Contents

Preface

On July 20, 1969, at the peak of our fantastic knowledge explosion, two men from the earth landed upon the moon. Already we are flapping our wings in preparation for greater accomplishment even further out into space.

When Mr. Armstrong and Mr. Aldrin stepped out of their landing craft, their feet touched a dead planet. The moon has no fertile topsoil, no atmosphere, no rainfall, no oceans, no forests, and no plant or animal life. There is not even enough air upon the moon to wave the American flag which the astronauts planted upon the lunar surface. So artificial supports had to be affixed to give our national banner its usual appearance of life and animation. Even the breath that the visitors breathed during their lunar stay had to be taken with them. So far as the space travelers themselves were concerned it may be that the most important part of their experience was their ability to pull away from the moon to begin their return trip home. However, one very prominent American has said that this 24-billion-dollar American venture into space, which placed two men on the moon for two hours and fourteen minutes, was the most important event that has taken place since the Creation.

Other people have reasoned that a far more important event occurred when the Son of God spent some thirty-three years upon our earth teaching us how to live. The Apostle Peter indicated that the purpose of Christ's mission was that "he might bring us to God." (1 Pet. 3:18.) But many people have become so interested in those things symbolized by our race to the moon that the gracious Being who has provided so much enrichment and benefit for our lives has largely been forgotten. Because of our crime waves, our dope addictions, our racial strife, and our atheism, we may even now be getting further and further away from the real purpose for which we were created and placed upon our earth. In spite of our space progress we may presently be no nearer to God than we were when the

Wright Brothers made their famous sixty-second flight at Dare-
devil Hill in Kittyhawk, North Carolina. And while we are all
very proud of the technology that has enabled us to pay a short
visit to that great orb of light that rules over our nights (Gen.
1:16-18), we ought not to allow this or any other interest to
thwart life's most important purposes.

In the beginning God looked out upon our earth and
pronounced it very good. And in preparation for our visit from
the Son of God, an angel came to our earth from the divine
presence. He introduced himself to Zacharias by saying: "I am
Gabriel, that stand in the presence of God; and am sent to speak
unto thee. . . ." (Luke 1:19.) He foretold the visit of the Son of
God who would come in his official capacity as the Redeemer of
our world and the Savior of the earth's inhabitants on condition
of their obedience.

Jesus announced his own mission by saying, "I am come
that they might have life, and that they might have it more
abundantly." (John 10:10.) And while we are all thrilled by the
wonderful material progress that we are making in so many
fields, what does it profit us if we gain an unproductive access
to the moon and fail in the purposes for which God placed us
upon the earth? Through our knowledge explosion we have
increased our substance and lengthened our mortal life expectan-
cy. We have multiplied both our sins and the headaches that
come as a consequence. While we have been trying to conquer
outer space we have seemed to be losing control over ourselves.
For some time our soul dangers have been getting greater, our
wars becoming hotter, our crimes growing more intense and more
numerous, and our sins getting more offensive in God's sight.
And we will bring an awful calamity upon ourselves if, while
reaching for a dead moon, we waste the opportunities upon the
earth which is so filled with life for our benefit.

On May 9, 1969, Mr. U. Thant, Secretary-General of the
United Nations, warned the peoples of the world that in his
opinion we have only about ten years left in which to solve the
problems pertaining to our earth. In speaking before a world
development conference at the U.N. Headquarters, the normally
optimistic Secretary-General said: "I do not wish to seem over-
dramatic, but I can only conclude from the information that is

available to me that the members of the United Nations have only about ten years left in which to subordinate their ancient quarrels, to launch a global partnership to curb the arms race, to improve human environment, to defuse the population explosion, and to supply the required momentum to our world development efforts." He continued somberly before the assembly of bankers, diplomats, and professors: "If such a global partnership is not formed within the next decade, then I very much fear that the problems I have mentioned will have reached such staggering proportions that they will be beyond our capacity to control."

It is apparent that the moon was not intended as a place of human habitation, as was the earth that we now occupy by the grace of God. But we have an increasing amount of evidence that God is becoming more and more disturbed by our serious violations of his laws of life and eternal success. By our unnecessary weaknesses, our ridiculous crimes, our willful diso- bedience, and our degrading sins we are at least partially nullifying the benefits for which this earth was created and for which the Son of God came here to serve us as an example.

Abraham Lincoln once suggested that we are only about as happy as we make up our minds to be. Likewise we are only about as successful and about as righteous as we make up our minds to be. And if our minds are set too much upon reaching for the moon or improving our material and political fortunes, we may so seriously offend God that we will miss the purpose of our eternal lives.

I am unaware of any revelation about any different kind of future designed by the Creator for the moon. But we do know that God has ordained a magnificent destiny for our earth. Those who are aware of the signs of the times are expecting the glorious second coming of the Son of God to this earth in the near future, and we will learn a lot more about space travel at that time, when the Lord will come "with his mighty angels, in flaming fire taking vengeance on them that know not God, and that obey not the gospel of our Lord Jesus Christ." (2 Thess. 1:7-8.) At that time the earth will be cleansed of its sins and increased in its status from its present telestial or fallen condi- tion to become a terrestrial earth in which the paradisiacal conditions of its Garden of Eden days will be restored. For its thousand-year millenium of peace, Christ will reign personally upon the earth. And at the end of that period the earth will again receive an increase in its status. It will then be celestialized and will become the permanent abode of those who qualify for the celestial kingdom.

This earth will then be inhabited by members of that order to which God himself belongs. In the meantime we have a desperate and urgent need to set our own houses in order and to greatly improve the quality of our individual lives. It is hoped that a weekly consideration of the following chapters will assist us in our need to get closer to God and thus help to secure our permanent place upon this great earth when it will be fully prepared for our eternal happiness.

The Three Infinities

The greatest responsibility that God has ever laid upon the shoulders of any individual is to make the best and the most of his own life. William James, the great Harvard psychologist, says that the deepest hunger in any human being is the desire to be appreciated. This divine craving to make our own lives worthwhile was placed in us to lift us toward God. God himself has decreed that the one business of life is to succeed. He has made our success and happiness the purpose of our lives. Certainly he did not create us in his own image and go to all of the trouble of placing us here upon this beautiful, wonderful earth, with our potentially magnificent brains and these miracle-producing personalities, and then expect that we should waste our lives in failure. The fact that we ourselves play a determining part in our own development is one of the important reasons why there is often such a wide difference between our potential and our actual accomplishment.

Probably the most inspiring fact in the universe is the idea that God created man in his own image and endowed him with a set of his own attributes and potentialities. But he has also given us the privilege of playing a major part in what we become. Actually each of us has two creators—God and ourselves. Someone has said that in this job of creation, God provides the capital but we are expected to furnish the labor. And in what was undoubtedly the greatest commission ever given, God said to us, "Thou mayest choose for thyself." The poet has said, "Know this, that every soul is free to choose his life and what he'll be; for this eternal truth is given, that God will force no man to heaven."

It is appropriate that our own salvation should be a kind of do-it-yourself project. And certainly the creation of man is not something that was finished and done with in the Garden of Eden six thousand years ago. The creation of man is still going on. It took place among us last month, and it is taking place here today, and it will also take place here next year; and we are the creators. Right now we are creating the faith, the righteousness, the enthusiasms, and the industry that will determine what our lives will be throughout an endless eternity. And if we deny our creative privilege or refuse our birthright for determining our own success, we nullify one of the greatest opportunities which God has provided for our use.

For a long time a Satanic doctrine has gone about in the world to the effect that "whatever will be, will be." Some people say, "We are what we are, and there is nothing that we can do about it." Nothing could be further from the truth. Shakespeare comes a lot closer to the facts when he says, "The fault, dear Brutus, is not in our stars, but in ourselves, that we are underlings." We have this tremendous privilege of spelling out our own futures, and the Lord has promised us that we may have every blessing if we are willing to obey the law upon which that blessing is predicated. We sometimes try to explain greatness in others by saying that someone is a natural-born teacher, or a natural-born salesman, or a natural-born leader, as though everything was in the package when he was born. But everyone has two personalities, the one that he was born with and the one that he develops after being born. It is always the acquired personality with which he earns his living, or becomes a good husband, does his church work, or effectively carries forward his part of the work of the world. A salesman once said to his sales manager, "But I am just not a salesman." The sales manager said, "Have you ever considered becoming one?"

We should thoroughly understand this important fact: our future is not in the hands of fate, it is in our own hands. The Lord has said, "For the power is in them, wherein they are agents unto themselves." (D&C 58:28.) It has even been suggested that sometimes life gives us a weakness in the place where we are expected to excel, in order to stimulate a more earnest effort on our part. For example, Demosthenes who became the greatest orator in the world was born with a very serious speech impediment. Julius Caesar was born an epileptic, and yet he became the conqueror of the world. Beethoven, the great musician, was deaf, and John Milton, the author of *Paradise Lost,* was blind. Usually by the time that we have developed the ability to overcome our handicaps, we have established enough good habits to carry us to an outstanding success.

To assist us on our way there is an interesting success formula which, if followed, can help us to work wonders of accomplishment. This formula is made up of what someone has called "The Three Infinities." The dictionary says that the word infinite means endless, inexhaustible, immeasurable, without limit or limitation, and capable of endless division. The three infinities of our formula can well serve us as the general headings under which all of our success is classified. Each one not only encompasses our endless possibilities, but is also attended by endless satisfactions and endless rewards. These interesting titles under which all of our success may be expected are:

TO KNOW TO DO TO BE

These abilities are all awarded to us by life as earned degrees. That is, knowledge is not a gift, it is an accomplishment. We are not born with a head full of knowledge. Neither is activity a gift. We learn to work, and to plan, and to organize, and to motivate. Neither is character a gift. Suppose, therefore, that we analyze our own situation so that we may order a greater success under each of these three headings. Instead of thinking of our success as impossible, or as dependent upon some mysterious radiation from the stars, we might more effectively think of it as subject to that tremendous power that we may exert upon our own infinities. We can study them one at a time and learn to utilize their powers to benefit ourselves.

Infinity number one is TO KNOW. Lord Bacon said, "Knowledge is power." What a thrilling experience to find someone who knows where he is going, and how he is going to get there! Jan Smuts, the late South African Prime Minister, said: "The greatest disease of the world is fragmentation. Too often we just partly know things." Just a little smattering of understanding and we close our minds and allow our knowledge to begin the traditional leveling-off process. Mr. Smuts said, "The cure of fragmentation is wholeism." We need to make our knowledge more complete. We need to know more about God and more about people and more about our own success procedures, and a lot more about our own souls. For who can tell why we do as we do when we believe as we believe?

Twenty-four hundred years ago Socrates said, "Know thyself." That is still about the best idea that there is in our world.

And to make a good start in mastering ourselves is a very good place to begin getting acquainted with our three infinities. The first question that Adam and Eve were asked to decide when they were placed in the Garden of Eden was whether or not they would eat the fruit from the tree of knowledge of good and evil. And after they had eaten, God said, "The man is become as one of us, to know good and evil." (Gen. 3:22.) And I would just like to point out in passing that the right kind of knowledge still tends to have that effect upon people. It still tends to make men and women become as God. Isn't it wonderful that we may know as much as we desire about the most important things in the universe!

A flaming sword was placed in the Garden of Eden to guard the tree of life. But fortunately for us there is no flaming sword guarding the tree of knowledge, and each of us may eat of its fruits to his heart's content. We may know more about ourselves, more about people, more about the work that life has given us to do and more about the procedures for getting it done, and more about God. Jesus said, ". . . This is life eternal, that they might know thee, the only true God, and Jesus Christ, whom thou hast sent." (John 17:3.) Many men and women have raised themselves to great heights of accomplishment by setting aside just a few minutes each day to eat the fruit from the tree of knowledge. Someone was recently praising a prominent United States Senator. It was pointed out that one of the significant secrets of his success was that he always did his "homework." He accepted his problems and then thought them through until he arrived at the correct answers. But life gives all of us a lot of important homework to do that success requires must be done.

The second of the infinities is TO DO. "Doing" is the process by which we convert our knowledge into action. It is also the way we convert our labor into rewards. Leonardo da Vinci once said, "Thou, oh God, doth sell us all good things at the price of labor." Nothing is ever denied to well-directed effort and nothing is ever achieved without it. There is no excellence without labor. And next only to my belief in God, I believe in industry.

Throughout the ministry of Jesus he was constantly calling for "doers." That is still our greatest need. We have plenty of talkers; we have many thinkers; we have lots of people with faith; we even have a fair number of listeners; but not very many who are really "doers." Brigham Young once said that anyone can preach, but it takes a good man to practice. Shakespeare expressed the same idea by saying "I can easier teach twenty what were good to be done, than be one of the twenty to follow mine own teaching." Yet even in eternity everyone will be judged according to his works. If a man isn't great in what he does, then he isn't great. Emerson said "Our greatest need is for someone to get us to do what we can." And certainly we need to catch up on a lot of our undone homework. We need to learn to develop initiative and vitalize our motivation with enough power to reach the desired accomplishments. One of the most important parts of any success is that internal pressure which makes us actually do things in a big way.

Alexander the Great set an interesting objective for himself in "doing" when he said, "What Aristotle is in the world of thought, I will be in the world of action." That kind of an involvement with the second infinity made him the conqueror of the world by the time he was twenty-six, and it will make any one of us anything that we want to become. All that we need is to learn "TO DO" effectively on our own power. There are some people who must depend on the goad, or the lash, or the bribe, to provide their stimulation. Others vitalize the spirit of "doing" within themselves and thereby develop better work methods and more effective accomplishment procedures. It is a very wise proverb that says, "We learn to do by doing." The best way for one to learn to skate is to get his skates on and get out on the ice. Constructive ideas, great ambitions, and high ideals are most effectively developed by actual performance. Solomon the wise man said, "With all thy getting, get wisdom." But someone who must have been considerably wiser than Solomon said, "With all thy getting, get going."

The basic problem in our world is inertia. This is a condition wherein we tend to run out of gas, causing our success to come to a standstill; whereas "genius" is the power to make continuous effort. To the members of the Church at Laodicea the Lord manifested the nearest thing to a divine disgust because of the inertia that had gotten into the people. He said, "I know thy works, that thou art neither cold nor hot. . . . because thou art lukewarm, and neither cold nor hot, I will spue thee out of my mouth. Because thou sayest, I am rich, and increased with goods, and have need of nothing; and knowest not that thou art wretched, and miserable, and poor, and blind, and naked." (Rev. 3:15-17.)

William James said, "Whenever life communicates an eagerness to him who lives it, his life becomes genuinely significant." Those spiritual vitamins effectively generated by our own activity will make our own lives genuinely significant.

This brings us to the third of our Three Infinities which is TO BE. It has been said that Washington won the independence of the American states not so much by what he did, as by what he was. Wealth isn't so much what you have, as what you are. We don't work merely to acquire; we work to become. Success in life is not just what you can get out of it, but what you can become by it. Every individual human being is also a human becoming; and what each of us will some day be, we are now becoming.

The writer of a financial column in discussing a business prognostication said that whatever is going to happen, is already happening. What we ourselves will discover on judgment day is already taking place. If we desire to be great souls in heaven, we should practice being great souls here. The most worthwhile of all development is self-development. We think of the immortality of our souls as being our greatest concept, but what about the immortality of those personalities that we ourselves are presently creating? Even God is engaged with these headings of the Three Infinities. God's power is infinite. He has all knowledge. His creations are infinite. His time is infinite and his ability is infinite. There is no end to his virtue or wisdom or truth or glory.

The poet said:

> We serve no God whose work is done,
> Who rests within his firmament.
> Our God, his work is just begun,
> He toils ever more with powers unspent.

Our job is to be like God. And so we come back again to the idea that the one business of life is to succeed. And one of our most effective formulas for success lies in the extent to which we master the Three Infinities. Then to get the total volume of our success we simply multiply our infinities:

TO KNOW   x   TO DO   x   TO BE

Abou Ben Adhem

Leigh Hunt tells an interesting story about a certain rich man of the far east whose wife had passed away and whose children had grown up and moved to far distant countries. He was a wise, kind-hearted man who loved people, and so he filled his large house with poor, homeless children whose grateful smiles gladdened him, and whose gay laughter filled his old heart with joy. He also gave comfort and cheer to the weary traveler, the poor outcast, the sick and the sorrowful whom he invited to sit around his heavily laden table. Then a kind of unspeakable joy entered his soul as cheer and gladness illuminated the heavy hearts of his fellow human beings, while they were under his hospitable roof.

One night he awoke from a peaceful sleep to see the room enriched with the subdued light of a beautiful angel presence who told Ben Adhem that his name was not recorded in the book of gold with the names of those who loved the Lord. "I pray thee, then," said Abou, "Write me as one that loves his fellow men." The angel did as he was instructed, and "The next night it came again with a great wakening light, and showed the names whom love of God had blessed, and, lo! Ben Adhem's name led all the rest!"

This interesting, helpful relationship that Abou Ben Adhem maintained with his fellow men was recognized by God as being the best test of a devout follower of Christ. This old patriarch's attitude toward other people gave him first place among all of those whose lives were blessed by God's love, and his treatment of others entitled him to the peace and happiness that comes from knowing that one lives in God's favor. In the inspiring lines of "Abou Ben Adhem" the poet gives us a more lofty look at the fact that loving and serving one's fellowmen is also the primary way for us to show our love of God, and to win his blessings and approval for ourselves. This story is in full harmony with the declaration of the Master himself that "Inasmuch as ye have done it unto one of the least of these my brethren, ye have done it unto me." (Matt. 25:40.)

Mr. Hunt has put this idea of serving one's fellowmen into the more forceful language of poetry. And as any philosophy is made more memorable, it becomes more easily adoptable by us. Mr. Hunt says:

Abou Ben Adhem (may his tribe increase!)
Awoke one night from a deep dream of peace,
And saw within the moonlight in his room,
Making it rich, and like a lily in bloom,
An Angel writing in a book of gold.
Exceeding peace had made Ben Adhem bold,
And to the Presence in the room he said,
"What writest thou?" The vision raised its head,
And with a look made of all sweet accord,
Answered, "The names of those who love the Lord."
"And is mine one?" said Abou. "Nay, not so,"
Replied the Angel. Abou spoke more low,
But cheerily still; and said, "I pray thee, then,
Write me as one that loves his fellow men."

The Angel wrote and vanished. The next night
It came again with a great wakening light,
And showed the names whom love of God had blessed,
And, lo! Ben Adhem's name led all the rest!

This poem is far more than some pleasant rhymes. It is a really great idea in its own right. Anyone who has had much to do with counseling troubled people knows that a kind of selfish self-centeredness is at the root of most of the unhappiness that devastates so many lives. No one can live unto himself alone. When human beings were created they were designed to live together, and it was intended that most of their primary satisfactions should come from each other. Instead of making each man a law unto himself, it was God who ordained that men should live together and be dependent upon each other. He also made his human creations male and female, officially joined them together in marriage, and pronounced that the twain should be one flesh. Then he organized them into families and made their most important employment that of creating and rearing

children, which God arranged to be a joint enterprise which
neither one could carry out by himself.

He also ordained that people should be joined in larger
groups such as communities, nations, businesses, and social organizations. Men and women are not supposed to be independent of
each other, neither are they self-sufficient within themselves.
Both sexes are necessary, and each has been given different
endowments, different abilities, temperaments, occupations, and
ideas about how to go about things. One of our highest abilities
is that of being able to live agreeably together and help each
other materially, mentally, spiritually, and physically. It would be
pretty difficult for a group of all doctors or all women or all
scientists or all school teachers or all Democrats to live happily
and successfully by themselves. When one individual, or even one
group, begins to care unduly about its own interests, or when
one tends to promote his own selfish programs at the expense of
others, then unhappiness takes over and the values of our human
lives begin to go downhill.

The selfish, unprofitable trait of thinking excessively about
one's own narrow interests and excluding the welfare of others is
the cause of most of our crime, vandalism, immorality, sin, and
laziness. It is a stimulating and helpful thing occasionally to hold
up before our eyes some such experience as that of Abou Ben
Adhem and let it penetrate our minds in the hope that it may
reproduce itself in us. We live in a world of opposites and we
seem to learn fastest by comparisons. The purpose of contrasts is
that we might learn as much as possible from both sides. In any
good play the villain usually teaches us as much as does the
hero. The hero incites our admiration, builds up our determination, gives us the desire to do right, and draws our interest
upward toward our highest goals. But the villain also helps us by
showing us the ugliness of wrong and the quicksands of sin
which we should shun. It is the function of the villain to show
us that failure and unhappiness always go with wrong-doing. We
sometimes get confused because the account of the villain
sometimes seems to show a profit temporarily. But the reason
for this is that God does not balance his accounts every
Saturday night. However, in the long run, wrong is always in the
red, and the life of Satan himself, brilliant as he once was, will
eventually show a complete loss.

There is a natural law in the universe that says that no evil ever goes unpunished, and one can no more do a good thing without at some time in some way receiving a reward, than he can do an evil thing without suffering a penalty. That is just not possible. God has never given us a commandment to which he did not attach a blessing for a good performance and a curse for disobedience. For example, he has said that we should pay our tithing. Through Malachi he said, "Bring ye all the tithes into the storehouse." That is the command, and the blessing is attached. He said, "and prove me now herewith, saith the Lord of Hosts, if I will not open the windows of heaven, and pour you out a blessing, that there shall not be room enough to receive it." (Mal. 3:10.) If we obey the law we will get such a great material reward that we will be unable to contain it, and we will get some good training in generosity thrown in besides.

From the top of Mount Sinai the Lord said, "Honour thy father and thy mother." That is the command, and he attached the blessing when he said, "That thy days may be long upon the land which the Lord thy God giveth thee." (Exod. 20:12.) Isn't it interesting that no one can even keep the Sabbath day holy without being paid for it, or think a good thought without receiving a reward? Certainly no one can keep those great laws of honesty, integrity, morality, and righteous industry without making a profit, and no one can violate them in the smallest fraction without suffering a corresponding loss.

There is an unseen avenger that constantly stands guard in the universe to make sure that no evil goes unpunished. Hate, dishonesty, sloth and immorality all bear a poison fruit. It is equally true that no good ever remains forever unrewarded. The fundamental law of the universe is that immutable, inexorable, irrevocable law of the harvest that says, "Whatsoever a man soweth, that shall he also reap." (Gal. 6:7.)

One of the most damaging sins, and the one that throws us for the biggest losses is the sin of selfishness. Almost every one of the Ten Commandments is a thrust against selfishness. When the Lord said, "Thou shalt not covet," he was trying to protect us against our own selfishness. When we bear false witness, we usually have some selfish self-interest as the motive. Stealing is also motivated by selfishness. This was the reason that Cain killed his brother, Abel. We usually violate the Sabbath day, use profanity, disobey God, and fail to honor our parents because of some selfish reason. This is also at the root of most of our family problems. Ignorance, immorality, and unhappiness are caused primarily by selfishness.

I know a family where the marriage and the entire family's welfare has gone on the rocks because of a ridiculous kind of selfishness in the husband and father. In many ways he is a fine person, but he has allowed himself to become very egotistical and extremely self-centered. He began his life amid humble surroundings, but because of a substantial financial assistance given by his wife, he became a professional man with a better than average income. But he has allowed his prosperity to go to his head, and he prides himself on virtues that he does not possess. At the first signs of prosperity, he became a dropout from church activity, as well as developing a tendency to be anti-social. Instead of showing appreciation to his wife and children, he indulges in some serious soul damaging criticism of the entire family. His immorality has broken his wife's heart, demoralized his children, and caused them all to suffer a serious loss of confidence in human nature.

He has given his wife so many problems that they have crushed her spirit and destroyed her joy in living. He has shamed, dominated, threatened, belittled, and depressed her until he has almost changed her from a person into a thing. This unbearable situation from which the family cannot escape has given them all some serious inferiority complexes. Their minds and souls are still being seared with the unfairness, distrust, depression, and the atmosphere of hate which contaminates their environment. It is a serious oppression to have to live with someone who is so deformed that his selfishness and immorality are more important to him than the welfare of his life's companion, as well as the little children that he is responsible for having brought into the world. What a great help it would be if in some way all of us could be given a few spiritual blood transfusions from Abou Ben Adhem to help us overcome this dark, dreary self-centeredness, and get a little more fairness and consideration for others into our hearts!

I know another man whose wife has been a near total

invalid for many years. But he lives for her, and "may his tribe increase." He takes the greatest pleasure in caring for her needs. Their children are uplifted by the power of love that they feel passing between their parents. The husband's love is so genuine that the wife is not made to feel unhappy or that she is a burden to anyone. Their devotion and mutual respect makes her sickness a mere inconvenience of minor consequence.

This great trait in the life of Abou Ben Adhem might well serve as a symbol to inspire us. Certainly a trait of such great importance should be cultivated, as few things could be more profitable than to destroy this deadly sin of selfishness. As harmful as it is, each of us is contaminated by this awful disease in some degree, and selfishness is the cause of much of the personal misery of most of us. Sometimes we behave like selfish children, where each tries to multiply the punishment of others and makes a full retaliation for every evil he receives.

One of the characteristics of every selfish person is that he always looks at his own sins through the little end of the telescope, but he reserves the big end, or the end that magnifies, through which to view the misdeeds of others. To a selfish husband a mote in the wife's eye often seems to be larger than a whole log in his own. It seems strange, but the primary motivation for many people is not what is right or wrong, but who is winning in the hard game of retaliation that demands an eye for an eye.

There is an old-fashioned proverb that says, "I will not let my enemy make me sin." That is, I will not let any selfish person make me selfish. If my enemy stoops to some unworthy deed, I will not allow him to seduce me down onto his level. To retaliate is merely to bring an extra condemnation upon ourselves. Retaliation has never cured a single wound, but only causes us to further degrade ourselves. There is no profit in hurting others. Certainly there is no satisfaction in tormenting ourselves. On the other hand, the great idea expressed by Jesus about loving people, even though they are our enemies, can be very profitable to us. Returning good for evil is one of the greatest ideas in the world. Then instead of doubling the damage, we increase our own blessing as well as wiping out some of our previous debits. And when, with Abou Ben Adhem, we use our

generosity and other abilities to lift up others, we also make
ourselves more successful and happy.

Allergies and Affinities

T here is an interesting physical problem that sometimes
bothers us that we refer to as an allergy. For some
reason the body frequently builds up objections to certain things
and has different degrees of susceptibility for particular foods,
articles of clothing, pollens, etc. The body has likes and dislikes
about the same as we do. And when it develops a severe
intolerance, it responds against that particular thing with a
violent reaction.

Our bodies, like ourselves, are often unfriendly to the very
thing that otherwise might be most beneficial. This was made
more than ordinarily clear to me a few years ago when I
contracted a common cold. The cold was not particularly severe
but because it lingered on a little longer than usual, I enlisted
the aid of the doctor to help my system throw it off. In
treatment the doctor gave me a substantial shot of penicillin. I
was pleased at the availability of this great modern medical
wonder drug. I knew that penicillin had worked miracles in
curing many people of their diseases. But what I did not know
was that my body didn't like penicillin, and in protesting against
the medicinal intrusion, it made a sudden and violent reaction
against it. It seemed difficult for me to understand why this
miracle drug should make so many people well, but make me
almost deathly ill. And from head to toe every inch of my body
broke out in a painful, ugly rash. While the disease had merely
caused me annoyance, the treatment put me completely out of
commission for several days.

The doctor who tried to cure my cold was not available
when the reaction set in, and so I asked another doctor to cure
me of the penicillin. At the end of the month I received the
bills from both doctors in the same mail, and the bill from the
doctor who treated me for the disease was only a fifth as much
as the bill from the doctor who treated me for the remedy. Our
bodies may have a lot of other allergies besides penicillin. Each

year many people have a reaction called hay-fever. Their noses run, their eyes become inflamed and their faces frequently swell up as the body lodges its protest against pollens or some other foreign element which in their case has the effect of a serious poison.

In trying to make up a list of the things that his body objected to, one man recently had fifty allergy tests. The doctor injected the cultures from pollens, clothing, food, dust, etc., into his blood. Of the fifty things tested he was allergic to twenty. Of course, his bodily reactions were more violent to some than to others. It is an interesting fact that there is not always a correlation between the things that we like and the things that are good for us. Sometimes the things that we like best may actually be the things that hurt us most.

It is interesting that our minds, spirits, and personalities also make some of these same kind of responses to life. We sometimes become allergic to certain people or to certain ideas or to certain standards of conduct. This would not be so disturbing if we only reacted against bad people or low standards or unprofitable procedures, but sometimes we have the most violent reactions against the very best things. Think how unfavorably many people react against religion, against their own parents, against their marriage partners, and even against God. What serious proportions this can assume is indicated by the scriptures telling us of Lucifer's unfavorable reaction against God in the council of heaven. God is all-wise and he is completely righteous. He is the eternal Heavenly Father of all of his spirit children. But in spite of all of this, Lucifer rebelled against him and against one of his greatest principles which is free agency.

Inasmuch as Lucifer was a very intelligent spirit, we might imagine that he would soon discover his error and repent and return to God and to righteousness. But an allergy is not like a cold that will cure itself or an emotional outbreak that, like a summer shower, spends its force and passes away. An allergy often gets worse as it goes along. Satan's dislike for God spread to others and the rebellion soon developed enough power to draw away from God one-third of all of the hosts of heaven. But like my body's antagonism to penicillin, Satan's attitude of bitterness and hate has continued to this day. In fact, his rebellion is still actually getting worse.

In our increasing crime waves there are thousands of additional people young and old whose lives are being more heavily loaded each year with rebellion and sin. Many who were formerly law-abiding citizens are now rebelling against law and order. People also rebel against decency, against their parents, against their wives, and against their own education and success. On a broad scale the communists have become experts in planting poison in many people with the aim of stirring up discord and trouble. Wherever possible they are making injections of hate, envy and fear into the hearts of people, and they try to get the most violent reaction going against the people and ideologies of the free-world population. The intensity of this enslaving passion circulating in the minds of the communists indicates how violently Satan and his followers are still reacting against God's great gift of free agency. It is something in me that causes my reaction against penicillin. And when sin and guilt get into us it sometimes causes us to react even more unfavorably against the best things. It is very unfortunate that my body reacts as it does. For otherwise penicillin would be one of my best friends instead of one of my worst enemies. But if taken under present circumstances it might destroy my life instead of saving it. A similar situation was created some nineteen hundred years ago when a howling horde of people crucified the best man who ever lived. His death was not brought about by anything he had done wrong, as he had lived a perfect life. They crucified the Savior of the world because of the evil in their own lives that caused them to react against his righteousness, even while he was trying to help them. However, we are following a similar course when we load ourselves up with so many wrong ideas and attitudes. Frequently, we not only react against the wrong things, but we also make our own spirits sick and unsuccessful.

I know of a man who is so seriously allergic to his wife that he makes her deathly miserable and keeps his own life a continual hell. This did not come about because of any wrongdoing on her part. At one time he thought that she was the most wonderful person in the world. But as this couple started down that straight and narrow path of marriage, his righteousness did not maintain a parallel course to hers, and as he began going beyond the bounds of morality and temperance, a poison began forming in him that caused him to react against her. Sin is always allergic to righteousness. It was Satan's unrighteous ambition that made God unacceptable to him, and this husband's evil causes him to react against his wife's prayers and faith. She works hard in the family interests, and the more she serves the children, the more she loves them. Whereas the more evil the husband tolerates in his own life, the more bitterness he develops, the more poison is produced, the more he hates his wife and the more unpalatable are the things for which she stands. Evil is always made uncomfortable in the presence of righteousness, and we tend to love other people more because of what we do for them, than because of what they do for us.

The people who love God are the people who serve God. When someone becomes bitter toward the Church, it is not always a sign that the Church has done wrong. The bitterness is more likely to be a sign of poison and inactivity developing in him. It is often true that a mother may have a deeper affection for an afflicted child because her greater service has developed a stronger affinity for that particular child. And a husband often loves his wife according to how faithful and how devoted he is to her. But in every field, hate and evil always build up allergies against good, whereas real love and genuine service always build up strong affinities for righteousness. Allergies can be built up by how we think. And what we do may so rearrange our personality chemistry that like Satan, we may react against good as a matter of course.

The scripture says that in the last days Satan shall rage in the hearts of the children of men. He rages in our hearts to the extent that he scatters evil all through our lives and makes us allergic to good. At first, we may merely be neutralized by evil, but when we have gone so far, we then begin reacting against good people and good ideas. An evil allergy even makes it unpleasant to hear good ideas discussed. No sinners like to hear discussions about their particular evils. And every wrong activity in us makes us dislike the right in others.

One would naturally think that the most serious sinners would be the ones who would have the greatest interest in their own education and repentance. But ordinarily it works exactly the other way.

The most difficult person to talk to about the advantages of repentance would be Satan himself. His affinities for evil are so strong and his attractions for good are so weak that there is no hope for him. Long ago he passed beyond the point of no return. Therefore, Satan and his angels must finally be turned over permanently to their own evil. John the Revelator saw their dreadful doom and pronounced their awful punishment when he said, "He which is filthy, let him be filthy still." (Rev. 22:11.) This may also apply to us. "Pure evil" is such a terrible thing that it allows us no pleasure in any good. Solomon says, "A fool hath no delight in understanding." (Prov. 18:2.) And Satan's sole satisfaction comes from doing wrong.

On the other hand, what a great delight to get pleasure from good, and joy from beauty, and happiness from godliness. Like things attract and opposite things repel, and those antagonisms and affinities that we develop in our souls will pull us either toward being the followers of Satan or the children of God.

There is a great deal of evidence that many people in our day are moving in the wrong direction. Nationally we are being accused of having departed from many of those important virtues that made our country great. Many people cannot feel the national fervor and patriotic zeal that characterized early-day, truth-seeking, liberty-loving Americans. But probably our most serious problems come because we have rearranged our religious affinities. As this lessening process continues to take place in our good behavior, we naturally become more tolerant of evil and less enthusiastic about doing good. Our society, including the Supreme Court, has been accused of wanting to help the criminal as against the law. And in our spiritual affairs we are tending to promote the interest of Satan as against God. As we develop a greater tolerance for evil, our affinity for ugliness, failure, and unhappiness increases. When our physical food doesn't taste good we know that we are sick. A little increase in mental and spiritual sickness can cause us to engage in all kinds of strange behavior. Then we actually promote sin, help our country's enemies, follow the devil and carelessly walk along that broad road that leads to hell. This is not only because our minds have deteriorated. It is because we have strengthened our evil allergies.

When we get all mixed up and get our hates where our loves ought to be then it seems natural to be disloyal and good to be indecent. Then we mistreat our families, abuse those who are trying to help us, become bitter toward the Church and fight against God.

Just think of the terrifying manifestations of our destructive allergies as they are exhibited in our wars, our race riots, and our industrial shutdowns. We not only try to kill each other, but we steal, burn, and destroy our own property, raise our own taxes, and delight in hurting innocent people. And with all of this trouble that we cause ourselves, we don't solve a single problem. A powerful communist nation serves us as an example of wrongdoing. Russia has taken upon itself to be the world's troublemaker. In their evil practices, they have become masters of deception, enslavement, force, and destruction. Armed with untruths, half truths, and evil propaganda, this nation has developed a great ability for making people hate each other. Their aims are the same as those of Satan. They want to stir up enough trouble that all nations may be sufficiently weakened to be subjugated by them. It is no mere coincidence that Russia has banished God and religion from that country. The aims of communism are almost completely antagonistic to God, religion, and freedom. What communism is trying to accomplish by force and enslavement has always been the pattern followed by Satan. And its worst aspects are the evil allergies that are being spread throughout the world among both nations and individuals. It is certain that the greatest opportunity of our lives is to live by the word of the Lord, and to develop within ourselves the strongest kind of affinities for good.

The Alternatives

One of the difficulties of our present world is that we have too many unsolved problems. And we frequently involve ourselves in additional troubles when we try to settle our difficulties in the wrong way. One of the most productive ways to improve our success procedures is to make sure that all of the possible alternatives have been carefully considered before we determine our course of action.

We are frequently led into failure and unhappiness because we attempt to solve our problems without knowing all of the available alternatives. Just suppose that we analyze our personal situation and see how many past mistakes we have made in our problem solving for this reason. Suppose that we make a post-mortem examination of each of our previous bad solutions, and in the clearer vision of our hindsight try to determine how much better we could have done if we had known a little more about some of those available courses that were not considered. Everyone must sometimes answer such important questions as: What kind of a person am I supposed to be? Whom should I marry? In what occupation can I make my greatest contribution? How should I invest my money, my enthusiasm, my energy, and my life?

One of our most fortunate circumstances is that everyone has a full set of choices and no one is limited to any one set of responses. It is thought that we can greatly improve the profit in our lives if we make a full canvass of our alternatives before taking action. In this way we can greatly improve the quality of our faith, our industry, our character, and our accomplishments. This will enable us to look ahead and understand consequences, and it will also teach us how we can best get along with other people, with ourselves, and with God. I have a relative who has an interesting procedure. When she reads a book, she always reads the last chapter first, because she wants to know before she gets started where she is going to be when she gets through.

And that is a pretty good idea for many of life's other activities.

We are frequently bothered by the great array of opposites in our world. Sometimes we wonder why God created weeds, rattlesnakes, and flies; or why he allows war, sin, failure, ignorance, misery, disease, and death. We might think that he himself could have had an easier time if he had allowed only the possibilities of success and happiness. But apparently God thought that there were some advantages to living in a world where we had choices. And only in the presence of opposites can we best strengthen our reason, improve our judgment, enhance our appreciation, give quality to our characters, and develop the power of our wills. Probably our greatest opportunity is to learn how to make effective choices after all of the alternatives are understood. We could take no credit for a virtue that was thrust upon us. And excellence would lose its meaning if mediocrity were unknown. Interestingly enough, there could not be any happiness if there were no misery. And while evil is important to serve us as a contrast, yet it is very unwise, as well as unprofitable, to make sin our life's choice.

Sometimes we lack in discrimination, and there are people who feel that they must make every mistake personally. With some enthusiasm, we frequently talk about sowing our wild oats and making evil and failure a major part of our lives by our own choice. However, as we more intelligently study the by-products and the consequences of our acts, we can see more clearly the advantages of carefully considering all of the alternatives.

In a little lighter vein, someone once told a story of a study in alternatives when a father said to his friend, "I have a problem. My son is ready to go to school, but if I tell the school authorities that he is age five, they won't let him in; whereas, if I tell them that he is seven, they will get after me because I did not bring him last year." The friend said, "How old is your son?" The father said, "He is six." His friend said, "Why don't you tell them that he is six?" The father said, "You know, I never thought of it." And while this story may exist primarily for its humor, tragically enough we often miss many of our own alternatives that are almost as obvious. Frequently some of our very finest possibilities are never thought of by us.

A man recently came in to talk about his marital problems. He was considering divorcing his wife and breaking up their home. He admitted to having many personal problems that had helped to bring his trouble on, but he also felt that his wife had made some mistakes. He thought that she could have been a better housekeeper. Their personal relations had also suffered a rather serious decline because she had not accepted him as enthusiastically as he thought she should have done. Because of the incompatibility that had resulted, this man had made the unfortunate decision that he didn't love his wife anymore.

On the other hand, there were some things that had made him hesitate to seek a divorce. One was the realization that his four small children needed both a father and a mother. In trying to make up his mind about his future course he was asking the following questions: (1) Should he stay married and suffer, or (2) Should he stay married and cheat on his marriage vows, or (3) Should he get divorced?

If these questions represented this man's only possibilities, then he is in a very different situation indeed, as the consequences of every one of these decisions are unpleasant, as well as being loaded with evil, and they will have a demoralizing effect upon everyone concerned. The restriction in the choices that he had placed upon himself is about like a situation which Abraham Lincoln once told about. A political antagonist once said to him, "You can either vote for me or go to hell." Lincoln said, "You don't really give a man very much of a choice."

It was suggested to this troubled prospect for a divorce that he had probably not made a very exhaustive exploration of the possible alternatives. There was one important way out of his troubles that somehow he had overlooked. Suppose that he should consider the possibility of staying married, re-falling in love with his wife, and re-learning to be a good father, as well as a happy, enthusiastic husband. That may seem like a big order to one who has become blinded by his own selfishness, and made unreasonable by his self-developed hate. However there are many things that a person can do if he really wants to do them and is willing to take the time to fully understand their possibilities.

A salesman once said to his sales manager, "Can you tell me how to get out of a sales slump?" The sales manager said, "I will tell you how to get out, if you will tell me how you got in." If one wants to re-fall in love with his wife, it can be very helpful if he can understand the process by which he fell out. Here is some of the case history in this particular case.

This man's wife had grown up in a religious home. She was a woman of excellent character. There was no question in the husband's mind but that she was an excellent mother. She was also serving as the head of a Church organization for young children. He himself had come from a good home, but he had always centered too much of his attention upon himself. Then as a little incompatibility began to develop, he had tried to drown his troubles with what he could get out of a liquor bottle. He did not stop to think that this procedure would not cure any of his problems, but would only increase them. He also admitted that he was naturally a little bit arbitrary and contrary. Some people outside the family had suggested to him that he was also a little disagreeable and hard to get along with in his business. Certainly most of his marital troubles were chargeable to himself. Yet it didn't seem to occur to him that a good place to begin in solving problems would be in changing his selfishness and eliminating the bad habits from his personality. He seemed to think that his own disagreeableness was unrelated to the main issue, and that his wife should be able to respond to him enthusiastically regardless of what he did. And while his wife had made an effort in this direction, she just wasn't strong enough to be enthusiastic about some of his sins that loomed so large in her eyes and so small in his.

It was suggested to him that because almost his entire life was at stake, maybe he should study the alternatives a little more carefully. Even if he stayed married and continued in his sins and misery, intolerable scars would be made upon the lives of everyone concerned. This foreseeable devastation made such a course unthinkable. But it would be much worse if he stayed married for the sake of the children and disregarded his marriage vows of faithfulness, love, and morality. He had tried to justify the consideration of this possibility on the grounds that many other people were living this way. But no matter how many people follow an evil course, it does not make it right. Nor can this impossible situation ever produce happiness or peace or success. Lawbreakers are never happy; sinners are never happy; drunkards are never happy; and haters are never happy. Happiness can only be found where there is righteousness, love, and excellence.

We always tend to be more happy when we do well. We like to get good grades in school. We would rather win basketball games than to lose them. In our occupations, we would rather get a raise in pay than be fired. There is always more pleasure in making other people happy than in making them miserable.

Satan suffers continual misery because he causes so much misery for others. It is a natural law of the universe that we get back, either in good or in bad, about what we give. And there can never be any genuine pleasure in any kind of wickedness.

My friend's third alternative was divorce, but this is also unthinkable. Marriage at its best is for eternity. The scripture says, "What therefore God hath joined together, let not man put asunder." (Matt. 19:6.) Four immortal souls have been born to this union. There is no possible way to transfer their maternity or their paternity to anyone else. And as God has said, "It is not good that the man should be alone." (Gen. 2:18.) But neither is it good for women to be alone. Certainly it is not good for children to be alone, neither here nor hereafter.

Just think what tragedies are caused when families are broken up. Hearts are damaged, personalities are twisted, attitudes become misshapen, instabilities are developed, and generally the feelings of insecurity and evil are greatly increased. Besides this, what possible satisfactions could come to any father that would compensate for the damage done to the immortal souls of these four wonderful little human beings that God had given him to be his own flesh and blood? Or what could compensate him for having a part in destroying the happiness of his children's mother whom he himself selected to be his companion for time and for eternity?

Even if this man gets a divorce, he will still have to choose whether he will remain single for the rest of his life or get

married again to someone else. In either event, there may be a
lot of problems arise. If he remains single, who will he live with
and how will he get along without a home and a family? Under
these circumstances, he himself might discover a hundred different reasons why it is not good for man to be alone. But if he
remarries, he may also have some problems. The cost of supporting two households will be much greater, and there may be some
problems in mixing up children and stepchildren. But besides
this, what chance will there be that his second wife will be any
more pleased with his liquor drinking than his first one was? Or
who can he find who will be enthusiastic about this hard-to-live-
with trait? No matter who his wife may be, he will likely have
to make some adjustment in his habits before he or she can
really be happy. He should probably make those adjustments
now before he sinks any deeper into his entanglements which are
already very serious.

The second wife may not be very enthusiastic about sharing
his income or his name with his first family. And almost
certainly she will have some personality and character traits that
may be as unacceptable to him as are those of his first wife. If
he should then fall out of love with his second wife, he would
be right back into his own little private hell again. And there
may be more problems living in two hells than in one. There are
many people who live in two hells simultaneously. If his second
marriage is not successful, he may even have to go through this
whole sordid, unhappy divorce and adjusting business with a
third wife. Sometimes the second marriage disintegrates faster
than the first one did. And this man's problems may be greatly
increased if he is unable to find a more favorable possibility than
those that he has considered. But in every situation there is
usually at least *one* good alternative to be found if those
concerned are willing to look for it and work at it.

If we want to enough, we can actually control our thoughts
and direct our lives where we want them to go. I know of a
salesman who once had a serious dislike for a certain man. But
when the salesman learned that this man was going to buy a
large amount of the salesman's product, his attitude toward him
completely changed. With a different attitude we can change
every bad situation in our lives to good. John Milton once said,
"The mind in its own place and of itself can make a heaven of

hell or a hell of heaven." When we fail to make the best use of our alternatives we can turn our heavens on earth into the most miserable hells. But it is also possible to change a hell on earth into a heaven. What is not possible, however, is to cheat, lie, hate, and booze and still remain happy. The result of every exercise of reason points to a solution that this man has completely overlooked, and that is that he should put his wife back up on the pedestal where he once had her and start doing things for her. You can't stay mad at anyone very long while you are doing nice things for them. And we can sincerely love whoever we really want to strong enough. How ridiculous for a man to train himself to love liquor and adultery and idleness, and then hate his wife and righteousness and God and his own children!

This man's wife is highly intelligent and deeply spiritual. One of her greatest desires is to build good character and genuine success into their children. On Sunday, she likes to see her family dress up in their best clothes and go to church and worship God. This is also the day for their traditional Sunday dinner, when they can all be together and feel the warmth and love of each other. And she would do anything that she possibly could to make her husband happy, except to wallow around with him in the abominations that he tries so hard to justify. But he has formed the habit of ignoring God and righteousness. On Sunday he likes to lounge around the house in his dirty clothes, or spend the day hunting or fishing. He devotes a sizeable portion of the Sabbath day to drinking, so that he provides little or no companionship for his wife or his children. No wonder he hates his wife when he does so much evil. But he still fails to understand why she doesn't respond to him as enthusiastically as he would like.

God is the author of our lives, and he has also told us how we should live them in order to be happy. And whether we like it or not, our final Judge will be this same God of righteousness. To get divorced and remarried a thousand times will never bring us happiness while we are living in moral dirt, disobedience, and incompatibility. Nor does it matter much what the "new moralists" say about what is permissible. God says that we must either be decent, or suffer the consequences. And the wisest alternative is always the one in which the program of God finds its fullest expression.

An American Religion

In 1892 Dr. Andrew D. White was serving as United States foreign minister in Russia. While there he became acquainted with Count Leo Tolstoi, the great Russian author, statesman and philosopher. A warm friendship grew up between the two and Dr. White often visited with Count Tolstoi, who had some very definite points of view about certain social and economic problems.

During one of these visits, Count Tolstoi said, "Dr. White, I wish you would tell me about your American Religion." Dr. White replied, "We have no state church in America." "I know that," said Tolstoi, "but what about your American religion?" Then patiently Dr. White explained to the Count that in America there are many religions, and that each person is free to belong to the particular church in which he is interested. Tolstoi said, "I know that, but I want to know about the religion that was born in America. Catholicism originated in Rome, the Episcopal church originated in England, the Lutheran church in Germany, Buddhism comes from India, Shintoism from Japan, Confucianism from China, Mohammedanism from Arabia, Brahmanism from India. The Baptists began in Switzerland, and the Methodists and Congregationalists in England. But there is a church commonly known as the Mormon Church which originated in America. What can you tell me about the teachings of the Mormons?" "Well," said Dr. White, "I know very little concerning that church."

Then Count Tolstoi, in his honest and stern but lovable manner, rebuked the ambassador. He said, "Dr. White, I am greatly surprised and disappointed that a man of your great learning and position should be so uninformed on such an important subject. As the Mormons teach the American religion, their principles not only teach the people of heaven and its attendant glories, but it also puts their social and economic lives on a sound basis." Then the Count gave it as his opinion that if the people would follow the teachings of this church, nothing could stop their progress. He said, "It would be limitless. If Mormonism is able to endure unmodified until it reaches the third and fourth generation, it is destined to become the greatest power the world has ever known."

In this interesting observation, Count Tolstoi has touched an important point. A church must have the truth in the first place, but the ability to remain unmodified has been one of the problems of ancient Christianity.

When the Lord established his Church in the meridian of time, he said through the Apostle Paul, "One Lord, one faith, one baptism" (Eph. 4:5), and the same apostle said: "Though we, or an angel from heaven, preach any other gospel unto you than that which we have preached unto you, let him be accursed." (Gal. 1:8.) And yet Isaiah had said: "The earth also is defiled under the inhabitants thereof; because they have transgressed the laws, changed the ordinance, broken the everlasting covenant." (Isa. 24:5.)

The people rejected Jesus, and with one exception each of the apostles he had appointed suffered a violent death. His doctrines became so modified that we now see its broken and splintered remains diverted into over 250 segments. There are some very important things taught by the Church to which Count Tolstoi refers that should be of tremendous interest to all Americans, and while there are many reasons for referring to this Church as the American Church, yet it is not! And while it was organized in America and gives us a great deal of new information about America, yet it is actually a universal Church and the scope of its teachings and mission are worldwide. The name Mormon is merely a nickname. The actual name of this Church is The Church of Jesus Christ of Latter-day Saints, and one of the interesting things about it is that it is the only Church ever organized in modern times in America, or in any other place, that claims to have been organized by the direct command of God, and claims that Christ himself not only selected the name of the Church but specifically directed that his name should be used. (3 Ne. 27:8; D&C 115:4.)

This Church also claims to be the only one that embodies

all of the teachings of that Church organized in Palestine some nineteen centuries ago. But the official doctrines of this Church pertaining to the land of America itself are also very interesting. It teaches that the Constitution of the United States was written by inspired men whom God himself raised up for that very purpose. The Prophet Joseph Smith said: "The Constitution of the United States is a glorious standard; it is founded in the wisdom of God. It is a heavenly banner; it is to all those who are privileged with the sweets of its liberty, like the cooling shades and refreshing waters of a great rock in a thirsty and weary land. It is like a great tree under whose branches men from every clime can be shielded from the burning rays of the sun." (DHC Vol. III, p. 304.)

This is the only Church that is familiar with the pre-Columbian history of our land. We have God's word for the fact that America has had a great history and it is destined to have a brilliant future. As a part of the official doctrine of the Church there is a direct revelation from God which makes known the startling fact that the Garden of Eden was located in what is now known as Jackson County in the state of Missouri, in the very center of what is now the United States. This period of our early world history was brought to its close by the universal flood in the days of Noah. The flood waters covered the earth for the biggest part of an entire year, and in the six-hundredth year of Noah's life, in the second month, the fountains of the great deep were broken up and the windows of heaven were opened. (Gen. 7:11.) The scripture says, "And God made a wind to pass over the earth." (Gen. 8:1.) Then the waters began to be assuaged "And the waters decreased continually until the tenth month: in the tenth month, on the first day of the month, were the tops of the mountains seen." (Gen. 8:56.) And in the second month of the following year Noah left the ark. (Gen. 8:14.)

It seems logical that the ark would not stand still during that long period. Rather it was moved by the winds and waters across the face of the earth and landed on Mount Ararat, which has been known to us as Armenia.

Religious records found in America indicate that many years later a new colony of people were sent back to repeople

America from the confusion of tongues at the Tower of Babel. These people were called Jaredites, and their scripture records the Lord as saying to their leader: "And [God] had sworn in his wrath unto the brother of Jared that [whatsoever nation] . . . possess this land . . . , from that time henceforth and forever, should serve him . . . or they should be swept off when the fulness of his wrath should come upon them." (Eth. 2:8.) Those who now live here are also promised great things if they will but serve the God of this land, who is Jesus Christ. In the meridian of time, the Savior came to the eastern continent. What little Christianity is still left on the eastern continent is functioning at a very low ebb, and is in a bad condition of repair.

The Communist powers in control of much of the eastern continent have already banished God and exiled religion. There is not much question that Jesus would get a cold reception if he should attempt to establish his Church in their sphere of influence. Even in the Holy Land there are almost no Christians. As we have watched the latter days unfold we have seen the center of religious gravity shift to America. We also know of the great commitment that God has always made to freedom. The liberty-loving refugees from foreign lands have gathered in America, and this nation has been established under God as a land of liberty, the citadel of freedom, with the divine mission to keep freedom, human dignity and righteousness alive in the world. Everyone is aware that America is a different kind of nation. We know that the greatest days of our earth's history are yet ahead. There are hundreds of Bible passages foretelling the glorious second coming of Christ to the earth. The Bible also speaks of his millennial reign, the great resurrections from the dead, and the final judgment. Anyone who is conscious of the signs of the times with their wars and rumors of wars, their disbelief and sin, is aware that the prophets were describing our day.

Prominent among those signs that should immediately precede his second coming, it was foretold that a fulness of original Christianity should again be preached upon the earth for the last time. As late as the last Tuesday of the Lord's life he said, "And this gospel of the kingdom shall be preached in all the world for a witness unto all nations; and then shall the end come." (Matt. 24:14.) John the Revelator actually saw the process of restoration as he looked down the years to our day and said: "And I saw another angel fly in the midst of heaven, having the everlasting gospel to preach unto them that dwell on the earth, and to every nation, and kindred, and tongue and people, saying with a loud voice, Fear God and give glory to him; for the hour of his judgment is come. . . ." (Rev. 14:7.)

It is the testimony of the Church that the church which Count Tolstoi referred to as the American Church is The Church of Jesus Christ of Latter-day Saints, and that the angel seen by John has come, and that he has come to America. His name was Moroni. He was the last of a long line of prophets who lived in pre-Columbian America. Then acting as God's messenger, he delivered to the Prophet Joseph Smith the Book of Mormon, which contained a fulness of the gospel as it was revealed by Jesus Christ to the ancient inhabitants of this land. It goes hand in hand with the Bible, which gives an account of the gospel as it was preached to the people of the eastern continent. The resurrected, glorified Jesus of Nazareth has also reappeared upon this earth to reestablish among men the fact that the God of Genesis, the God of Sinai and the God of Calvary is also the God of the latter days. He has reestablished his Church upon the earth with apostles and prophets, and has renewed his ancient commission, saying, "Go ye into all the world, preach the gospel to every creature. . . . He that believeth and is baptized shall be saved, and he that believeth not shall be damned." (D&C 68:8-9.)

Everyone knows how the United States came into being. Many people were led away from the eastern hemisphere where despotism and kingcraft sought to control the minds of men. But this same condition has also existed in modern times in Russia, China, Hitler's Germany, and elsewhere. Even England has largely departed from its Christianity. America is about the only place where the gospel could have been restored, and certainly this is now by far the most outstanding Christian nation in the world. By long odds more Bibles are sold in the United States than in all of the rest of the world put together.

The early settlers were led here where they might be free to worship God according to the dictates of their own conscience. And our nation was built upon a foundation of law. Every thoughtful person is aware that America is a different kind of nation. We have never had the Stalin blood purges, the Hitler gas ovens, or the attempts to dominate others that have been made by such old world despots as Genghis Khan, Napoleon, Mussolini, Hitler, Stalin, and present world dictators. We have never had that impulse to "bury" everyone else that has always character-ized Communist nations. And while we have many problems, yet we pledge allegiance to one nation under God, with liberty and justice for all. We still cling to our motto, "In God we trust," and we still recognize the American mission to keep freedom, righteousness, and human dignity alive in the world.

The scripture says, "Except the Lord build the house, they labor in vain that build it." (Ps. 127:1.) The United States has become the center of our world knowledge explosion. We know that the center of accomplishment for our world in these last days has shifted to America. It is also the center of invention, culture, science, military power, and religion. And while America has not honored freedom, righteousness and Christianity as it should have done, the people of America are far ahead of anyone else in these important matters. Russia, China, and their satellites may be serious competitors to America in their willing-ness to destroy the world. They are far ahead of all others in their desire to subjugate all other peoples. However, they are not serious competitors in their desire to worship God and to promote freedom, religion, peace, and human dignity.

No other church in or out of America except the one mentioned by Count Tolstoi makes any claim of any knowledge of the fulfillment of the great prophecies concerning America. But this Church with great anxiety proclaims the fact that by divine decree the God of this land is Jesus Christ, that it is an ancient law that there shall be no kings upon this land, and that our success will be determined by how well we obey the principles of the gospel of Christ. At the present time the United States is playing an important role in world affairs. The United States is the only nation that has prevented a Communist world take-over.

It was foreseen that not all of God's children upon the earth would be successful or righteous in our day. Many prophe-cies foretell that Christ will come in great power, with his

mighty angels in flaming fire to cleanse the earth of its wickedness at the end of the sixth one-thousand-year period. Then the
earth's stature will be increased, and its paradisiacal conditions
will be restored, and for the earth's sabbath of one thousand
years the earth's inhabitants will enjoy peace and happiness.
Following this the earth will be celestialized. And those who
qualify for God's highest kingdom will dwell upon it.

In the meantime we need to honor and serve the God of
our land, who is Jesus Christ. And we need to belong to his
Church and follow the religion that he has ordained not only for
Americans but for his children in Russia and China and every
other nation in the world.

The Beatitudes

O ne of the important parts of the teachings of Jesus is known as the Beatitudes. This word itself is not found in the Bible. It has been coined to fit the nine conditions of blessedness mentioned by Jesus in the Sermon on the Mount. These blessings which he pronounced upon people were to be fulfilled by their own virtues and righteousness. And someone has named these blessings the "Beatitudes" or "the beautiful attitudes." There is another word that is closely related to "beatitude" and that is "beatify." The dictionary says that beatification is one of the prerogatives of the Pope, and is a part of the process of canonization. It means to ascertain and declare by a public process and decree that a deceased person is one of the blessed. The word beatify means to endow with beatitude and to make one extremely happy. But this is also one of our own prerogatives while we are yet alive.

Dryden mentions beatified spirits—these are spirits that are beautiful and happy. Certainly one of the best ways to be happy is to have enough beautiful attitudes. God himself is the author of beautiful attitudes. God has also made happiness the purpose of life. The gospel is an expression of good news, and each human being has been endowed with a kind of joy instinct, so that every genuine success makes us feel good and every evil brings us a depression.

God is also the God of beauty. As God is a magnificent person, it was intended by creation that his offspring should be beautiful also—not only in their attitudes, but in every other way. When a baby is born we usually make something of a fuss about its beauty. Unfortunately as we grow older our beauty sometimes fades, and we experience one of the tragedies of life when we lose any of our beautiful attitudes. Of course the experience that mars more beauty and disfigures more characters than anything else is sin. We can beautify our own lives by living beautiful attitudes. The Psalmist said, "Let the beauty of the

Lord our God be upon us." (Ps. 90:17.) The Lord said, "Blessed are the pure in heart: for they shall see God." (Matt. 5:8.) Purity and all of our other virtues make us beautiful. Socrates was a very homely man and he prayed to God saying, "Make me beautiful within." We can make ourselves beautiful by holding in our minds and hearts beautifying thoughts. We have all seen plain people who have become beautiful by the working of a radiant spirituality. A godly spirit will make the plainest body beautiful. Great mental and spiritual qualities transform our bodies into their likenesses.

God loves beauty in all of its manifestations. And we might judge him by using his own standard of appraisal, wherein he indicated that a tree should be judged by its fruits. We might even try to understand what is in God's mind by thinking about the beauty that he has placed in the flowers, the landscape, the mountains, and the sunrise. Certainly the heaven that God has prepared for his children must be a beautiful place, as the Apostle Paul indicates that it is glorious beyond our imagination. He said, "Eye hath not seen, nor ear heard, neither have entered into the heart of man, the things which God hath prepared for them that love him." (1 Cor. 2:9.)

The poem "Beautiful Zion Built Above" is an attempt to stimulate our imagination in that direction:

> Beautiful Zion, built above;
> Beautiful city that I love;
> Beautiful gates of pearly white;
> Beautiful temple—God its light;
> He who was slain on Calvary,
> Opens those pearly gates to me.
>
> Beautiful heav'n, where all is light;
> Beautiful angels clothed in white;
> Beautiful strains that never tire;
> Beautiful harps thro' all the choir;
> There shall I join the chorus sweet,
> Worshipping at the Savior's feet.
>
> Beautiful crowns on ev'ry brow;
> Beautiful palms the conq'rors show;

Beautiful robes the ransomed wear;
Beautiful all who enter there;
Thither I press with eager feet—
There shall my rest be long and sweet.

Zion, Zion, lovely Zion,
Beautiful Zion,
Zion, city of our God.

The most beautiful creation in the universe is God himself. He is also the most intelligent, the most wise, and the most powerful. The scripture makes many references to "the glory of God." We are told that God is such a glorious being that no mortal in his natural state could be in his presence and live. When Moses was with God in the Mount, the glory of God rested upon Moses... "and he saw God face to face and he talked with him, and the glory of God was upon Moses; therefore Moses could endure his presence." (Moses 1:2.)

One of the most important ideas in the universe is that God created man in his own image and endowed him with a set of his attributes, with the objective that the offspring of God may eventually become like their eternal parents. To achieve this end, we must make our own lives beautiful—not only on the inside, but on the outside as well. Washington Irving once said, "It is the divinity within that makes the divinity without." But this law works in both directions. Clean hands help to make a clean heart. It is easier to have beauty in the soul when one has beauty in his mind and in his activities and in his body.

Schlegel says, "There is no more potent antidote for a low sensuality than the adoration of beauty." Aristotle says, "Beauty purifies the thoughts as suffering purifies the passions." The earth itself is a place of boundless beauty and endless fascination. The great beauty in Nature can put one in tune with the infinite, so that the spirit of peace grows in his soul. Think of the inconceivable variety of color and the beauty of design in God's creations. In combining beauty with utility, God gave us red cherries, yellow peaches, blue plums, black blackberries, green gooseberries, and purple grapes. We have oranges, apples, watermelons, dates, and figs all done in the most inspiring harmony and good taste. When God dresses his creations in such beauty we cannot imagine him dressing himself in any distortion of personality or slovenly, unattractive attire.

In attempting to describe his vision of the Father and the Son, the Prophet Joseph Smith said, "I saw two Personages whose brightness and glory defy all description, standing above me in the air." (Joseph Smith 2:17.) On another occasion the Prophet said, "His eyes were as a flame of fire . . . his countenance shown above the brightness of the sun." (D&C 110:3.)

In speaking of one of his visits with the Angel Moroni, the Prophet said: "He had on a loose robe of most exquisite whiteness. It was a whiteness beyond anything earthly I had ever seen; nor do I believe that any earthly thing could be made to appear so exceedingly white and brilliant." He said, "Not only was his robe exceedingly bright, but his whole person was glorious beyond description, and his countenance truly like lightning." (Joseph Smith 2:31-32.)

Some time ago Eugene Burdick and William Lederer wrote a book entitled *The Ugly American.* They pointed out some of the things that tend to give others a bad impression of America and some Americans. For the purpose of making a more terrifying image some half-savage, half-naked, original Americans painted grotesque designs on their faces and bodies in order to send a shudder of terror through those who were attacked. And it is thought that one of our greatest present-day problems is that some of God's more modern children are also turning away from beauty in favor of ugliness, not only in dress, but also in deed and in thought. We know that all evil, crime, and immorality make ugly scars in our faces and on our spirits. The puffy bloated face, addled brain, and scrambled speech of an alcoholic have never been cited as being beautiful. Neither are our ugly tempers, our hateful moods, nor our perverted spirits that are loaded with ungodliness.

There are many people in our fair land who identify in appearance and ambition and accomplishment with such groups as the "Nothings," the "Devil's Disciples," and the "Hell's Angels." What we are becoming is a natural result of the ugliness we watch on the screen and read about in our books. We seem to delight in filling our minds with the ugliness of violence,

crime, and sin which we ourselves create. We patronize a great
many horror movies where we intently watch some ugly, Frank-
enstein monster act out his feelings of depravity and crime as
entertainment for our lower appetites and passions. Sometimes
the more filthy or abhorrent a movie or a crime is, the more
our interest is glued to it, and consequently the more we are
influenced by it.

We frequently applaud a certain ugliness in art and we have
a so-called music that incites our frenzy, and puts us in the
mood of the jungle out of which it came. Many of the things
that we do and say and think are often designed to arouse the
worst in us. And there are many thousands of people who
deliberately put ugliness in their dress, and just as deliberately
make their persons ugly. In many ways we follow the savage
people of the earth, as we minimize and worsen our clothing,
pick our eyebrows, and paint our faces. The kind of dress worn
and the personal appearance of people have always had an
important influence in helping to form their self-image. We don't
dress up like clowns or villains for a masquerade ball, and then
go around acting like wise men and good citizens.

Recently I was driven through a kind of hippyland, in one
of our large cities, where hundreds of strangely dressed, queer-
acting people were assembled. Instead of using care in the
quality, cleanliness, and arrangement of their dress, they seemed
to have deliberately tried to make themselves as unattractive as
possible. Their long, uncut hair was dirty and in disarray. All of
the indications were that the inside of their lives was about as
disorderly as was the outside. They resorted to an extensive
addiction to dope, immorality, and uncleanness to make their
behavior as unattractive as their physical appearance. The great
eternal laws saying that "cleanliness is next to godliness," and
that "order is the first law of heaven," seem to have been
unintelligible concepts to them. How to account for this volun-
tary and unnecessary degeneration is beyond my understanding.
Whether this is a Satanic inspired rebellion against God and
decency, or whether the degeneracy is brought about for some
other reason, I do not know. Whatever its cause, this reversion
to ugliness seems to be a part of the spirit of our times.
Although it is an effective way to make "ugly Americans," it is
not something of which we should be proud. We should be

aware that people do not act the same way if they are properly dressed as they do when they are improperly dressed.

A female musical student recently came to her university class dressed in sloppy, unbecoming, unladylike dress. The instructor said to her, "Fanny, I would like to have you look at me, and tell me whether or not you think I am properly dressed. Do I have on clean clothing? Is it properly cared for and in good taste? Do I have on a shirt and a necktie? Is my clothing harmonious, modest and attractive?" To all of these questions she answered, "Yes." He said, "Does my clothing offend you?" and she answered, "No." Then he said, "Fanny, will you look in the mirror and answer these same questions in regard to yourself, and if you are not satisfied with your appearance, we will be glad to excuse you while you go home and get yourself dressed as becomes a lady and in a spirit appropriate to the great art that you are studying."

Proper dress, cleanliness, and order are important for many reasons. One is that we naturally tend to materialize our own self-image. We also tend to become like those with whom we identify. And we should destroy as far as is possible this disease of ugliness that is drawing so many of us in the wrong direction. On the other hand, one of the greatest opportunities of our existence is to build beauty, dignity, splendor, and glory into our own and other people's lives. "A thing of beauty is a joy forever." As far as I know, the idea of keeping our bodies, minds, and spirits clean, orderly, attractive, and progressive, are among the most profitable and praiseworthy of the beautiful attitudes, and will bring on one of the most commendable conditions of blessedness.

Jesus said, "Blessed are all they which do hunger and thirst after righteousness, for they shall be filled with the Holy Ghost." (3 Ne. 12:6.) And those who hunger and thirst after righteousness shall also be filled with the right conduct. Their lives will be filled with order and beauty, and their futures will be filled with righteousness and the glory of God.

Sometimes when we go to an important dinner we dress ourselves in evening clothes. When people get married, they dress in clothes appropriate to the occasion. On these important occasions we want to make ourselves as attractive as possible. But *every* occasion in life should be a great occasion. Someone has said that the clothes don't make the man, but they can help. It helps the morale of the army when soldiers are properly uniformed. Certainly it helps soldiers to be dressed in attitudes of patriotism and loyalty, and in order to make the best and the most of our lives we ought to allow no exceptions in properly dressing ourselves outside and in. Certainly we should always dress ourselves in beautiful attitudes, fill our minds with beauty, and carry on a process to beautify our spirits. Emerson has said that "beauty is the mark that God sets on virtue." And certainly we should all be beautiful in the sight of God and in our own sight.

Behold the Man!

In Austria there is an interesting bridge spanning a beautiful river. As one crosses the bridge he passes twelve statues of Christ spaced a few paces apart. Each of these likenesses represents the Master in his relationship to some occupational or special-interest group. As herders cross over this bridge with their flocks they usually tarry for a few moments before the statue picturing Christ as the Good Shepherd. Farmers stop and meditate before the statue depicting him as the sower. Horticulturists and gardeners think of Christ in his described functions of pruning out the wild branches or as the good husbandman dressing the vineyard. Fishermen stand in reverence before the representation of Christ stilling the tempest and telling his fishermen friends how to catch fish and causing their nets to break with their heavy load. Those travelers who are sick either in body or in spirit wait before the image of Christ the healer, and by rethinking his inspiring thoughts they can be made whole of their infirmities.

A great benefit can be transferred to any worshipper as he feels that Christ understands his occupational as well as his personal problems and always stands ready to help. One of the statues on the Austrian bridge represents the Great Teacher. Jesus was the greatest teacher because he looked with clearest insight into human lives and knew what should be done about their problems. Better than anyone else he understood the effects of those common everyday events on which our life successes continue to depend. Most of us have a tendency to isolate our religion by putting it in a special compartment whereas we put our daily activities in another. Jesus made them one. And as the Great Teacher he used the simple experiences of people to illustrate those profound truths which still determine every accomplishment. Jesus did not always use theological ideas in teaching religious principles. He used those practical ideas that everyone understood. As George A. Barton has said:

He spake of lilies, vines and corn,
　　The sparrow and the raven,
And the words so natural yet so wise
　　Were on men's hearts engraven:
And yeast and bread and flax and cloth
　　And eggs and fish and candles—
See how the most familiar world
　　He most divinely handles!

Jesus presented his lessons with as much freedom and
confidence to the wise men in the temple as to the unlearned
fishermen working at their nets. The inspiration of his life is
indicated by a kind of statue which J. A. Francis built of words
when he said:

"Here is a man who grew up in an obscure village, the child
of a poor peasant woman. He worked in a carpenter shop until
he was thirty, and then for three years he was an itinerant
preacher.

"He never wrote a book. He never held an office. He never
owned a home. He never had a family. He never went to college.
He never put his foot inside a big city. He never traveled two
hundred miles from the place where he was born.

"While still a young man, the tide of popular opinion
turned against him. His friends ran away. One of them denied
him. Another betrayed him. He was turned over to his enemies.
He went through the mockery of a trial. He was nailed upon the
cross between two thieves. While he was dying his executioners
gambled for the only thing he owned, which was his cloak.
When he was dead, he was laid in a borrowed tomb through the
pity of a friend.

"But since then nineteen wide centuries have come and
gone, and today he is the very center of the human race. I am
well within the mark when I say that all of the armies that ever
marched, and all of the navies that were built, and all of the
parliaments that ever sat, and all of the kings that ever reigned,
put together, have not affected the life of man upon this earth
as powerfully as has this one solitary life."

Now just suppose that as we cross the bridge of life we utilize our own representations of the Master to inspire us in those places of our greatest need. A few years ago an article was written about the Bible as "The Book That Has Helped Most in Business." Most of the scientific books written fifteen years ago are now out of date. And while the Bible was written when the camel was the most modern means of communication, it still is the most helpful book in creating our business success. By stopping before Jesus and having some devoted meditations, businessmen can absorb his honesty, his industry, his fairness, his faith, and his leadership. What an upsurge our economy would receive if we pruned out all of our harmful activities and devoted ourselves fully to those goals which he has indicated would make our lives most successful and worthwhile!

Beginning in his early youth, Jesus was engaged in the greatest of all enterprises which he referred to as "my Father's business." This is the business of building character, integrity, and eternal life into the lives of God's children. The Creator has invited each of us to have as large a share as we desire in the affairs of this most important family concern which he has organized. And when we feel a little bit discouraged and are tempted to do less than our best we might listen to this young "businessman of the centuries" as he went around saying to people, "Be of good cheer," "Be not afraid," "Why are ye troubled?" "Why do thoughts arise in your hearts?" "Rejoice and be exceeding glad."

The golden rule made up of seventeen words is probably the greatest formula for success in our public relations that has ever been prescribed. And as we pass along our own bridge of accomplishment, we might learn from him about how to be more responsible workers, more effective planners, more dependable self-motivators, and wiser judges of our human values. One of the greatest of all of life's lessons is that "man does not live by bread alone." We need a lot more of the word of the Lord. We need a good dose of inspiration occasionally. We need to build up our faith and recharge our love of life. Above all other interests we need to remember that we are the children of God formed in his image, endowed with his attributes and heir to his glory. And we should be constantly reaffirming our destiny through our daily duties.

As we cross this river of life we need to stop occasionally before the representation of Christ, the Great Physician. Each of us has an important responsibility for his own health, and we can perform some of the greatest cures if we understand the possibilities of that great command saying, "Physician, heal thyself."

The world is presently making itself sick by wrong thinking, yet there is a great power at our disposal capable of making us well physically, mentally, morally, and socially if we would just utilize the ideals and ideas Jesus taught. He gave his greatest success formula in two words when he said, "Follow me," and everyone ever born into this world must finally be judged by how well he carries out that single direction. If we meditate effectively enough upon his role as our example we can actually follow him. We can follow him in his faith, and in his righteousness, and in his industry, and in his doctrines, and in his obedience to God.

But Christ has some higher titles than those of physician or shepherd or teacher or businessman. He is also the King of kings. We must not repeat that mistake made nineteen hundred years ago when one group announced their own downfall by proclaiming, "We have no king but Caesar." Caesar's subjects and serfs have they remained ever since that time.

To serve our own best interests we might erect upon the bridge of life a special divine representation to be designated as "the Christ of the latter days." The scriptures tell us a great deal about Christ's occupational assignment for the cleansing of the earth, the destruction of the wicked, the universal resurrection, the millennial reign, and the final renewal and glorification of the earth. The scriptures make clear that the miracles and wonders of the latter days will be among the most important events that have ever taken place on this earth.

Many people place a very serious handicap upon themselves when they think of Christ only in his ancient setting of "sowing" and "teaching" and "suffering." In describing the Christ of the latter days, the scripture says, "Behold, I will send my messenger, and he shall prepare the way before me: and the Lord whom ye seek shall suddenly come to his temple, even the messenger of the covenant, whom ye delight in: behold, he shall come, saith the Lord of hosts. But who may abide the day of his coming, and who shall stand when he appeareth? for he is like a refiner's fire and like fuller's soap." (Mal. 3:1-2.)

On our bridge of life the representation of him who will come to cleanse the earth of its sins should hold more than ordinary interest for us, inasmuch as they will be our sins that are being purged. Someone once painted a famous picture entitled "Christ before Pilate." It represents Jesus being judged and condemned by Pilate and the people Jesus came to save. But some day another picture may be painted entitled "Pilate before Christ." This will concern his second coming, when with his mighty angels in flaming fire he will come to judge the world and take vengeance upon them that know not God and that obey not the gospel of the Lord Jesus Christ. (2 Thess. 1:7-8.)

About this event the Apostle Paul said, "But I would not have you to be ignorant, brethren, concerning them which are asleep . . . even so them also which sleep in Jesus will God bring with him. For this we say unto you, by the word of the Lord that . . . the Lord himself shall descend from heaven with a shout, with the voice of the archangel, and with the trump of God: and the dead in Christ shall rise first: then we which are alive and remain shall be caught up together with them in the clouds, to meet the Lord in the air: and so shall we ever be with the Lord." (1 Thess. 4:13-17.) What a great day to look forward to, and what a disaster for those who are still unprepared!

Even nineteen hundred years ago Jesus knew a great deal about our own personal and community needs. He looked forward to our day and was greatly concerned about what he saw. He gave a comparative appraisal of our times when he said, "As the days of Noe [Noah] were, so shall also the coming of the Son of man be." (Matt. 24:37.)

As the Great Teacher one of the specific things that most disturbed him about our present world was its false teachings. Our newspapers give us a day-to-day account of the many areas in which we are leading ourselves astray. But some nineteen centuries before we were born, Jesus projected our future image by saying: "And many false prophets shall rise, and shall deceive many. And because iniquity shall abound, the love of many shall wax cold." (Matt. 24:11-12.) Some of these false prophets are now saying that God has lost interest in us and that the canon of scripture is full and that he no longer reveals himself to men. They say that it doesn't matter any more what we believe or what we do, because all roads lead to the same place. But Christ says there is "one Lord, one faith, one baptism."

Jesus projected our greatest opportunity when he said, "And this gospel of the kingdom shall be preached in all the world for a witness unto all nations; and then shall the end come." (Matt. 24:14.) And in the latter-day fulfillment of his own promise he has reestablished his Church and has revealed anew a fullness of his original doctrines including the greatest of all truths—that God lives, and that the God of Genesis, the God of Sinai, the God of Calvary, is also the God of the latter days.

Christ organized one Church and placed his own name upon it. He taught the one set of doctrines necessary for our salvation. To help us get ready for "the Christ of the latter days," he has said, "For I the Lord cannot look upon sin with the least degree of allowance." (D&C 1:31.) He has tried to make it clear to us that God is his Father and that he is also our Father, and that he is the real tangible Person in whose image we were created. He taught the great doctrines of the atonement and eternal progression. He personally initiated the literal bodily resurrection. And he foretold his own glorious second coming to the earth, and the gospel restoration that should precede it.

As we pass along the bridge of our lives we ought to understand that our greatest latter-day need is not for bigger industries or more oil wells or greater power plants or a more ample gold supply. Our most critical problems are not our population explosions or our projected food shortages. Our primary concern should center itself in getting a sufficient love of God and truth enshrined in our hearts and a more devoted will to obey all of God's commandments.

Christ is the Good Shepherd and the Great Teacher, but he is also the Savior of the world. He is the rock of our eternal exaltation. He is the Lord of truth, the Prince of Peace, the Son

of God and the giver of all good things, and he is also the
"Christ of the latter days." And if we properly meditate before
him, we may be inspired to make the best and the most of our
own lives.

The Big Two

One of the two most serious problems limiting our success, is the inclination we often indulge in to disbelieve in God. Since time began, most of the people of our world have followed the program of rejecting God's messages and killing his messengers. God is not only the giver of all good things, but he is also our eternal Heavenly Father who has a most intelligent, helpful interest in our success. There are thousands of personal testimonies, confirming his existence and the value of his program, if practiced in our lives. Yet we seem to turn away from him in favor of drunkenness, immorality, nicotine, and dishonesty. Many people seem like natural-born law-breakers, and even under the extreme threat of losing our own souls we continue to load ourselves down with atheism and many kinds of those soul-destroying sins. This ridiculous traffic with evil is reported to us daily in ten thousand newspapers. However, as serious as this number one problem is, the second is almost as bad, and that is the tendency that most people have of disbelieving in themselves.

It has been said that the most widespread disease in the world is the inferiority complex. Our errors and negative attitudes seem to give us a subconscious tendency to think of ourselves as cowards, weaklings, sinners, and failures. Last year in the United States alone, over twenty thousand people became so unhappy with themselves that they took their own lives. And many others would have "followed suit" if they had had a little more courage. Unresolved conflicts sometimes neutralize the good opinion we might have of ourselves, and leave us fearful, guilt-ridden, discouraged, and unhappy. We often recognize these seeds of failure in even the greatest men.

For example, Moses was personally selected by God to free the Israelites and to build up among them a great nation. But even Moses had trouble with these two big problems. Moses had spent the first part of his life as the adopted son of Pharaoh's daughter. Apparently, he grew up in the palace and had all of the advantages of royal education and training.

When Moses was grown he killed an Egyptian and was compelled to flee from Egypt. He settled in the land of Midian, where he married the daughter of Jethro, the priest, and tended his flocks. One day on the desert, God spoke to Moses and introduced himself as the God of Abraham, Isaac, and Jacob. Then God told Moses about the problems involved in the Egyptian bondage of the Israelites. It was his desire to reestablish them in the land that had previously been given to their fathers. God also explained that Moses had been selected to lead the people in carrying this project forward. But Moses didn't respond to the call very enthusiastically. He said, "Who am I, that I should go unto Pharaoh, and that I should bring forth the children of Israel out of Egypt?" (Exod. 3:11.) This sounds much like some of our own traditional responses. We say, "Why me?—Why don't you get someone else?—There are a lot of other people who are better qualified for this assignment than I am; why not get them to do it?"

We remember that Jonah had a similar attitude about his divine call to go to Nineveh and warn the people of their impending destruction. Because Jonah didn't want to go, he got on a ship headed in the opposite direction. But the Lord caused a severe storm to arise which almost sank the boat, and at his own suggestion Jonah was thrown overboard. He seemed to feel that to drown would be better than doing what the Lord wanted him to do. Only after his experience with the whale was he willing to go to Nineveh and deliver his message.

Moses not only seemed negative but, for one with such a good education and such a superior background, he also seemed to feel seriously insecure. God tried to reassure him by saying, "Certainly I will be with thee . . ." (Exod. 3:12.) But Moses still had a lot of excuses. He was afraid that the children of Israel would not believe him, and that he would not know what to say to them. The scripture says that, "Moses was very meek, above all the men which were upon the face of the earth." (Num. 12:3.) That is pretty meek.

The Lord tried to tell Moses how to handle all of these

problems. But Moses was hard to convince. He said, "They will
not believe me, nor hearken unto my voice: for they will say,
The Lord hath not appeared unto thee." (Exod. 4:1.) In trying
to persuade him, the Lord performed the miracle of turning his
rod into a serpent. But Moses still didn't want the assignment.
He said, "I am not eloquent, . . . but I am slow of speech, and
of a slow tongue." (Exod. 4:10.) It seems a little strange that a
former member of the royal family should feel incapable of
leading a group of Egyptian slaves. The Lord said to Moses,
"Who hath made man's mouth? . . . have not I the Lord? Now
therefore go, and I will be with thy mouth, and teach thee what
thou shalt say." Moses continued to argue until the record says
that "the anger of the Lord was kindled against Moses." (Exod.
4:11-12, 14.)

Finally the Lord made a kind of compromise in which he
suggested that Moses take along his older brother Aaron, to do
his speaking for him. And the Lord also outlined how he should
proceed. He said to Moses: "Thou shalt speak unto him, and put
words in his mouth: and I will be with thy mouth, and with his
mouth, and will teach you what ye shall do. . . . and he shall be
to thee instead of a mouth, and thou shalt be to him instead of
God." (Exod. 4:15-16.)

When the Lord asked Moses who had made man's mouth,
he was probably hoping that Moses would get the idea of
learning to use his own mouth, instead of having to depend
upon the mouth of someone else. God gave all of us our
potentialities undeveloped but he also supplied us with the means
for their improvement. However, most of us have a tendency to
bury our talents in the ground. Of course, we have had some
notable exceptions to this rule. Demosthenes was also slow of
speech, but by working at his problem his impediment was
overcome, and he became the greatest orator of his day.

There is a great deal of evidence supporting the idea that
frequently God gives us a weakness in the very place where we
are expected to excel. He has said that he gives weaknesses in
order that we may become strong. A weakness can sometimes
become so annoying that it arouses in us a sufficient power to
overcome almost any handicap. God sometimes gives us very
difficult assignments to stimulate our development and enable us

to solve all of our problems. However, if we do nothing more than throw up our hands and quit trying, then we are licked before we start. Sometimes the Lord has to provide a whale or some other unusual motivation in order to get us to go forward.

When we try to justify our failures, or make excuses by saying, "I was not cut out to be a leader," or "I don't know how to be an orator," or "I don't want to be a worker," or "Who am I that I should go into Egypt?" then we greatly increase the Lord's troubles, as well as our own. But like Demosthenes, many of the world's greatest men have excelled in the place of their most serious weaknesses. A salesman once said to his sales manager, "I am just not a salesman." His manager answered, "Have you ever considered becoming one?"

John Milton was blind, Beethoven was deaf, the Apostle Paul had a disabling weakness which the Lord refused to relieve him of. Julius Caesar was an epileptic and was often taken in a seizure before his men. It has been said that many people are presently drawing total and permanent disability benefits who are in better physical condition than Caesar was while he was conquering the world. The man who, in my opinion, is the best salesman in the world was once a backward, timid introvert. And it was largely because of this annoying feeling of inferiority that, like Demosthenes, he went to work on his problem. He felt that he had to keep proving to himself every day that he could do the job as well as anyone else. And now he loves it more, and does it better, than any of his former superiors, so that now everyone calls him a "natural-born salesman."

Weaknesses were never intended to make us weaklings. They were given to challenge and sting us into greatness. And while we may not understand everything about Moses, yet we know that the Lord became disturbed because of his excuses, which seems to indicate that the Lord thought that he could do better. And many of us cheat ourselves out of our intended blessings because we lack faith in God's program and in our own possibilities.

The Lord pointed out to Moses that God had made Moses' mouth, but God also made *our* mouths. God promised to be with Moses, and he will also be with us. It is one of the greatest ideas in the world that if we try hard enough, we can develop our abilities and overcome almost any defect. There is no justification for anyone saying, "I am what I am and there is nothing that I can do about it." Everyone was created subject to the eternal laws of growth, and God wants us to have a big hand in our own creation. Certainly we would not appreciate our own success if everything was done for us. Many people are slow of speech and slow in many other ways, when actually they don't need to be.

I thought about Moses the other day while in a foreign land with a translator serving as *my* mouth. And I felt how tiresome it would be to be dependent upon this kind of mouthpiece on a permanent basis. God agreed to tell Moses what to do, and then Moses had the job of getting the ideas over to Aaron. But sometimes it is pretty difficult effectively to pass one's spirit, or enthusiasm, or even one's ideas on through a translator. Even after God had done much of Moses' thinking for him, Moses still had to hunt up Aaron and inspire him to get these ideas over to the people. Many of us seem to need an "Aaron" to do our speaking for us. There are many things that we need to talk about to our families and friends and others, where we imagine that we need someone else to do the job for us. And we should remember that Demosthenes could never have become a champion orator had he spoken through an interpreter. To begin with, everyone got better grades than Demosthenes. And if *he* could learn to do his own speaking, then so can we.

God not only made our mouths, but he also made our brains, our personalities, our ambitions, and our spirits just as he did those of Demosthenes. It is also important to understand that we can learn to do a lot of wonderful things with this equipment that God had given us if we just believe in it, and then work at the job hard enough.

If we take the attitude that we were not cut out to use our mouths effectively, then we don't have much chance, but we should remember that substitute mouths are sometimes pretty inconvenient also. I know of one man who has never yet learned even to operate the gadgets on his own television set. He thinks that he was not cut out to be a television operator.

The scripture, as well as our own observation, indicates that most of our difficulties come in one of these two places. Either we don't believe in God or we don't believe in ourselves, even though we are his chief handiwork and greatest creation.

The problems of Moses continued even after he was out of Egypt. When the people complained to him about their burdens, Moses said to the Lord, "Wherefore hast thou so evil entreated this people? Why is it that thou hast sent me? For since I came to Pharaoh to speak in thy name, he hath done evil to this people; neither hast thou delivered thy people at all." (Exod. 5:22-23.) And on other occasions Moses continued to ask the Lord why he had been assigned to this particular mission.

For the following forty years there was a lot of murmuring about why God had led the people out of captivity, only to endure the greater discomfort of the desert. Moses became one of the greatest men who ever lived, and like him God gives us all difficult problems to solve. Certainly he did not intend that we should become weaklings or cowards, sinners or pygmies, incompetents or failures. He created us in his image and endowed us with a set of his own potentialities. God made our mouths and our brains and our ambitions, and he has given each of us a share of the work of the world that he expects us to do effectively. And the most important of all our tasks is the inestimable privilege of helping him to develop us that we may become like him. We must not profane his image by making ourselves less than we ought to be. Great power will come to us, if we keep in mind these two big factors of success. Number one is to have faith in God, and number two is to have faith in ourselves as God's chief creation. And with the right attitudes he will bless us to achieve both of these important objectives.

Cain

O ne of the important parts of our literature comes under the heading of biography. Biographies are the written histories of the lives of people. And the history of the world is made up largely of the biographies of men and women, both good and bad. However *all* biographies may be used for our benefit, as the villain shows us the quicksands to be avoided while the hero points out the way wherein our lives should travel.

One of the most tragic of our biographies centers in the life of Cain, the son of Adam and Eve. To Cain goes the credit of starting the first crime wave. He seems to have done nearly everything wrong. He was one of those unfortunates who seemed to make all the mistakes personally. The scriptures say that Cain was a tiller of the ground and his younger brother, Abel, was a keeper of sheep. These two brothers were very different in character, and when they made their offerings to the Lord, Abel's offering was accepted and Cain's was rejected. We are told that the Lord had respect for Abel and his offering, but for Cain and his offering the Lord had not respect. Then Cain made a mistake. Instead of correcting his unfavorable situation he became angry. The scripture says, "And Cain was very wroth and his countenance fell. And the Lord said unto Cain, Why art thou wroth? And why is thy countenance fallen? If thou doest well, shalt thou not be accepted? and if thou doest not well, sin lieth at the door." (Gen. 4:5-7.)

Cain also made another mistake when he became jealous of his brother. Because the unfavorable comparison with Abel was offensive, Cain decided to try to solve his problem by slaying his brother. Then the Lord said to Cain, "Where is Abel thy brother?" In an attempt to conceal the facts Cain made the mistakes of lying and trying to deceive God. He said, "I know not: Am I my brother's keeper?" (Gen. 4:9.) The Lord then asked Cain a question that might be a good one for us to remember. He said to Cain, "What hast thou done?" And giving a partial answer he continued, "The voice of thy brother's blood crieth unto me from the ground." (Gen. 4:10.) Most people act thoughtlessly, and it might well have been that Cain didn't actually realize what he was doing. Certainly he didn't understand what the consequences of this act would be, as no one had ever killed anyone before.

I have always felt sorry for Cain. He lived when the earth was new, and he had none of the mistakes of others to restrain him from his evil. When we see tragedy invading other lives it should tend to make us more cautious. But because no one had ever before wrestled with those powerful forces of anger, jealousy, disappointment, and hate, Cain had no idea where they would take him. The scripture says that Cain loved Satan more than God (Moses 5:18) and Cain made a covenant with Satan and he gloried in his wickedness. And yet in all of these evils we are Cain's beneficiaries, as his mistakes should stimulate us to anticipate what it would be like to hear this question in our own ears: "What hast thou done?" We can put ourselves in a much stronger position for preventing evil by thinking about the answer before it becomes necessary for the Lord to ask us this personal question.

Upon the cross Jesus said: "Father, forgive them; for they know not what they do." Four thousand years after Cain the people committed an even more serious crime without realizing what they were doing. And even in our day almost all of the sins of the world are the sins of ignorance. We still allow ourselves to get involved in the evils of jealousy, hate, atheism, drunkenness, and immorality. We are still making covenants to serve Satan without realizing that, as a consequence, our lives are being radically changed on a permanent basis.

When Judas began to understand what *he* had done in betraying the Master, he wept bitterly and then went out and hanged himself. We can avoid some problems for ourselves by an advance understanding of the penalties that are always inflicted in consequence of evil deeds.

In pronouncing sentence upon Cain, the Lord said: "And now art thou cursed from the earth, which hath opened her mouth to receive thy brother's blood from thy hand; when thou tillest the ground it shall not henceforth yield unto thee her strength; a fugitive and a vagabond shalt thou be in the earth." (Gen. 4:11-12.) We can feel the terrible despair in Cain's reply as he said: "My punishment is greater than I can bear. Thou hast driven me out this day from the face of the earth, and from thy face shall I be hid; and I shall be a fugitive and a vagabond in the earth; and it shall come to pass that everyone that findeth me shall slay me. And the Lord said unto him, Therefore whosoever slayeth Cain, vengeance shall be taken on him sevenfold. And the Lord set a mark upon Cain, lest any finding him should kill him." (Gen. 4:11-15.)

Cain enacted this dreadful tragedy nearly six thousand years ago, and he has been paying its awful penalty ever since. The record indicates that Cain's posterity has also been bearing his heavy burden with him. It is the law that "the sins of the fathers shall be visited upon the children," and the scriptures tell of one of Cain's descendants by the name of Lamech, boasting of being a murderer. He said, "If Cain shall be avenged sevenfold, truly Lamech seventy and sevenfold." (Gen. 4:24.) How terrible it would be to have to live with Cain's hates, his feelings of inferiority, the knowledge of his disobedience, and the awful awareness that he was a criminal before God! And it would be even worse to realize that through his example of ungodliness he was transmitting these evils to his own posterity.

When the Lord said to Cain, "What hast thou done?" he coined a verbal instrument that might be of great assistance to us, if we used it early enough and with sufficient frequency.

When Cain discovered that his offering was not acceptable, he should have found out the reason why. It would have been much more profitable for him to have made a correction then, instead of getting angry and letting his countenance fall. How much better it would have been if Cain had been able to anticipate the Lord's question so that when he felt these emotions of anger and jealousy stirring his heart, he could have said to himself, "Cain, do you know what you are about to do? Do you realize what will happen to Abel as well as to yourself and your posterity if you don't correct your negative attitudes and learn to offer an acceptable offering?" With an effective advance consideration he could have saved his brother's life and his own soul.

Every hater is a potential murderer. It was not the Lord who placed the curse upon Cain. Cain himself committed the deeds that brought on their inevitable consequences. This situation has not changed since, as we all still live in a world where evil consequences always follow evil deeds. If we were considering jumping over a cliff or hugging a million volts of electricity, we could, with a little forethought, accurately predict what the result would be. And when we let our own countenance fall and get entangled in hatreds we may be sure that we are bringing curses upon ourselves and putting unsightly marks upon our children.

Some time ago an unwed mother gave birth to a baby that did not have any arms. Upon investigation it was discovered that the father had been a user of drugs. This child will probably suffer a far worse fate than Abel's. And as the sins of these parents are visited upon their baby, they will also be confronted with God's question saying, "What hast thou done?"

This sin of putting marks upon ourselves and others is a pretty serious business. Every sin has its own marks. Lung cancer and heart disease are some of the marks left by nicotine. Alcoholism leaves a score of terribly disfiguring marks upon its victims.

If we are unable to look ahead and discipline ourselves, our punishment may also be more than *we* can bear. And as the Master said, "Every tree that bringeth not forth good fruit shall be hewn down and cast into the fire." (Matt. 7:19.) And that fire may burn for a long time.

We are sometimes offended by these stern "Thou Shalt Not" commandments found in God's law. But if only Cain could have gone back and had another chance, he might have found that this command of "Thou shalt not kill" would not only have given him great pleasure but, if he could have obeyed it, it might have saved his soul. If he understood the consequences in advance he might also have taken delight in some other commands saying, "Thou shalt not be wroth, thou shalt not let thy countenance fall." To keep ourselves safe from these sins, we need to fall in love with God and righteousness. We should get the greatest satisfaction from obeying those great commands designed for our happiness. I suppose that murder today is as serious as it was when Cain originally committed it. The marks left by every other crime cause as much misery now as then. Yet with all of our added experience the people in the United States committed murder last year over twenty thousand times. The records also show that last year 414,433 people were arrested for breaking that command saying, "Thou shalt not steal." One-tenth of these were for stealing automobiles, 211,000 were arrested for drunken driving and there were probably over ten thousand times that many cases of drunkenness. If we add the Sabbath day violations, those dishonoring their parents, and those being disobedient to God we should have a staggering total of disfigured people. Think of the marks left by anger, jealousy and hate, and the suffering that must be endured in hell because of these sins that we thoughtlessly commit! There is no credit or satisfaction that comes from doing wrong, or from fostering the crime wave started by Cain so many years ago.

It is customary for every railroad crossing to have some big cross-arms saying, "Stop, Look and Listen." But saving a life is always big business. And if it helps to put up "Stop, Look, and Listen" signs at railroad crossings, and a skull and crossbones label on bottles of poison, maybe we should also put some caution signs on anger, jealousy, hate, selfishness, and those other emotions that got Cain started off on the wrong foot. It may have taken Cain only two minutes to kill Abel, but the penalty will last forever. Cain's problem began when he did those things that made him offer an unacceptable offering.

Wherever Cain may presently be, we can be sure that he is still dragging with him the dead weight of his awful suffering. And he must often say to himself, "Cain, what hast thou done?" "How did you ever get yourself into this awful mess?" And I expect that his thoughtful posterity may also be asking these same kind of questions. However, his misery will not be a total loss if it helps some of us. Many people are aided by this vicarious process whereby a benefit can be transferred from Cain's experience to protect us. We can learn far more profitably and pleasantly from Cain's deed than we can by having a similar experience of our own. We may relive Cain's crime and come out of it better off. But when we can only learn from committing our own evil, then the experience may be so destructive that we may not survive it.

Unless we are extremely unobserving or seriously retarded mentally, we can learn from others that sin is the most unprofitable and miserable activity that there is in the world. How terrible when of our own free will we load up our own lives with these damaging kinds of sin, where, like Cain, we will be compelled to pay its awful price forever!

Jesus said, "Follow me." But there is a set of skull and crossbones warning us against following Cain. The circumstance that gives this fact significance is that the lives of everyone, both good and bad, are eternal and the consequences will last forever. The Savior of the world is more alive today than he ever was, and so is Cain and so is Abel.

God wants every one of us to be happy. Therefore he has made every true success pleasant, hoping to encourage us to do well. We enjoy winning a basketball game, getting good grades in school, or deserving a pay raise. Doing good things for others makes us happy. Righteousness is happiness, and happiness is the goal of life. God himself has said, "Men are that they might have joy." The Lord has given us the principles of the gospel to teach us the way of success and happiness. It also gives a lot of satisfaction to repent, and to cleanse our minds of guilt. There is great joy in heaven when the most humble turns the course of his life upward toward more worthwhile things. But this joy is greatest in the one who brings it about. What great satisfaction can come from being baptized, receiving the Holy Ghost, and living the golden rule!

On the other hand, sinners are always miserable. Satan is miserable. And Cain is one example of what happens when we violate God's laws and follow Satan. But even these bad examples can be used by us to move us away from sin. The life of Cain can give us a benefit without the penalty, and we get the profit without the pain. There is no fun or profit in hate, anger, lying, arguing, cheating, or killing. Criminals are not happy. Sinners, weaklings, failures, and ne'er-do-wells are not happy.

And one of the greatest opportunities of our lives is to use the scriptures, the Church, our own conscience, and our ability for self-discipline, to bring about the greatest success and joy in ourselves.

The Cemetery of Neglect

I t is always a very interesting experience for me each Memorial Day to spend a few hours in the cemetery. For this day the Veterans organizations provide a worthwhile Memorial Day program. They have some stirring drum and bugle music, and a thought-provoking talk. A rifle salute is fired as a means of paying tribute to the soldier dead. The cemetery itself covers a large area at the foot of the mountain, and is beautifully landscaped. There are many acres of attractive lawns, and each of the graves is identified by a headstone with the name, dates, and other information, including a fitting personal tribute made to the individual whose body lies buried beneath it. The thirtieth day of each May is set aside as a special day for remembering and thinking about those who have taken their departure from this life.

Because I have been around for a rather extended period, this experience is of particular interest to me. Many of the names on the headstones identify people with whom I have been personally acquainted, and I am able to recall many of the events that have distinguished their lives. It also adds to my pleasure to have a Memorial Day visit with other friends who are still living.

The dictionary says that a cemetery is "a sleeping place" or "a burial ground." It is an area set apart for the graves and tombs of those people who die. It is interesting, however, to remember that there are other kinds of sleeping places and burial grounds. The government has a burial ground at Fort Knox, Kentucky, where our national gold reserve is buried. And we remember the parable of the unprofitable servant who buried his talent in the ground. There are also some mental and moral sleeping places where we produce in ourselves a condition somewhere between life and death. Someone once wrote an interesting epitaph that might fit many of us. It said, "Died at thirty, buried at sixty-five."

Many years ago Arthur Brisbane wrote a syndicated column which was read with great interest by thousands of people. On one occasion he said: "The greatest losses to the human race have *not* been caused by floods or fire. They have not been brought about by the epidemics that have filled the cemeteries by mowing down millions of people with the scythe of the grim reaper. Nor have our greatest losses been caused by the wars, and earthquakes, or the financial panics that have wreaked so much havoc in the economy of so many people. Our greatest losses have come about because so many good people have been following the lead of the unprofitable servant and have been burying their talents in the ground." Then Mr. Brisbane asks some interesting questions. He says, "Is there anything more tragic than to see a trained teacher who will not teach Sunday School? or a trained voice that will not sing in a choir? or an effective businessman who will not give the benefit of his knowledge to God's work? or a good lawyer who will not serve in church councils so that his fellow men may have some use of those talents which God has given him? In every walk of life there are richly endowed men and women who refuse to use their talents to help others."

When someone dies we take him to the cemetery and bury him. But when we allow a talent to go unused or an opportunity to be wasted, we bury some part of ourselves alive. Over the years, we bury so many of our opportunities. We bury our virtues, we bury our friendships, and we bury all of those abilities that we allow to go unused. There is a great burial ground in our subconscious minds where we lay out a lot of important personality traits for their final sleep. The physical diseases that put so many people in the cemetery each year are not so detrimental to our best interests as those conditions that consign our virtues, our talents, and our great personality traits to their eternal rest. We allow our virtues to be destroyed by sin, but our abilities themselves are cut down by disuse. We build much of our lives to resemble a vast cemetery filled with victims of our own neglect.

The dictionary says that we become guilty of neglect when we fail to pay effective attention to some important thing. To neglect a person is to slight or disregard him. Frequently, we neglect a great human genius in his own day and only honor him after he is dead. It is impossible for anyone to qualify for the American Hall of Fame until he has been dead for twenty-five years. Usually we don't even appreciate the members of our own family until after they are laid away in the cemetery.

The religious history of our earth indicates that we honor the dead prophets, but we kill the living ones. And by abuse and neglect we also kill many of the most important and finest feelings, not only in members of our own families but in ourselves as well. We neglect our education. We neglect our spirituality. We neglect our Church opportunities. We neglect our personal appearance. We are all depressed by those people who at one time took such great pride in themselves but who now because of neglect have lost interest in themselves and in their own success. Some people have allowed themselves to become so seriously run down that they now appear in some variety of their role as a physical, mental, or spiritual hippy, or other brand of ne'er-do-well. Through mere neglect people sometimes bury the most important parts of themselves. Then they mill aimlessly around with empty faces and glassy-eyed expressions which bespeak the futility they feel. The sad outlook, dirty attire, and long unkempt hair announce the partial death that has turned them into unwashed, smelly refugees from life and success.

The dictionary says that "to neglect" is to omit through indifference, carelessness, indecision, or ignorance those things that we should give attention to. It may be that we ought to make up a written inventory of those things to which we should properly give a great deal of more serious attention. We are guilty of an awful sin of neglect when we fail to carry out life's highest orders in the interests of our eternal welfare, or when we neglect to perform those duties on which our own success and happiness inevitably depend.

One of the chief problems of murderers comes in getting rid of the body. That is also one of the chief problems of the hippies and of ourselves. What a tragedy it sometimes is to have our badly neglected selves on our hands! The waste that we see in damaged souls is often because we have neglected our faith, our industry, and our high standards of morality. Each year by our inattention and negligence, we fill up a few more graves in that vast cemetery of our lives.

Sometimes we try to get rid of some of the bodies of our responsibilities by attempting to shrink them into invisibility. There is a word called "negligible" that is frequently involved as a part of our problem. Negligible is described as a state where something is so small or trifling that we think it can be safely disregarded. Sometimes we even sprinkle some of this shrinking powder of neglect on our important duties and then in our minds these duties soon become so small that we merely forget about them. The Communists are shrinkers. They try to belittle the points of view of their opponents. They have shrunk up their own belief in God until to them he no longer exists. Then in their minds it becomes unnecessary for them to keep his commandments or practice his success principles.

Speaking for the Communists, Mr. Khrushchev once threatened to bury us, and they have actually buried many of those righteous principles that would inhibit them in this and their other unholy courses. But many of us individually do many of those same things that the Russians are trying to do as a nation. We even bury ourselves a little bit at a time. We dig our own graves by our negative thinking, by our alibiing, our procrastination, our mediocrity, and our feelings of inferiority.

A poem pertinent to this idea was once written by Alice Bennett, who says:

I have no voice for singing; I cannot make a speech.
I have no gift for music; I know I cannot teach.
I am no good at leading; I cannot organize.
And anything I write would never win a prize.
But at roll call in the meetings, I always answer "here."
And when others are performing, I lend a listening ear.
After the program's over, I praise its every part.
My words are not to flatter, I mean them from my heart.
It seems my only talent is neither big nor rare—
Just to listen and encourage and to fill a vacant chair.
But all the gifted people could not so brightly shine,
Were it not for those who use a talent such as mine.

Under the right circumstances, to be a listener and to fill up a vacant chair is all right. But it is pretty difficult to really encourage someone else very much, unless we have a substantial

amount of success inside of us. God expects us to be doers and
thinkers, as well as sitters and listeners. In fact he has made an
irrevocable law to the effect that if we are to retain the talents
he has given us they must be used. When the "works" are taken
away from any accomplishment, the "faith" dies also. There is
no such thing as preserved faith. No faith can live in isolation.
Neither can virtue, nor ability, nor spirituality. We lose all of
those things that we abuse, disuse, misuse, or neglect. Then, in
whole or in part, we soon find ourselves buried in our own
cemetery.

Great experiences come not only because of what happens
to us, but it is much more important what we *do*, about what
happens to us. A small deed carried out is far better than a
great deed that is merely planned and then unconsciously abandoned to our own neglect. Someone has written what might
apply to us when he said:

> If all the sleeping folks will wake up,
> And all the lukewarm folks will fire up,
> And all the dishonest folks will confess up,
> And all the disgruntled folks will sweeten up,
> And all the discouraged folks will cheer up,
> And all the depressed folks will look up,
> And all the estranged folks will make up,
> And all the dry bones will shake up,
> And all the Christians will stand up,
> Then we can have God's paradise upon this earth.

Every one of us always carries within himself the very
things that he seeks. If we seek faith, we need only look within
ourselves, for God has already planted within each of us the
seeds of faith, waiting only for us to make them grow. If we
seek courage, we need only to develop that which we already
have. God has already endowed our lives with greatness, just as
he has endowed our arms with muscles, and our heads with
brains. However, if we neglect to use them they may never
amount to very much. I know of one man who has one of his
legs buried in the cemetery. But I know of another man who
has most of his faith and ambition also buried there.

It might be a pretty good idea to make an inventory of
those abilities and virtues that we are neglecting, so that we can

give them a more effective daily exercise. The other night in the movie I saw a trainer of some famous Kentucky racehorses putting these valuable animal charges through the daily hard workout that is necessary if they are going to win future races. We can imagine what mere neglect could do to a racehorse. And if we also understand what it can do to us, we will be well on our way to win the important race of our life. God gave us our brains, our hearts, our hands, and our eyes, and he expects that we will use them properly and regularly. As soon as we begin neglecting our faith, our enthusiasm, our imagination, or our industry, we start laying them away in some nice little grave in our cemetery of neglect.

Neglect is one of our greatest sins against God. It is also one of our most serious sins against ourselves. God is a Creator, but he is also trying to make creators out of us. He gave us life in heaven, and he has enabled us to be born here. But our power to grow has given us the tremendous ability to put muscles on our arms, and abilities in our brains, and faith in our hearts, and good attitudes in our personalities, and habits of success in our bloodstream.

At the resurrection God will open our graves, but the kind of people that will come forth will largely depend upon what we have done with ourselves. We can't have a glorious resurrection unless we have first opened some of those graves in our own cemetery of neglect. God can only fully redeem us if we have already redeemed those godly traits which he has entrusted to us to develop.

It has always been a very exciting thought for me to contemplate the resurrection. That will be the occasion when God's angel will sound his trump as the signal for us to come forth. But in preparation for that event we should be blowing a few bugles of our own, in order to make sure that our own great qualities will not still be asleep in the cemetery of our neglect.

The Chambered Nautilus

O ne of the distinguishing characteristics of great men and women is that they usually have a larger than average number of sources from which they can learn. People have trouble when they don't progress effectively, and no matter how favorable the environment may be, learning presents a difficult problem for some people. Even in a great university where conditions are made as favorable as can be, many students have problems. Some fight learning by cutting classes. They put off study and resist any enthusiasm to work at their own education. Some have only half made up their minds to learn and some allow distractions to seriously upset their progress.

Only a comparatively small percentage of those who begin college are still there to finish the course. And even many of those who stick it out get only a small fraction of the possible benefit. And so it is in life. We miss many of our opportunities almost completely, and drag our feet on many others. We reach a learning plateau very early in our careers from which we never progress substantially. Many of us are no farther ahead at sixty than we were at fifty. Frequently we don't have any better attitudes at forty than we had at thirty. Our faith may be no greater at seventy than at sixty, and we are often farther away from God at eighty than we were at seventy.

It is a sad fact that some people make very little progress during their entire lifetime, yet others learn from everything and everyone around them. James Watt invented the steam engine, after watching a boiling teakettle. Eli Whitney invented the cotton gin, after seeing a cat try to pull a chicken backwards through a picket fence. Robert Bruce built up enough determination to win freedom for the Scots, while watching a spider persist after repeated failures until it reached its goal.

Shakespeare pointed out some of these effective learners as those who found tongues in trees, books in running brooks, sermons in stones, and good in everything. Jesus himself was the greatest master of this art of observation that leads to learning. As far as we are aware, Jesus had no extended formal schooling. In his lifetime he probably never traveled any great distance from his home, and yet from the most simple experiences he learned some of the greatest lessons which present-day wise men are still studying.

In his parable of the sower, he gave us some of the thoughts that went through his mind as he watched the farmer sowing his wheat. He also taught great lessons out of the experiences of the prodigal son, the good Samaritan, the wise and foolish virgins, the tax money, the tribute money, the ten talents, and the pearl of great price. Whether an event was good or bad in itself, Jesus made a lesson of good from it. He even drew strength from his own temptation, and every other experience he ever had was made to promote some useful purpose. Even Satan himself is permitted in this world to serve our best interests. For as we resist evil and struggle against weakness, we develop our characters and become stronger and more determined. Every failure should recharge our determination to rise *above* failure, and every success should build up our enthusiasm to increase the volume of our total accomplishment.

The Apostle Paul said, "All things work together for good to them that love God." What a great idea! That is, if we love God, if we think right, if we have the right attitude, then everything works for our benefit and we learn from everybody and everything.

In 1858, Oliver Wendell Holmes published a stimulating poem entitled "The Chambered Nautilus." It is the story of the life and development of a little shelled animal called the pearly nautilus, which spends its life in a series of successively enlarging physical compartments. As the nautilus grows, it builds an ever widening spiral shell which is divided into chambers by transverse curved partitions of shelly matter. As it increases in size, its former habitation becomes inadequate, and therefore it moves into the larger and more suitable house, the need for which it has foreseen and provided for. As each change is made it occupies only the last and outermost compartment.

On one occasion, a little girl visited Dr. Holmes. His study contained many of these beautiful sea shells that had previously served as homes for these little animals. In order to more clearly explain his poem to his young visitor, Dr. Holmes took one of these shells and sawed it in two crosswise. Then he could clearly display to her the vacated sections to illustrate the animal's expanding way of life. Because we are all interested in life's profound meanings, Dr. Holmes' poem serves us as a kind of symbol or pattern for our own lives. In its first stanza the author relates some of the traditional fancies that the poets have built up around the nautilus. In their poetic imaginations, this little craft is a ship of pearl which sails through enchanted seas where beautiful fabled sirens sing songs of unheard-of sweetness. And in the imagination, it might be an echo of these siren songs that can be heard when one puts an ocean shell up to his ear.

The second verse pictures the discarded lifeless shell. The occupant has now gone, and its dwelling-place has been sawn asunder so that onlookers may more clearly understand the marvelous growth program with which God has endowed this humble result of his creation.

The third verse is a flashback to the life of the nautilus, and suggests the excellence of the toil that took place during its growing period. This after-view of the chambered nautilus' success may serve us as a preview of the possibilities of our own lives.

The fourth stanza is a rhapsody of thanksgiving for a heavenly message of progress and success. The fourth stanza also serves as a prelude to the fifth stanza, which might well become the prayer of every aspiring human soul. Every child of God has been endowed with his own divine right for fulfillment through a thrilling series of growth experiences. "The Chambered Nautilus" is a beautiful poem and has a delightful philosophy, a message of appreciation, and an uplifting eternal challenge. Our own lives take on meaning as we are able to translate the music, aspiration, and spirit of accomplishment into our own hearts.

When John Greenleaf Whittier first read this exquisite poem he pronounced his own verdict of its worth by saying that it was "booked for immortality." And Dr. Holmes himself prized this poem as one of the best he had ever written. He says:

This is the ship of pearl, which poets feign,
    Sails the unshadowed main,—
    The venturous bark that flings
On the sweet summer wind its purple wings
In gulfs enchanted, where the siren sings,
    And coral reefs lie bare,
Where the cold sea-maids rise to sun their streaming hair.

Its webs of living gauze no more unfurl;
    Wrecked is the ship of pearl!
    And every chambered cell,
Where its dim dreaming life was wont to dwell,
As the frail tenant shaped his growing shell,
    Before thee lies revealed,—
Its irised ceiling rent, its sunless crypt unsealed!

Year after year beheld the silent toil
    That spread his lustrous coil;
    Still, as the spiral grew,
He left the past year's dwelling for the new,
Stole with soft step its shining archway through,
    Built up its idle door,
Stretched in his last-found home, and knew the old no more.

Thanks for the heavenly message brought by thee,
    Child of the wandering sea,
    Cast from her lap, forlorn!
From thy dead lips a clearer note is born
Than ever Triton blew from wreathed horn!
    While on mine ear it rings,
Through the deep caves of thought I hear a voice that sings:—

Build thee more stately mansions, O my soul,
    As the swift seasons roll!
    Leave thy low-vaulted past!
Let each new temple, nobler than the last,
Shut thee from heaven with a dome more vast,
    Till thou at length are free;
Leaving thine outgrown shell by life's unresting sea!

I thought of a contrast to the chambered nautilus the other day as a discouraged salesman was telling about some of his problems. For the first three years his occupational record had shown that, like the nautilus, he had also made steady improvement, so that each period found him substantially ahead of where he had previously been. Then he began allowing some distracting occupational sins to take his mind from what he was doing, and consequently his shell stopped expanding and began to shrink. If he had been a pearly nautilus, he would have had a pretty tight squeeze trying to live in a financial house that was only half the size of the one he had occupied during the previous year. These distractions had also done a considerable amount of damage by shrinking up the personality house in which he had lived. The discouragement and lethargy caused by his distractions had started a backward movement, making him smaller and weaker than he had formerly been. As this belittling process continued, he lost a considerable amount of his faith and self-confidence.

For the next few months he made a forced effort in trying for a comeback, but he had lost the spirit of growth and the beautiful songs of success no longer echoed in his heart. When one has a broken spirit, a comeback is sometimes pretty difficult. God can resurrect a dead body, but who can resurrect a dead faith, or powerize a sick attitude, or cleanse a sinful heart? Many alcoholics, criminals, and other sinners have frequently so belittled themselves that they have found it difficult to get back the growth spirit of the chambered nautilus.

Success is always so much more simple when one makes steady year-by-year progress in building up his faith and getting greater power into his self-confidence. For after one lives in a rut for a long enough time, or cultivates too many reverse attitudes, he loses the spirit of that song of success that is often pretty hard to recover. We don't take much joy in any accomplishment that doesn't have an expanding pattern. There can be a lot of fun in working one's way from a hovel to a mansion, but there is no joy in having to hide one's pride and move out of the mansion to again occupy the hovel. Life has been given to us as the greatest gift that even God can provide. And our days represent that precious time allotted to us in which to go forward. It is a serious misuse of life when we spend our inheritance floundering around or thrashing up and down without progress or direction. We should never permit any situation where a clear view of our lives would disclose that a worsening process was making our living compartments smaller and less desirable.

In speaking of some of those who follow the opposite course of deterioration, the scripture says "It had been better for them never to have been born." We need a particular control over both our life's compass and its speedometer. Sometimes we grow very rapidly at certain periods, and then we allow adverse influences or a series of demerits to send us back toward zero.

Homer, the ancient author the the *Odyssey*, tells the story of Ulysses and his men visiting the magic isles while returning from the battle of Troy. As a punishment to some of these men for what they had done, the story says that they were turned into swine. But we often perform a similar feat by turning our lives into something less than they were and thereby we bring upon ourselves a punishment that is most unpleasant.

In the financial and occupational departments of our lives our progress is often promoted by the urging of necessity. But in the mental and spiritual fields we frequently do not have the same pressure from behind and we therefore frequently pick up some bad habits that turn our course downward. At one time King Saul was the goodliest person in Israel, but his disobedience to God and the evil spirit that it engendered brought on a serious retrogression, and he died a suicide. Solomon was once the wisest man who ever lived. He saw God twice, but when he began violating the laws on which his wisdom had been granted, the blessings were withdrawn, and he too began that long, hard journey downhill. He provided an idolatrous mother for his son Rehoboam who would follow him upon the throne. He led his own people into atheism and slavery, and he himself died a partial idolator, very much out of favor with God.

Lucifer, who was once a son of the morning, ended up as Satan, and Judas the apostle of Jesus Christ became his Master's betrayer and finally hanged himself. There is no benefit or happiness in walking down that broad road toward making our lives into zeros. And most of our ultimate success will depend on how well we have lived the philosophy of the chambered nautilus. If each year we can fill a little bigger compartment than we did the year before, we will always be looking in the right direction. This involves the processes of eliminating evil, and filling our lives with faith and the kind of righteousness, industry, devotion, obedience, and service that will help us to reach our destiny in becoming like God. Therefore we again offer up our own life's prayer as we sing:

Build thee more stately mansions, O my soul,
    As the swift seasons roll!
    Leave thy low-vaulted past!
Let each new temple, nobler than the last,
Shut thee from heaven with a dome more vast,
    Till thou at length are free;
Leaving thine outgrown shell by life's unresting sea!

Come Up Higher

Some 3,460 years ago one of history's most important events took place upon Mount Sinai when God said to Moses, "Come up to me into the Mount." (Exod. 24:12.) Then, after a memorable forty days in the divine presence, Moses received the law by which our world was to be governed.

It is interesting that a great many of the world's most important events have been enacted in high places. The greatest discourse ever given was the Sermon on the Mount. Jesus was transfigured upon a high mountain. He died and rose from the dead on Mount Calvary. And when he ascended into heaven he took his leave from the top of the Mount of Olives.

God's ancient invitation for Moses to meet him on a higher level has been repeated to us many times in many ways. Jesus spent his entire ministry trying to change the mental and spiritual level of men's lives. When he said to his disciples, "Follow me," he was trying to lead them upward. To a group of ancient Americans the resurrected Jesus said, "What manner of men ought ye to be?" And then in answer to his own question he said, "Verily I say unto you, even as I am." (3 Ne. 27:27.)

As John the Revelator was serving out his lonely exile on the Isle of Patmos, he beheld a door opened in heaven; and a voice said, "Come up hither, and I will shew thee things which must be hereafter." (Rev. 4:1.) To help us make the best and the most of our lives, God has planted a divine development instinct in us. We are given a holy ambition to climb upward toward our eternal destiny. We have a divine hunger for accomplishment, a natural passion to increase the dimensions of our lives. We seem to have in our blood an ambition to climb mountains. Our spirits have a comparable urge to scale those lofty spiritual heights that God has placed before us. And in accepting this challenge to improve ourselves we need to follow the Master in his faith, in his righteousness, and in his devotion to God. When we are at our best we rise above the ordinary levels of life and approach that door in heaven which is always kept open for our benefit.

Every good parent has a desire for all of the good things of life to be enjoyed by his children. The primary message of the gospel is to extend to us an invitation to have a part in God's program for our eternal progression, and the plan contemplates that as offspring of God we may eventually become like our eternal parents. The primary focus of the divine message has always been, "Come up higher," "Be more faithful," "Follow me."

Jesus taught his disciples to pray saying: "Thy Kingdom come. Thy will be done on earth, as it is in heaven." (Matt. 6:10.) In the Sermon on the Mount he said, "Be ye therefore perfect, even as your Father which is in heaven is perfect." (Matt. 5:48.) And in contemplating his atonement he said, "And I, if I be lifted up from the earth, will draw all men unto me." (John 12:32.) In making our response it is important that we understand who we are and what our own inheritance and destiny mean. Frequently we have only a limited vision or we tend to keep our eyes too securely glued to the earth.

In "The Pilgrim's Progress," John Bunyan tells the story of a man with a muck rake. This man had spent his life thinking only of those values that are upon the ground, as he raked unto himself the chaff and muck of the earth. There was an angel standing over his head with a celestial crown in his hand offering to exchange the crown for the muck rake, but this man could look in no direction but down, so he disregarded the offer of the angel as he continued to rake unto himself the chaff and dust of the earth. There is also an angel standing over our heads offering us a celestial crown if we can only look up. All of us can be outstandingly successful and supremely happy if we can only look up to God and righteousness and faith.

The animals were created to go down on all fours and thus their vision is thrown upon the ground. But man was created to stand upright in the image of his Maker so that his vision might reach up to God. Inside heaven's open door a great reception has been arranged awaiting our arrival. Each of us is an important part of God's family. And even if there is only one vacant chair, there will be an incomplete family circle. Because we are the children of God we should not spend our lives acting like orphans or weaklings or foreigners or sinners. It is one of our most profitable possibilities to trade in our muck rakes for a celestial crown. God himself has said, "Let the wicked forsake his way, and the unrighteous man his thoughts: and let him return unto the Lord, and he will have mercy upon him; and to our God, for he will abundantly pardon." (Isa. 55:7.)

The scripture says that Jesus was the first begotten son of God in the spirit and the Only Begotten Son of God in the flesh. But we are also the sons of God destined to become even as God himself is. Jesus said, "I have said, Ye are gods; and all of you are children of the most High." (Ps. 82:6; see also John 10:34.) Instead of accepting his invitation to elevate their thinking, those to whom he spoke accused him of blasphemy and tried to kill him. It has always seemed about as difficult for us to believe in our own glorious destiny as it is to believe in God our Eternal Father.

In our antemortal experience we walked by sight. We have all seen God. He is our Father. We lived with him. And when during mortality we are given a very necessary assignment and asked to learn to walk a little way by faith, God is saying to us, "Come up higher." We became more like God when we were "added upon" with these beautiful, wonderful mortal bodies capable of a literal resurrection and a glorious eternal life. We climb a little higher when we organize our families and by the power of the priesthood have them sealed together for eternity. This is the time and place where we are tested and proven and developed. And we lift ourselves upward when we satisfactorily pass our final mortal examinations. Only then do we qualify to have glory added upon our heads forever and ever. Then we will pass through heaven's door to receive our "inheritance among all them which are sanctified." (Acts 20:32.)

Mortality is only a temporary condition. And actually we are strangers here even to ourselves. In referring to man, the inspired psalmist said, ". . . Thou has made him a little lower than the angels, and hast crowned him with glory and honour." (Ps. 8:5.) Another translation of this scripture says, "Thou hast

made him 'for a little while' lower than the angels." The Apostle
Paul points out that in some ways even Christ was made
temporarily a little lower than the angels. (Heb. 2:9.) But the
facts are that God, angels, spirits, and men are all of the same
species in various degrees of excellence and different stages of
development. Our antemortal life is a kind of infancy for our
immortality and our present life is where we prove ourselves and
secure our eternal destiny in the presence of God.

No one could adequately understand the life of Jesus if we
saw him only as the man of sorrows walking the dusty roads of
Palestine. We also need to hear the description of him as given
by John the Revelator some sixty years later when John saw
him in his glorified, resurrected state. Think what progress a man
may make within the narrow limits of this life as he may go
from rags to riches, or from log cabin to president, or from
plowboy to prophet! Then what wonders may we expect for
ourselves at our best as we live throughout eternity with God
our eternal Heavenly Father as our guide and teacher!

In redeeming us from death, Jesus was saying to us, "Come
up higher." His whole life and his entire teachings were devoted
to that purpose. In one of his parables he used the words,
"Friend, go up higher." (Luke 14:10.) And if we were to search
for some short phrase that could best sum up the entire meaning
of the divine message, it would probably be found in these three
simple words. Our response should be a more determined effort
to comply with all of the requirements. We should be more
thoughtful in our righteousness, more industrious in developing
our abilities, and more faithful in the good example we set for
others. Certainly we should be more devoted to God and more
obedient in following his directions. For as we move up higher
in our accomplishments we will also move up higher in our
satisfactions and in our other eternal rewards.

To give ourselves an additional lift, just suppose that in our
minds we turn back the calendar and stand upon the top of the
Mount of Transfiguration and contemplate that great event which
Matthew records as follows: "And after six days Jesus taketh
Peter, James, and John his brother, and bringeth them up into
an high mountain apart, and was transfigured before them: and
his face did shine as the sun, and his raiment was white as the

light. And, behold, there appeared unto them Moses and Elias talking with him." (Matt. 17:1-3.) Moses and Elias had served their own period in mortality many years before. They had once been mortal men just as we are now. Moses and Elias then differed from Peter, James and John only in that they had gone ahead of them into their next stage of development. Jesus was then still in mortality, yet his body and spirit were capable of being transfigured so that "his face did shine as the sun, and his raiment was white as the light." There were other occasions during the life of Jesus when other messengers from the presence of God came and ministered to him and who also discussed with him matters of importance pertaining to the welfare of God's work upon the earth.

Of course the glory of God has also rested upon other mortals. After Moses had been in God's presence on Mount Sinai, he came down to make a report to the people. The record says: ". . . Behold, the skin of his face shone; and they were afraid to come nigh unto him. And till Moses had done speaking with them, he put a vail on his face. But when Moses went in before the Lord to speak with him, he took the vail off, until he came out . . ." (Exod. 34:30, 33, 34.) As we elevate our own standards we can also add a little extra glory to our lives, both while we are here and afterwards.

On one occasion Paul said to the Romans ". . . Be ye transformed by the renewing of your mind . . ." (Rom. 12:2.) We can raise ourselves to a higher level of living by transforming our thinking and revitalizing our spirituality.

Of course, we should keep in mind that "up" is not the only direction in which our lives may travel. There is also a great down-draft in operation in our world which is constantly lowering our levels of life. One of the most important events in the history of our earth was the fall of man. When our first parents disobeyed God they became less than they had previously been in some ways. Then the earth also fell. Instead of the earth continuing in its paradisiacal state, it began bringing forth noxious weeds. However, the fall of man was not something that was finished and done with in the Garden of Eden six thousand years ago. The fall of man is still going on. If you put your ear to the ground at any hour of the day or night you can hear the steady thud, thud, thud, of the fall of man.

Cain started our first crime wave by killing his brother, Abel. The influences of this downward movement were continued and brought on a flood, the confusion at Babel, the crucifixion of Jesus, the great apostasy from God, the dark ages, and the gigantic deluge of crime, sin, war, atheism, and disobedience which characterizes our own day. The signs of the times indicate that through this lowering process we may be about to call down upon our world the terrible cleansing that will mark the end of this particular period of our earth's history.

But each person may choose the direction that his own individual course will take. God never forces anyone to do right, and Satan has no power to force anyone to do wrong. It has been said that God always votes for us and Satan always votes against us, and then we are asked to vote to break the tie. It is how we vote that is all important. It is interesting that no one is ever sent to hell by someone else. No one is being held down except by himself. And no one is required to remain on his present low level of life, even for one more minute. If we are presently headed downward, we may reverse our course and go in the other direction. The great power of repentance is available for our immediate and unrestricted use. And with a very loud voice the Author of repentance is saying to every one of us, "Come up higher." The power of faith is also trying to make us more successful. Our conscience is pointing us toward better things. The scriptures join hands with our success instincts and say to us, "Come up higher."

As Nancy Hanks lay on her deathbed she said to her nine-year-old son, "Abe, go out there and amount to something." And that also is exactly what life is saying to us. That also is what God is saying to us. And that is why he has placed this divine instinct for self-improvement at the very core of our individual lives. It was the Creator himself who planted in us this natural tendency to grow. And it was he who decreed that the attaining of success should cause our most pleasant emotions. All of us have been given a divine discontent with our lives as they are, to encourage us in this upward reach, thus enabling us to overcome our inferiorities and our weaknesses. If we effectively motivate this natural hunger for eternal improvement we may reach our eternal goal where we, the offspring of God, may eventually become like our eternal parents.

COME UP HIGHER

I saw the mountains stand.
Silent, wonderful and grand,
Looking out across the land.

When the golden light was falling
On distant dome and spire,
I heard a soft voice calling
"Come up higher, come up higher.

"From the lowland and the mire,
From the midst of earth's desire,
From the vain pursuit of pelf,
From the attitude of self,
Come up higher, come up higher."

Thomas J. Shelton

A Committee of One

One of the interesting developments of our day is the trend toward the use of committees in solving our problems and in carrying on the important work of the world. Our affairs are so large and complicated that the specialized services of many people are required if the desired accomplishments are to be attained. Boards of directors that carry the responsibility for the welfare of a great business interest or some other enterprise usually divide themselves up into committees so that specialized duties can be met with specialized skills, and thereby bring about the desired success in the shortest possible time. This is also a usual procedure with legislative bodies, educational groups, social organizations, and even families.

The dictionary describes a committee as a body of persons appointed or elected to consider, investigate, or take action on some matter that has been assigned to it. The committee may be asked to report back its findings and recommendations to a larger group, or under some circumstances it may be authorized to take direct action.

There are many kinds of committees. There are steering committees, and committees on rules. There are finance committees, ethics committees, program committees, and entertainment committees. In the Senate of the United States they have a committee on committees. This committee selects the members of the various other committees. In the House this function is performed by the Ways and Means Committee.

This idea of using committees for carrying on the work, play, progress, or entertainment of people is a very good one. It utilizes the time and special abilities of particular individuals for the good of all. An effective committee pools the wisdom, experience, and know-how of its individual members. It conserves time and makes greater progress possible. To use the judgment of several people also makes mistakes less likely. Then as the several

committees pool their efforts, the total accomplishment is greater
than if each item had been worked on by the entire group. Of
course some committees are given more important work than
others. One of the most important committees is usually the
executive committee. Under certain conditions the executive
committee is given power to act for the entire group. The
executive committee is assigned to think, initiate, reason, and act
for the benefit of all. Sometimes another important committee is
appointed called the Committee of the Whole. Then the entire
group is constituted as a committee in order to fulfill some
specified assignment.

There is another kind of a committee that also has the
greatest possible importance. It is called a committee of one.
Sometimes a single individual is selected to carry the responsibility and do the work of an entire committee, or even the
whole organization. There are many advantages in a committee
of one. One advantage is that a one-man committee is less bulky.
It may be more maneuverable, and it gets the job done faster.
There is an old adage that says, "He travels fastest who travels
alone." A one-man committee loses no time bringing committee
members up to date, or reconciling opposing viewpoints or
differences. Some committee members may think negatively and
waste the time and efforts of the others. Also, when full and
complete authority is centered in one individual he may feel his
responsibility more keenly and do his work better. It is reported
that after Lindbergh made his solitary flight across the Atlantic a
lady said to her husband, "Isn't it wonderful that he could do it
alone?" The husband replied, "It would have been a lot more
wonderful if he could have done it with a committee." A
divided responsibility sometimes results in a lessened responsibility.

There is an old story to the effect that one boy is a boy,
two boys are half a boy, and three boys are no boy at all. And
someone once described a committee as a body that keeps the
minutes and wastes the hours.

The greatest and most important responsibility that is ever
laid upon the shoulders of any human being is to make the best
and the most of his own life. Of course this is an assignment in
which we need all of the help we can get, and yet the primary

responsibility must be pinpointed and placed in the hands of the concerned individual himself.

Sometimes people lay the blame for their failure upon someone else. We frequently blame our employers for our lack of opportunity, our teachers for improper instruction, our wives for lack of support, and our friends for our bad habits. Many of us would like to have, and actually need, one powerful committee to be responsible for our righteousness, another for our progress, another for our faith, and another for our prosperity. It would be an especially good idea if we could place all of these committees under a heavy bond so that if they didn't produce the right results in us we could collect some handsome damages. It is a great idea to be able to get effective help from wonderful, capable people. But every aspiring individual must have a dependable "committee of one" made up of himself, and he must be capable of guaranteeing his own personal success.

The President of the Church carries great responsibility for the welfare of the Church. The President of the United States has a load of responsibility for the welfare of his country and its people. All of us have a share in the responsibility for many things. But God has appointed each one of us as a committee of one, to be primarily responsible for ourselves. And to each of us, as a person, God has given great authority in saying, "Thou mayest choose for thyself." No one else can do our choosing for us. No one else can do our learning, or our growing, or our progressing for us. Many people rank above us in political, occupational, and religious authority. But when it comes to the important consideration of our own lives, we have been constituted a "committee of one" with almost unlimited authority and responsibility. Upon our shoulders had been placed the need and the duty for making decisions, the power to act with full authority, and the job of carrying all of the responsibility for the consequences. And we might very profitably build up within ourselves the attitude of being fully answerable to ourselves.

The dictionary says that responsibility is the state of being responsible. That is, we must be financially, morally, mentally, spiritually, and socially accountable to ourselves, and capable of producing a full measure of success within our own lives. To be fully responsible, we need to be bigger than our job. And we need to be stronger than anything that can happen to us. Other people around us may fall, others may be irresponsible and undependable, but we must succeed. One of the greatest joys of life is to be able to fully trust ourselves. A great salesman once said, "One of the things I appreciate most is that I am not in competition with me." How lucky it is for us that we may have ourselves on our side limitlessly. If we are properly integrated and persuaded, we can, if we like, take our own part and foster our own interests on an unlimited twenty-four-hour-a-day basis.

I recently talked with a man who had nearly all of the problems. He spent most of his energies working against himself. He was divided in his allegiance to right and wrong. He was vaccilating, uncertain, unstable, and unpredictable. It would have taken a whole group of committees to keep him in business successfully. He needed a committee on marriage relations, on finance, on personal relations, committees on spirituality, planning, efficiency, and one to help him make up his mind. Many people are as difficult to integrate as two antagonistic races. We always have serious problems when we are not really interested in our own welfare. Probably our greatest ability is to get ourselves all in one piece, and take sides with ourselves. If we don't believe in God, the universe still goes along anyway. But when we don't believe in ourselves, our world soon comes crashing down around our ears. Our primary duty while serving on our own committee of one is to see that our own interests are promoted, including our own confidence in ourselves. Someone has said:

Trust in thine own untried capacity,
As thou wouldst trust in God himself.
Thy soul is but an emanation from the whole.
Thou dost not dream what forces lie in thee,
Vast and unfathomed as the grandest sea.
No man can place a limit in thy strength.
Such triumphs as no mortal ever dreamed
May yet be thine—if thou will but
Believe in thy Creator and thyself.
At length, some feet shall stand on
Heights now unattained—
Why not thine own?—press on;
Achieve! Achieve!

Because we are only one, that does not mean that we are unimportant. Many people fail to vote in an election because they think that their one vote doesn't make much difference. But our one vote is about a hundred percent of the total when we cast it in our own interests. It not only should have a lot of influence in our lives, but it also represents a majority in other areas of influence. Both Thomas Jefferson and John Quincy Adams were elected to the office of President of the United States by a margin of one electoral vote. Rutherford B. Hayes was also elected President by a one-vote margin. His election was contested and the matter referred to an electoral commission, where again he won by a margin of a single vote. The man who cast the deciding vote for President Hayes was a congressman from Indiana who himself was elected to Congress by a margin of just one vote. That vote was cast by a client of his who, though desperately ill, had insisted upon being taken to the polls. Just one vote gave statehood to California, Idaho, Oregon, Texas, and Washington, and today all of the millions of people living in those five states are Americans because of this one-vote majority.

But these one-vote margins are not all in the distant past. The draft act of World War II passed the House by just one vote. But the most important one-vote margins come when we really vote in our own behalf. It has been said that God always votes for us and Satan always votes against us, and then *we* are asked to vote to break the tie. It is how we vote that makes the difference, and it can also make a great difference outside ourselves. It has been said that, if he will, one man can change the morale of a whole community. Oscar Hammerstein said "a heart can inspire other hearts with its fire," and Edward Everett Hale said,

> I am only one, but I am one.
> I can't do everything, but I can do some things.
> What I can do, that I ought to do.
> And what I ought to do, by the grace of God,
> I will do!

If we always did what we ought to do, one man could just about remodel any society. Jesus was sent into this life as a Committee of One to save the world and redeem all mankind

from sin, and before he died he was able to say, "It is finished."
We have also been set apart as a committee of one to set the
world right, and finish some jobs that until now have been left
undone. The most important one is to make an outstanding job
of our own lives. If everyone would effectively take care of that
single job, this earth would be God's paradise. If we can conquer
ourselves, everything else is easy. Since capacity and power walk
hand in hand with responsibility, Tyron Edwards says that
"when we sin with the multitude, our guilt is as great as if we
alone had done the wrong." We cannot hide our responsibility
by mingling with a group. The Pied Piper of Hamelin was only
one, but he led many others to destruction, and in one way or
another, good or bad, everyone becomes a pied piper. One poor
basketball player may cause his entire team to lose the championship. One pilot can wreck an entire plane-load of people.
When one man loses the spirit of success, those who follow him
may also pile up in the ditch.

Abraham Lincoln was only one, but he changed the course
of millions of lives. It was said that while George Washington
was fighting for the national life of America, he seemed like a
man possessed. It was as though the freedom of America rested
upon him alone. By hard, continuous labor he became a kind of
Atlas balancing his own world of work on his own broad
shoulders. He loved success with the same kind of passion with
which a miser loves money, whereas one who is a spendthrift of
his time and wastes his spiritual forces is as profligate as the one
who squanders his patrimony on liquor and cards.

One of the greatest ideas that I know of in the world is
that God has appointed each of us as a committee of one to set
the universe in order and make our own lives outstanding. Major
Martin Treptow was killed in the Battle of Chateau Thierry in
1918. After the battle his diary was found on his body, and in
it he had written these words: "I will work, I will save, I will
sacrifice, I will endure, I will fight cheerfully, and do my utmost
as though the entire conflict depended upon me alone." And so
it does. May God help us to help ourselves.

Coping

Abraham Lincoln once said that the Lord must have loved the common people because he made so many of them. Following this line of reasoning we might conclude that the Lord must have loved to see people solve problems, as there are so many problems needing solutions. In fact there are many more problems to solve than there are people to solve them. Each Sunday morning for many years it has been my privilege to look into the faces of a large congregation of church attenders. They are dressed in their best clothes, they have on their brightest smiles, and are wearing their finest attitudes. However, in counseling with some of them during the week, I have become aware that all people have problems, and some still remain unsolved. It seems that the enemy has gotten into all of our fields by night and has sown many tares among the wheat. Everyone has several varieties of cares that are covered up by the Sunday suits and smiling faces. There are many goats that have not yet been separated from the sheep, and a few serpents are still hiding among the flowers. There are many deep wounds that have not yet been healed, and some heavy hearts are still beating out a symphony of pain.

Most of the resources of the world are devoted to helping people solve their problems. Medicine is concerned with solving the problems of our health; good lawyers are problem solvers. Agriculture teaches us to get our food out of the soil. We also have an assortment of mental problems, social problems, sex problems, financial problems, and personality problems that are badly in need of solutions. Every year in America we pay psychiatrists millions of dollars to dig down into the dark subconscious regions of our minds to ferret out those hurtful experiences and wrong attitudes that have become embedded in our lives and are causing us difficulty.

The Church was organized to help us solve those moral and spiritual problems that so upset our lives and cause an awful turmoil in our souls. The critics of Jesus seemed to feel that he spent a disproportionate amount of his time with the sick and heavily burdened. The importance which he himself attached to this phase of his ministry is indicated by his parable of the shepherd, who left the ninety-and-nine and went to help the one that was in trouble. In justifying the time he spent with sinners, Jesus said, "They that are whole have no need of the physician, but they that are sick." (Mark 2:17.) But all of these ancient problems have not yet been properly disposed of, and we still speak of our "sick world." A very large percentage of our population spend some of their lives in the classification of being mentally ill, and a still larger number have serious spiritual problems that have not yet been resolved. However, a great deal of the problem-solving of our world has been put on a do-it-yourself basis.

Jesus was pointing us in this direction when he said, "Physician, heal thyself." When Shakespeare's Lady Macbeth went to the psychiatrist seeking "some sweet oblivious antidote" to cure the guilt sickness that had gotten into her mind because she had helped to kill the king, he said to her, "Therein the patient must minister unto himself." That is, in spite of the large numbers of people whose business it is to help us, the deciding factors in solving most of our difficulties are in our own hands. There is a key word in this interesting self-help program called "coping." It refers to that important process of wrestling success-fully with the vital problems having to do with our own welfare. The dictionary says that to cope is to "strike" or to "fight." It is to enter into a contest and then to struggle for mastery. To "cope" is to contend, whether the opponent is a friend or an enemy. To the degree in which we cope successfully, our lives become fruitful and happy, and each individual must come to terms with his environment in his own personal way. It is in our coping experiences that we discover the real solutions to our problems. And as we make our abilities superior to our diffi-culties, we become victors.

There are many unfortunate people who have an unpleasant weakness that Roger Price refers to as "copelessness." These folks don't have enough strength to prevent them from being pushed around by their impulses. Some have a kind of person-ality rigidity that makes them unmaneuverable and unskillful in life's battle. A lack of accurate information about themselves and their problems is one of the significant stumbling blocks that problem-troubled people have in "coping." Other difficulties root in some kind of an emotional block, or some unrecognized conflict between their conscious and subconscious minds that prevents them from solving their difficulties.

Some time ago a man came in to discuss a serious sex transgression. I asked him why he had done as he had. He said he didn't know. No one is in a very good position to cope with any problems that he doesn't understand. Aristotle once said that we never know a thing until we know it by its causes. Every failure has a cause and every success has a cause. Indigestion has a cause, overweight has a cause, immorality has a cause, and happiness has a cause. If you can find out what causes success, you can reproduce the cause. If you can find out what causes failure, you can eliminate the cause. In this man's conscious mind he told himself that he was doing nothing wrong. More or less he had dissociated his opinion of himself from those uncontrolled sex energies that were preparing to cause him even more serious difficulties. He didn't want to lower his opinion of himself, so he merely placed himself in a position where his unrighteous acts would take place with as little censure on his part as possible. Many people like to think that they are being forced into something that subconsciously they desire to do, and yet they want to be able to tell themselves that it is not their fault. This man did not want to be immoral, but he refused to sufficiently recognize his problem, or to arouse enough of his fighting forces to overcome it. Many people do wrong because they have never really made up their minds *not* to do wrong.

It is pretty hard to cope with any situation when one has serious conflicts within himself, and where half of his own powers are fighting against him. When one does not or will not recognize his problem, or when he gives the voices of the body as much authority as he gives to the voices of his mind, then he can expect to encounter many failures. And when we fail to recognize an enemy as such, then we fail to build up the proper fortifications against it. Subconsciously many people *want* to be overcome by those evils that they have a strong attraction for. Sin has much more power over us when we deny the blame or claim that we did not recognize the enemy or know what made us do as we did. We increase our "copelessness" when our methods of self-analysis deteriorate, or when the power of our self-control is weakened.

When we have weak motives, or let ourselves run down in mental health, our coping problems increase. Even for a professional problem-solver to help a troubled person most effectively, he almost needs to crawl inside the troubled mind to get a clear understanding of what is upsetting the tranquility of the patient.

Each of us has some powerful heart hungers that need to be fed. We long for appreciation and recognition that we may not be strong enough to earn. If we are to maintain a sound mental health, we need to love and to be loved. It has been said that our three most essential personality needs are (1) to love, (2) to be loved, and (3) to feel that we are worthwhile both to ourselves and to others. We can increase our coping ability by establishing more worthwhile ambitions and by strengthening those motivations that can bring them about. The feelings of guilt and inferiority that follow some people like a shadow should be overcome by an actual record of righteousness and proven ability. Most guilt feelings can be effectively dissolved by the six-stage process called repentance. It is made up of confrontation, confession, restitution, forgiveness, reconciliation, and a successful performance. But sometimes we get exaggerated feelings of inferiority and guilt from our own imagination. We usually see others at their best and we know so much more about our own weaknesses that we frequently magnify our problems out of all proper proportion. "Guilt has a Siamese twin by the name of 'alienation'." This alienation frequently destroys constructive belief in important things, including ourselves, and it therefore makes all of our battles harder to win.

God has promised us that if we repent he will forgive us. He has said that "though your sins be as scarlet they shall be white as snow." He has promised us that he will wash our sins out of his mind and forget them. But what good does it do for God to wash our problems out of *his* mind if we keep running them through the delicate tissues of our own.

There is some guilt that is like an open wound, and is easily recognized and treated, but there are other kinds of guilt that are not only hidden from other people but frequently we even keep them hidden from ourselves. Wrong always produces a miserable feeling, and when we lay the blame on others, give excuses for ourselves, and pretend that we don't know what is causing our trouble, then this paralysis of copelessness is seriously increased.

Recently I witnessed the final breaking up of what could have been a fine family. The husband was unduly impressed with his own importance, and would recognize no wrong in himself. He had previously been married and divorced but in both cases, in his opinion, the problems were caused entirely by others. He had an ability to magnify the weaknesses of others out of all proportion, and shrink his own into invisibility. He had capitalized on his wife's retiring nature, and had almost worn her out in serving his selfish and unappreciating demands. He had subjected her to all kinds of indignities by threatening to break up their home and leave her and their four little children if she did not cater to his every whim. Because she had allowed him to wipe his feet on her, so to speak, it never seemed to occur to him to be fair and honest with her when he didn't have to.

When we keep our problems hidden, they often fester and pour poison into our blood stream without our knowing it. At this moment many vicious marital conflicts and personality assassinations are taking place where the criminals have no recognition of themselves in their roles as villains. Even when problems are discovered, we sometimes continue feeding our dislikes and blocking all possibilities for a happy solution because we won't make the effort to take up arms against our sea of troubles.

Lawrence S. Kubie points out that men and women can become very ingenious in finding new ways of being unhappy together. We cripple ourselves with dislike, and we do irreparable damage by defending our faults instead of correcting them. One can cope most effectively only after he has built up enough fairness and righteousness to make him a worthwhile responsible person who loves a few other things besides himself. Proper morals, high character, good standards, and worthwhile values in behavior are all necessary to the genuine fulfillment of our needs for a real feeling of self-worth. One must also develop some ability for self-correction, and be able to make effective and enforceable plans for his own personal improvement and success.

Our surface problems may be only manifestations of the existence of the deeper psychological difficulties that lie buried below the surface of so many lives. A human being is complicated because he has so many parts making up the one whole. And even a small disease in one part of the body can make the whole person sick. A little cancer of the liver can put the whole body out of order, even though the patient has perfect health in every other organ. Plato once said, "As you ought not to attempt to cure the eyes without the head, or the head without the body, so you ought not to attempt to cure the body without the soul—for the part can never be well unless the whole is well—and therefore, if you would make the head and the body well you must begin by curing the soul."

Our industry, our motives, our faith, our moods, and our personalities are all dependent to some extent upon each other. And what Melville calls "a damp, drizzly November in my soul" can dim the luster of all other virtues. Frequently we are bored and nauseated by the empty meaninglessness of our own existence, and it is thought that the most constructive way of handling our problems is to have that authentic and effective religious life that God intended for those whom he had formed in his own image. One great psychologist said, "Among all of my patients there has not been one whose problems in the last resort have not been a deficiency in his religious outlook on life." Real religion makes us aware of the fact that we are the actual children of a living God, and are called to be active partners with him in the perfecting of our own lives.

Each one of us should confront himself occasionally with the great questions, and then get some satisfactory answers to the important objectives of life. We need to ask ourselves such searching queries as:

1. Are the urgent things crowding the important things out of our lives?

2. How much are we investing in the more unprofitable kinds of success?

3. Are we getting rid of those activities that bring no adequate gains on a long-term basis?

4. Do we know what our problems are and can we cope with them effectively?

We must not be seduced by superficiality, or hide from life's real issues, or try to dodge our coping with responsibilities. Spiritual growth takes place most rapidly when we have committed ourselves to religious values and become members of the Church that God has organized to foster the greatest values in our lives. In our minds, we should not tamper with God's laws, or substitute our own ideas for his, and some good reading and living assignments based on the goals that God has established can be invaluable in helping us to cope effectively.

Death and Taxes

There is an old proverb to the effect that nothing is certain but death and taxes. And we might add that nothing is quite as difficult to deal with effectively. In recent years the amount of our taxes has been multiplied many times. But in addition, the number and variety of the things taxed has also been greatly increased. There are income taxes, property taxes, sales taxes, gasoline taxes, luxury taxes, inheritance taxes, and gift taxes. Taxes are levied against our automobiles, our real estate, our securities, and our success. We have many examples of double taxation and triple taxation. Taxes are placed on our industry, our thrift, and our pleasure. The harder and more effectively we work or the greater our thrift becomes, the higher our taxes go. Someone has said that if our founding fathers thought that taxation *without* representation was bad, they should be here now to see what it is like *with* representation.

We are taxed continually from the time we are born until the time we die. And some of our heaviest taxes are imposed upon our estates after we are dead. Both during our lives and after our deaths, taxes are levied by the federal government, the state government, the county government, and the city government. In addition to all of the visible taxes, we also have many hidden taxes. Some of these are assessed against our property, and some are assessed against our lives themselves. But the number and variety of our deaths have also been going up. And some deaths and some taxes have a very close association. For example, excessive taxes frequently tend to kill our initiative, our industry, and our ability to provide for our families.

But we not only worry about our increasing taxes, we also worry about the new causes of death. For example, we presently have on hand more than enough atomic bombs to kill everyone upon the earth. These are under the control of antagonistic nations who for a long time have been threatening to use them upon each other. Our cold wars are doubling our taxes, but they are also killing off our prosperity. And they are giving us enough jitters to send many people to their graves. The strikes, riots, wars, crimes, student revolts, and racial conflicts are also causing a great increase in both death and taxes. But on top of all of this we load down our lives with gangsterism, labor disputes, senseless marches, and many people even resort to suicide. We get both death and taxes from war, strain, disease, crime, accidents, sin, and failure. We have some physical deaths, cultural deaths, financial deaths, spiritual deaths, and deaths involving our comfort and peace of mind.

As we bring all of these things upon ourselves, we make our lives unpleasant and unprofitable. Life is the most important commodity in the universe, and the primary purpose of the great science of medicine is to lengthen and strengthen it, and make it free from pain and unhappiness. This is also the purpose of that great science called religion. The Savior of the world announced his own mission by saying, "I am come that they might have life, and that they might have it more abundantly." (John 10:10.) That is directly opposed to some of our deaths and some of our taxes. Of course, the interest of Jesus was not confined to that part of life that lies within the narrow limits of mortality. His concern was also centered in the benefits that come with eternal life. In fact he has made it clear to us that one of the primary purposes of this life was to prevent death and taxes in the next life. Jesus said, "Fear not them which kill the body . . . but rather fear him which is able to destroy both soul and body in hell." (Matt. 10:28.)

This idea is closely related to the philosophy of William James, who pointed out that the greatest use of life is to spend it for something that outlasts it.

Apparently eternal life is like almost everything else, and it can be a lot more satisfactory if we ourselves have had an important part in bringing it about. However, the two chief problems involved, even in gaining an eternal life, are death and taxes. It is obvious that all deaths are not equally serious, and some taxes are much worse than others. Actually we get some very great benefits from paying some kinds of taxes. For example, the government uses some of our money to fight our enemies and keep their troublemaking activities contained within as small an area as possible. The ungodly Communist leaders who pose such a serious threat to our welfare have boasted that they would like to bury us. And there is no secret about the fact that they would enslave every person in the world without a moment's hesitation, if they thought they could. Of course, serving in Russian subjugation would be much worse than paying American taxes. For as Emerson once said:

> Of what avail is plow or sail,
> Or land or life, if freedom fail?

The money that we pay to the government is also used in an attempt to control crime, curb delinquency, and protect us from vandalism. If we did not pay our taxes, we would have no courts, no policemen, and no armies. Then our ridiculous riots, our criminal racial strife, and the bitter hate that causes us so many problems would soon get so out of hand that we would be likely to lose everything. In addition our taxes furnish us with a convenient way to provide schools and hospitals for ourselves. They also enable us to assist those who are mentally and physically unable to take care of themselves. We live in a land of the most ample abundance, and if we all cooperate effectively together we can provide a large measure of success and happiness to many people, and still have enough left "after taxes."

However, there are some taxes that are much harder to bear and have fewer benefits than the taxes required by the government. Yet for these we are not even required to fill out a tax return. These are among our hidden taxes.

Benjamin Franklin was a very wise man and he pointed out that we are taxed many times more by our waste, our sloth, our weakness, our errors, and our sins, than we are by the government. There is a very heavy tax that is levied against our dishonesty. I know of one man who spent twenty years in Ohio State Penitentiary for robbery, and the most money that he ever got at any one time was $63.20. Paying his tax on dishonesty took his entire income for twenty years, and yielded a net return of only a few hundred dollars.

But for many people who are out of jail this hidden tribute

is constantly being exacted because of our dishonesty. Sometime
it would be interesting to try to figure out the tax burdens that
are frequently placed upon us because of our ignorance, our
indifference, and our procrastination. Think what we lose because
we can't make up our minds, or don't do the right things when
they ought to be done. We often lock the barn door only after
the horses have all been stolen. Or suppose that we got some
efficiency expert to try to calculate the amount of the tax
burden imposed upon us by our bad judgment, or our weaknesses, or our transgressions. Take the example of a person who
buys a quart of liquor. To begin with the cost would probably
be about thirty dollars, whereas he could get a quart of the
finest water, or a quart of grade A vitamin-enriched milk, or a
quart of the best orange juice—all of which are superior products—and the cost would be only a few cents. Of the $30, he
may pay a tax of about $7.50.

But it is when the purchaser drinks the liquor that the real
tax is imposed. If he drinks rather generously, then in addition
to what he pays the state he may have an absenteeism tax
imposed by his employer that would wipe out his entire income
for a week. He may also be charged for a wrecked automobile, a
bad hangover, a few hardened arteries, and maybe even an
accidental death or two.

The liquor bill that some people pay in cash each year is
often much bigger than their total taxes to the government. But
think of the tax placed on people for their bad judgment caused
by the liquor. If this money had been invested in good securities, or in education, or in character, it may have made him rich
in a few years in many ways. A chain smoker also gets off easy
so far as the state and federal taxes on his tobacco are
concerned. Even if he smokes two packages a day, he only has
to pay about eighty cents a day for cigarettes. And only about
20 cents of this is for taxes. But the Surgeon General's report of
1964 indicated that a tax of many billions is placed upon the
health of American smokers by cigarettes to pay for their lung
cancers, heart disease, emphysema, bad nerves, and the whole
group of their miscellaneous tobacco illnesses. This is not to
mention foul breath, discolored fingers, and atmosphere filled
with the unpleasant odors of stale tobacco smoke. The American
tobacco industry also places a giant tax upon the nation itself, as

it withdraws from its productive uses many hundreds of thousands of acres of our best American soils. It also takes up the time of a whole army of American workers to produce, process, and merchandise this destructive product. In a day when many people in the world are starving or suffering from malnutrition, this is very important.

When Columbus discovered America, he found the tobacco plant growing here as a poisonous weed. And some half-naked, half-savage Indians were going around with rolls of its leaves burning in their mouths. We have made a number of rather serious mistakes in America. And one was made when we didn't spray all of the tobacco plants with some good, strong weed-killer.

Suppose we get some experts to figure out the burdens imposed on our great country by its dope addiction, its student rebellions, the wastes of manhood and womanhood caused by "hippyism," and our other varieties of negative thinking and subnormal living. What a tax we lay upon ourselves by our ignorance, our disloyalties, our immoralities, and our irresponsibilities. We have the richest country in the world with the potentialities of being a paradise, and yet we make ourselves poor and miserable by taxing ourselves with our hates, our race riots, our strikes, our idleness, and our selfishness. However, we impose the most serious taxes upon ourselves by our sins. Whenever we violate the laws of God, we lay an unbearable tax upon our souls.

Our greatest wealth is never counted in terms of what we have, but always in terms of what we *are*. We don't work merely to acquire—we work to become. Success in life isn't just determined by what we can get out of it, but by what we can become by it. And again we see the close relationship between death and taxes. As Paul points out, "The wages of sin is death." (Rom. 6:23.) We are punished *by* our sins as well as *for* our sins. A drunkard not only pays a penalty for what he does wrong, he pays another bill for what he becomes because of what he does wrong.

The ancients used to have an unusual system for punishing crime. When someone committed a murder, the sentence was that he should be chained to the corpse of his victim. Then wherever he went forevermore he must drag with him the victim's putrefying remains. The sentence was permanent, and there was no possible way for him to disentangle himself from the results of his evil act. Then if he should decide to kill again, another dead body would be added to his oppressive burden. This punishment seems severe, but life has a plan of retribution exactly like that. We are chained to the corpse of every evil. If one chooses to become an alcoholic, his punishment is that a ruinous driving thirst attaches itself which drives him further and further down the road to despair. If one tells lies, his sentence is that he becomes a liar. If one doesn't study, he is chained to his ignorance. The smoker is chained to his lung cancer, his poisoned blood stream, and his diseased organs, and all of the taxes that go with them. And even after the cup of his iniquity is full, he may be chained forever to an eternal death. Then like Cain he may cry out in vain, "My punishment is greater than I can bear."

The taxes that we pay to the government are grievous, but how horrible our situation will be if a writ of eternal bankruptcy is attached to our souls. Life is the most valuable of all commodities, and God's greatest gift to man is the opportunity to achieve an eternal life. Jesus said, "Lay up for yourselves treasures in heaven, where neither moth nor rust doth corrupt, and where thieves do not break through nor steal." (Matt. 6:20.) There aren't even any taxes on treasures in heaven. In the beginning God created man in his own image, but what may be even more important, he endowed him with a set of his attributes and potentialities. And it was decreed that the off-spring of God could someday become like the parent. All of our eternal values are tax free, and God has made it impossible for anyone to rob us or reduce our own eternal values except ourselves. There is no earthly government, Communist or otherwise, that can invade our heavenly store. And no one can ever be sent to hell by someone else. Each one commits himself to misery and death by the taxes imposed by his own deeds.

And so again we come back to that thrilling idea that life is the greatest of all commodities. We can cut out any eternal taxes by our faith, and we can forever banish death by our righteousness.

The Devil's Advocate

Most people are familiar with the religious customs involved when deceased Catholic persons are elected to sainthood. There are some procedures involved referred to as beatification and canonization, by which the deceased persons are elevated to places of high praise and veneration. The dictionary says that in beatification, the Pope officially blesses the person concerned to enjoy the supreme happiness of heaven. His eligibility is first ascertained by a public investigation, and an elaborate process of inquiry concerning his worthiness is carried on in thirteen or fourteen stages, often covering a period of many years. If he is finally approved, he is entitled to the greatest Catholic honor. It is thought that by this beatitude he may be rewarded with many blessings in heaven. After investigation, beatification, and canonization, his name is placed in the catalogue of saints, and thereafter he is entitled to enjoy perpetual veneration and invocation from Roman Catholics.

The dictionary points out that, as a part of the investigation for sainthood, an official is appointed called the "devil's advocate." It is his duty to present arguments *against* the proposed beatification, or to point out errors in the evidence on which the claim for canonization rests. It is also his responsibility to uncover any defects in the character of the person for whom the honor is sought. The term "devil's advocate" also has some general meanings, including those of a person who champions inferior causes for the sake of the argument. Or this term may refer to a critic who picks out flaws in various situations in order to evoke a controversy in an attempt to bring out more truth. This process hopes to insure that one's judgment will not be based on one-sided, incomplete, or incorrect information.

However, this idea might also have some suggestions that could be used in perfecting us individually while we are still alive. I suppose that in a little different way the major political parties serve each other as a kind of devil's advocate. Apparently the Democrats feel that it is their duty to point out the defects and weaknesses of the Republicans. And the Republicans try to prevent the sainthood of the Democrats. And while there are many disadvantages in the mudslinging and name-calling that usually takes place during a political campaign, yet this "devil's advocate" idea sometimes uncovers facts and brings out points of view that would not otherwise be known. Inasmuch as one's judgment is no better than his information, it is helpful to know all of the facts before taking final action. We would not want to elect someone to a high office and put our welfare in his hands, before finding out about his defects and weaknesses. Nor should an individual be canonized, and later have some major faults uncovered. We see many instances of the operation of this interesting idea.

In a court of law a prosecutor is appointed to assemble all of the evidence concerning the defendant's guilt, and do what he can to secure a conviction. Naturally there is a lawyer on the other side to see that all of the favorable facts are also clearly presented. These opposing legal representatives are encouraged to cross-examine witnesses and to get all of the testimonies possible, so that an accurate and intelligent decision can be made by the judge and jury.

This idea also has some applications in scientific research, in our personal religion, in our family relationships, and in our individual lives. It is the duty of parents, teachers, employers, friends, etc., to render this service to those for whom they have responsibility. The effectiveness with which hidden facts are brought out can very frequently determine the quality that our lives themselves will assume. This is especially true if we can uncover in advance enough of the adverse evidence to prevent any serious harm from being done. If you are going to hire a lawyer, it should be done early enough that he can help you to avoid making any mistakes in the first place. And those who have any ambitions to become worthy of high honors or great happiness might think it a good idea to get some kind of "devil's advocate" to point out their wrong attitudes and hurtful procedures before those have time to turn into deeds.

For example, a lawyer can figure out one's income tax advantages better before his client makes his report to the government than he can by trying to correct the mistakes afterwards. And instead of each of us waiting until judgment day to find what is written down in our book of life, it may be to our advantage to make sure as we go along that the catalogue is being filled up with only good deeds. Some unprejudiced procedures for checking up on ourselves as we proceed may upset our complacency a little more at the time, but in the long run it might be more profitable if the candidate had someone to help him detect his errors rather than being surprised when this information is used against him in the final judgment. Then it may be more difficult to persuade the judge and jury to change their opinions. Any action in correcting an error can be more easily handled when the investigation is done as far in advance as possible.

This program for an early and impartial check-up on ourselves is a little more difficult, inasmuch as we must usually serve as our *own* devil's advocate. In such a case our prejudice sometimes prevents us from getting unbiased facts It is certainly much more difficult to accurately pick out our own defects and weaknesses. Yet that is the most rewarding field for our investigation, and developing such an ability is something that we should work at vigorously.

The story is told of a man who traded some blankets to an Indian for a pony. However, the white man made a mistake and the Indian got too many blankets. The next day the Indian returned the surplus merchandise. The white man said, "Why didn't you keep them? I made the deal and I would probably never have discovered the mistake." The Indian put his hand on his heart and said, "I have a good man and a bad man in here. Good man say take blankets back, and bad man say keep blankets. I try to go to sleep but good man and bad man talk all night so I get no sleep. Now that I bring blankets back I feel good." The good man in the Indian's conscience was acting as his devil's advocate. Bringing out in advance the arguments that the Indian's bad man would not want mentioned, gave him peace. A good conscientious conscience can produce a great many favorable situations in our experience.

Every good action tends to beatify our lives. The action of the Indian's good man at least brought him a little closer to some kind of a canonization in the mind of the one he was doing business with. It is also important that we make ourselves worthy of bestowing some blessings and honors upon ourselves. We do ourselves a serious dishonor when we close our eyes to our own evil. There are several unpleasant worsening processes by which we Satanize ourselves, instead of getting our names in the catalogue with people worthy of great honor and happiness. The difference in people often comes because some fail to make an honest self-investigation, or allow their prejudices so many privileges that they can't tell right from wrong when they themselves are involved.

A woman once wrote to Ann Landers about one of her problems. She and her husband were both heavy smokers. They both decided that they should quit smoking so that they could set their small son a better example than they were doing as nicotine addicts. The husband quit as he had agreed, but his wife just couldn't put her resolution into operation. Instead she went underground with her bad habit, and indulged her practice only when no one was around. In presenting her problem to Miss Landers she said: "My deception is making a wreck out of me. Do you think it would be all right for us to find some good couple that didn't smoke and let them adopt little Earl?" Miss Landers wrote back and said, "If you can't stop smoking for your son, I think the next best solution would be for your husband to get rid of you and keep little Earl." Miss Landers was acting as a "devil's advocate" in getting a critical opinion to help a weak mother.

Abraham Lincoln employed a kind of devil's advocate when he kept two of his most bitter enemies in his cabinet because he wanted their frank criticism to test his own arguments, keep him on his toes, and prevent him from making too many mistakes for want of an opposite viewpoint. Some kings have been known to keep only friendly counselors to advise them. Others keep counselors who are not afraid to disagree with their monarchs. One such counselor used to present himself to his sovereign as "your Majesty's loyal opposition." If the counselor always agreed with his chief, there would likely be no reason for keeping that particular counselor. Many kings and other people have been saved from serious blunders by the "loyal opposition" of someone else, and of course the best time to correct any costly errors is always before they have been committed. This is one of the reasons why everyone should train a good conscience.

A good conscience serves as a built-in judge who has a great natural knowledge of right and wrong. It is also one of the best of the "devil's advocates," as it always has an intimate knowledge of both sides of our lives and can remind us of our wrong without fear of giving offense. Our conscience can also most effectively weigh our actions against our possibilities. But the conscience must not slight any of the evidence, for if only one side of the argument is presented, or if we use all of our resources arguing on just one side of the issue, then our judgment itself will be inaccurate. It is for this reason that we sometimes criticize the proceedings at funerals. Sometimes funerals are made up of nothing but extreme eulogies and one-sided presentations. Because we feel no need for revealing weaknesses or calling attention to a person's problems at his funeral, the service may get a little bit out of balance. But the most dangerous off-balance takes place when we assume a one-sided view of ourselves in either direction.

With an extreme statement, a husband was once praising his wife before a group of his friends. He said that she was the most wonderful person in the world and that she had no bad habits of any kind. He was so completely and highly favorable that his listeners became a little bit suspicious. One friend questioned him and said, "But she must do something wrong." The husband said, "Well, she does cuss right smart when she's drunk." There may be nothing seriously wrong with one-sidedness when one is praising his wife, or giving eulogies at the funeral of his friend, but prejudice and one-sidedness do not serve a very practical purpose when they are indulged in by a court of law, or in the process of dealing with ourselves. It is difficult to live very successfully when we set our nets to catch all of life's compliments, while we carefully let all of the criticisms go by without consideration.

There is in every man something that has been called an impenetrable mystery so far as he himself is concerned. We never see ourselves as others see us. And we always seem to be able to speak endlessly about ourselves without giving a complete or accurate picture. We spend a great deal of time alibiing for ourselves, and covering up our errors and mistakes with excuses and rationalizations. But when we stand before God we may get our feelings hurt, as he is very likely to insist on having a fairly accurate balance in the evidence. We may even feel an overwhelming humiliation if we discover then for the first time that we are not what we thought we were, nor what we wanted and hoped to be. We can easily be misled when our evidence is loaded with prejudice. How much more helpful it might be for us, if we insist on "the truth, the whole truth, and nothing but the truth" as we go along!

A lot of time may be spent after one is dead in collecting the favorable and unfavorable evidence concerning his life, but in our own situation it may be more profitable to get any adverse evidence before we die. Then by correction we might increase our own chances for favorable post-mortem action. The truth is much more easily available to us when we ourselves take an intelligent interest in it and work at producing it a little more vigorously. If we plan and work for our own forgiveness and success in advance, God's grace will be more abundantly available to us.

Elijah's Raven

One of the very interesting events recorded in the Old Testament centers in the life of the prophet Elijah. King Ahab had married the idol-worshipping Jezebel, and together they had imported several hundred of the priests of Baal, who almost destroyed Jehovah worship in Israel. The greatest influence preventing their complete success was the fiery old prophet Elijah.

As a part of God's punishment for Israel's wickedness, a divine decree was sent forth that there should be a three-year national famine in which no rain should fall in Israel. To protect Elijah, the Lord said to him:

"Get thee hence ... and hide thyself by the brook Cherith, that is before Jordan. And it shall be, that thou shalt drink of the brook; and I have commanded the ravens to feed thee there. So he went and did according unto the word of the Lord ... and the ravens brought him bread and flesh in the morning, and bread and flesh in the evening; and he drank of the brook.

"And it came to pass after a while, that the brook dried up, because there had been no rain in the land. And the word of the Lord came unto him saying, Arise, get thee to Zarephath, which belongeth to Zidon, and dwell there: behold I have commanded a widow-woman there to sustain thee. So he arose and went to Zarephath. And when he came to the gate of the city, behold, the widow-woman was there gathering of sticks: and he called to her, and said, Fetch me, I pray thee, a little water in a vessel, that I may drink. And as she was going to fetch it, he called to her, and said, Bring me, I pray thee, a morsel of bread in thine hand. And she said, As the Lord liveth, I have not a cake, but an handful of meal in a barrel, and a little oil in a cruse: and behold, I am gathering two sticks, that I may go in and dress it for me and my son, that we may eat it, and die. And Elijah said unto her, Fear not; go and do as thou hast said: but make me thereof a little cake first, and bring it unto me, and after make for thee and for thy son. For thus saith the Lord God of Israel, the barrel of meal shall not waste, neither shall the cruse of oil fail, until the day that the Lord sendeth rain upon the earth. And she went and did according to the saying of Elijah: and she, and he, and her house, did eat many days. And the barrel of meal wasted not, neither did the cruse of oil fail." (1 Kings 17:3-16.)

The scriptures are filled with special blessings given by the Lord to those helping to accomplish his purposes. But we sometimes do ourselves great injury by assuming that the Lord is also going to do that work which he expects us to do. This can produce in us a kind of personal irresponsibility and mental laziness that destroys our chances for success. There are some people who feel that because inspiration and revelation are important factors in the work of the Lord, our own efforts are not necessary.

And we may be more or less inclined to feel that if Elijah lived out of the widow's barrel of meal and received meat from the ravens, why shouldn't we? Because God spent forty days in the Mount with Moses, that does not mean that he is going to spend an equal time with each of us. Some of us must learn from the experiences of others. Jesus had something to say about this idea in the first lesson given in his hometown after the beginning of his public ministry. The scripture says:

"And Jesus returned in the power of the Spirit into Galilee: and there went out a fame of him through all of the region round about. And he taught in their synagogues, being glorified of all. And he came to Nazareth where he had been brought up: and as his custom was, he went into the synagogue on the sabbath day and stood up for to read. And there was delivered unto him the book of the prophet Esaias. And when he opened the book, he found the place where it was written, The Spirit of the Lord is upon me, because he hath anointed me to preach the gospel to the poor; he hath sent me to heal the broken-hearted, to preach deliverance to the captives, and recovering of sight to the blind, to set at liberty them that are bruised, to preach the acceptable year of the Lord. And he closed the book, and he gave it again to the minister and sat down. And the eyes

of all them that were in the synagogue were fastened on him."
Apparently a discussion followed, and Jesus said to his hearers,
"This day is this scripture fulfilled in your ears."

The people said, "Is not this Joseph's son? And he said
unto them, Ye will surely say unto me this proverb, Physician
heal thyself: whatsoever we have heard done in Capernaum, do
also here in thy country. But I tell you of a truth, many
widows were in Israel in the days of Elias, when the heaven was
shut up three years and six months, when great famine was
throughout the land; but unto none of them was Elias sent, save
unto Sarepta, a city of Sidon, unto a woman that was a widow.
And many lepers were in Israel in the time of Eliseus the
prophet; and none of them was cleansed saving Naaman, the
Syrian." Then something happened to upset them, as the scripture says that "all they in the synagogue when they heard these
things were filled with wrath, and rose up, and thrust him out
of the city, and led him to the brow of the hill whereon their
city was built, that they might cast him down headlong. But he
passing through the midst of them went his way." (Luke
4:14-30.)

I suppose they were disturbed because they weren't all given
an inexhaustible barrel of meal or a raven to deliver them some
T-bone steaks. I thought of this principle the other day as a
discouraged salesman was telling me how faithfully he had
prayed that the Lord would make him successful in his sales
work. He seemed to think that if he prayed he wouldn't need to
follow through on his training course, or make any serious effort
to solve his own personal problems. Because of his extreme "call
reluctance" he hoped that the Lord would make regular effort
on *his* part unnecessary. Substantially he was praying for a barrel
of success that would not waste, and an unfailing cruse of oil to
go with it. Subconsciously he hoped that Elijah's raven would
bring him a brief case full of signed orders with checks attached.
Many of us share in this vice of irresponsibility.

Even when a farmer does a good job in teaching his Sunday
School class, it is still required by the Lord for him to fertilize
the soil and keep the weeds out of the onions if he expects to
get a good crop. We are entitled to the greatest blessings of the
Lord when we are obedient to him and have done all that we

can do personally. The Lord expects us to work and study and be resourceful. Any father, especially a rich and powerful one, might easily make hot-house plants and weaklings out of his children by doing everything for them and thereby robbing them of their responsibility. The wisest father is the one who teaches his sons to help themselves. God could do everything for us if he desired. It isn't necessary for birds or animals to go to school or get jobs. But if we are to think and grow we should exercise in the sweat of our own faces and not depend too much upon the ravens. We may not know why only Naaman was cleansed out of all of the leprous people, and we should not be too badly upset if all of the great miracles are not performed for us personally.

In some periods of the world's history there have been numerous revelations sent from God, while other periods have been characterized by comparative silence. However, that does not mean that God is dead or is disinterested in us. It does not mean that God has gone out of business merely because a raven is not waiting on our doorstep every morning with our breakfast and a blueprint for a day of successful activities. God has given us the great blessing of life. He has also given us the privilege of living it as we choose. We have the holy scriptures as our guide, including detailed instructions as to exactly how our lives should be lived.

But it is not necessarily true that those who receive the greatest number of special manifestations are any better off than those who obey God because of the revelations given to someone else. Many of those who personally saw and heard Jesus turned away from him and refused his message. The people of his own hometown tried to throw him over a cliff. The Lord said to Thomas, "Thomas because thou hast seen me, thou hast believed: blessed are they that have not seen, and yet have believed." (John 20:29.)

I know of an office worker who, when a problem comes up, would rather ask the office manager or some other associate for the answer than look it up for himself. Because he is unwilling to personally have this learning experience, he never learns very much about his own office procedures. There are a lot of us who behave like that with the Lord, whereas God is pleased when we put on our thinking caps and get some of the answers for ourselves. He has said, "Behold, I say unto you, that you must study it out in your mind." (D&C 9:8.) The Lord has already answered most of our questions in saying: "Search the scriptures; for in them ye think ye have eternal life: and they are they which testify of me." (John 5:39.)

With the scriptures and our brains the Lord has given us an ability to answer many of our own prayers. If we wanted a drink of water from the stream, we would not ordinarily write to the Governor or to the President, or ask the Lord to handle the job by sending a raven. If we desired to strengthen our arm muscles, we would not ordinarily pray that the raven would have them there when we woke up in the morning, as this procedure would be contrary to God's laws of diet, exercise, and growth. Through the establishment of his natural laws he has made us aware of how to build good arm muscles and get a lot of hard work done at the same time. There may be no particular point in asking God to forgive our enemies, because we can do that ourselves even better than he can. It may also be pretty difficult for him to make us honest, kind, and faithful, without a substantial effort on our part. Since time began God has been praying for us to answer that prayer for him.

At the wedding feast at Cana, the people involved ran out of wine and an appeal was made to Jesus. By some process that we do not yet understand, he changed the water into wine, enabling the feast to go on without interruption. But like the miracle of the raven, the miracle of changing water into wine has only been performed once in the history of the world. Yet when some of the most ordinary farmers get hold of a little good real estate, the right climate, and some young grape plants they can turn millions of gallons of water into wine every year. This takes a little longer and may require some extra effort, but up until now this is the only method that the Lord has approved for general use. And when we do it this way he throws in a good set of muscles and some extra horticultural know-how free of charge.

The scriptures say that the raven brought bread and flesh to Elijah in the morning and in the evening. But I suppose that even then Elijah had to cook the meat and make the sandwiches himself. And by the Lord's program of self-help we can bring about almost any blessing that we desire. People who are successful are likely to speak of themselves as self-made. And when we have someday qualified for God's highest kingdom, we may take an even greater joy in having played an important part in bringing about our own eternal exaltation.

The animal creations all operate under a set of instincts which permit them no choices. Only to man did God say, "Thou mayest choose for thyself." Not only are we obligated to make our own choices, but we are the engineers in building our own bodies out of the dust of the earth. By our own thinking we also determine the kind of minds and attitudes that we will have. God has atoned for our sins and redeemed us from death, but he has also ordained that we must finally be judged according to our works. The Apostle Paul points out that everyone is required to "work out your own salvation with fear and trembling." (Phil. 2:12.) Each will qualify for the celestial or the terrestrial or the telestial glory according to his own merit. And the lowest kingdom which is not a kingdom of glory will be inhabited by those who have brought the most demerits upon themselves.

We are grateful to God for our lives, our possibilities, and our opportunities. We are grateful for our freedom and that awful responsibility that has left some part of our final exaltation in our own hands. May we be inspired to do our best and make the most of our opportunities.

An Episode With a Sequel

Canada has just finished celebrating her centennial year. During the last one hundred years this gigantic half-continent has been explored, developed, and linked together as a great nation. In terms of population, Canada ranks twenty-sixth among the nations of the world. However, in land area she ranks third, and her possibilities for development are unlimited. Canada is one of the great exporting nations. She also provides one of the most desirable places in which to live.

During her centennial year many conventions were held in Canada, and many important studies were made concerning her future possibilities. The political leaders and industrial representatives of many nations visited Canada during her one hundredth year, and gave lavish commendation for her accomplishments. Then in its November monthly letter, the Royal Bank of Canada presented an interesting article under the title of "Whither now?" And this is always a very good question. It is not uncommon in the lives of nations and individuals for someone to work up to a high point of achievement, and then suffer a letdown in proportion.

In fact, our accomplishments sometimes actually become stumbling blocks that get in the way of our progress. Nations, like individuals, can sometimes lose their lives while trying to find them. When we over-relax to repair our strength, we are sometimes unable to get going again. Our complacency, or the sins that may be brought on by our success, can often destroy our future without our realizing it. Many temporary successes have touched off some cases of permanently arrested development.

So after Canada's centennial celebration, a forward-seeing editor asks Canadians, "Whither now?" That is, what should we do after the excitement is over, and the dignitaries have gone home? This question reminds us of Rudyard Kipling's poem, the

"Recessional." In 1897 Mr. Kipling put into verse his famous philosophy that was inspired by the sixtieth anniversary celebration of Queen Victoria's ascension to the British throne. Britain had had a wonderful sixty years and had fully earned the right to be called "Great Britain." A magnificent celebration was appropriately held in recognition of her tremendous accomplishments. Mr. Kipling addressed his prayer to God that all Britishers might remember that a damaging recession can sometimes take place not only among nations but also in business, religion, and individual honor.

The dictionary describes a recessional as a withdrawal or a retreat. In some churches a recessional hymn is sung as the clergy and the choir withdraw from the chancel for their return trip to the robing rooms. And while the withdrawal of the world's great men from England was taking place, Mr. Kipling addressed the Creator and prayed that Britain would not withdraw from those qualities that had originally brought her greatness about. He says:

> God of our fathers, known of old—
> Lord of our far-flung battle line—
> Beneath whose awful hand we hold
> Dominion over palm and pine—
> Lord God of Hosts, be with us yet,
> Lest we forget—lest we forget!

> The tumult and the shouting dies—
> The Captains and the Kings depart—
> Still stands thine ancient sacrifice,
> An humble and a contrite heart.
> Lord God of Hosts, be with us yet,
> Lest we forget—lest we forget!

> Far-called, our navies melt away—
> On dune and headland sinks the fire—
> Lo, all our pomp of yesterday
> Is one with Nineveh and Tyre!
> Judge of the Nations, spare us yet,
> Lest we forget—lest we forget!

If, drunk with sight of power, we loose
Wild tongues that have not Thee in awe—
Such boasting as the Gentiles use,
Or lesser breeds without the Law—
Lord God of Hosts, be with us yet,
Lest we forget—lest we forget!

For heathen heart that puts her trust
In reeking tube and iron shard—
All valiant dust that builds on dust,
And guarding, calls not Thee to guard,
For frantic boast and foolish word,
Have mercy on Thy people, Lord! Amen!

This great poem advises caution in our successes. This is also what the Canadian bank letter does. It suggests that Canadians beware lest their centennial year should represent—and I quote—"an episode without a sequel."

Canada has only one close neighbor. And because a neighbor's success can sometimes be about as important as your own, all citizens of the United States join in congratulating Canada on her century of outstanding progress. We are all very grateful that living on the other side of our three-thousand-mile border, we have such a wonderful, friendly, prosperous nation. We are grateful that Canada ranks at the very top of the list so far as trustworthiness, honesty, and righteousness are concerned. Canadians are devoted to the highest ideals of freedom, and they set an outstanding example in good conduct.

Canada also has a stable, dependable government. We are very pleased that unlike some other nations, Canada is not trying to bury us. Nor is she sending out hordes of troublemakers trying to exhaust us into failure. We have no fear that Canada would ever permit its territory to be used to build atomic launching pads from which an enemy nation could attack the United States. We are also grateful that it is not necessary to defend our extensive Canadian borders. We know that Canada is not inclined to any kind of national blackmail, or a desire to rule other people by force. And we are particularly happy that Canadians are the kind of people they are, and we feel confident that they will continue their wonderful upward progress.

This idea of "Whither now?" should never be lost sight of by any nation, or by any individual. Everyone is always faced with the possibility of a recessional. In the words of the bank letter, everyone's life may become "an episode without a sequel."

The dictionary says that an episode is one section in a series. It may be one chapter in a narrative, or one incident helping to make up the experience of one's life. The sections in some movie and television serials are called episodes.

The dictionary goes on to describe "a sequel" as some literary work that continues the narrative from the one that preceded it. The sequel has to do with the subsequent happenings. It refers to the events and circumstances that follow. In our national and individual affairs, our present loses much of its importance, unless what follows continues the good quality and high order. Certainly we have no desire to become "one with Nineveh and Tyre."

The present condition of mother England herself is not a happy sequel to her great past. A part of the glory that was Britain's has vanished from the earth. Great Britain is no longer as great as she used to be. Her present condition may indicate that something went wrong so far as Mr. Kipling's prayer is concerned. The vast British empire once covered a quarter of the globe. Britain was probably the world's leading sponsor of orderly government, education, religion, trade, prosperity, and progress. Britain and her offshoot nations are the only nations that have made this idea of democracy and free enterprise work on a large scale over a long period. More than any other nation, it was Britain under the leadership of Winston Churchill that saved the world from the mechanized might of the tyrannical, murderous, German madman, Adolf Hitler. How unfortunate it is that British greatness has not continued in full measure! Britain has had many great episodes that do not have sequels of corresponding excellence.

In recent years Britain has been called the sick man of Europe. Some people now see her as a sin-laden, morally compromised ghost of the great nation that she formerly was.

She may have forgotten some important things about greatness and her ghost lacks much of the pride, power, influence, and honor that she once possessed. We are accustomed to speaking of the fall of past nations. But Great Britain is our own flesh and blood and is now very ill with some serious moral, educational, and financial diseases. Nations in the past have sickened and died when their recessions have gone beyond the point of no return. And when one nation falls, every other nation suffers a loss. Think of the world tragedy involved in the fall of the ancient nation of Israel. That nation was organized by God himself, and designed to be a "chosen generation, a royal priesthood, an holy nation, a peculiar people." (1 Pet. 2:9.) But Israel fell because she failed to follow through on God's program.

She had some wonderful episodes, but instead of equally wonderful sequels her great episodes were followed by long recessions, serious rebellious periods of degrading captivity, and a highly regrettable apostasy from God. Her sequel was spoiled by her own sins. The pattern of having great beginnings followed by future failures has also been a course pursued by millions of individuals. Very often our lives are built on a steadily rising plateau. But if we take too much time out to celebrate, or over-relax our effort, or change the success formula, we may start a long downward recession. There are a great many ways to destroy a high grade continuity in national or individual lives. Sometimes our episodes are thrown out of balance by our letdowns. Sometimes we lose interest when we imagine that we have arrived. We often become careless and reverse the process that brought our original success about. Sometimes we get peevish or arrogant or proud. Sometimes, like some ancient and modern nations, we turn our backs on God. Because the Israelites wanted to be like other nations they lost their sense of identity. And it's always pretty dangerous for a nation sponsored by God to forget who they are.

However, our most serious concern does not now center in other nations. Presently the United States is also being accused of losing its sense of identity. In our fear of the Communists, we have tended to adopt too many of their procedures and techniques. Instead of clinging to our own standards as a Christian nation, we are trying in some instances to excel the Communists on their own grounds. Neither nation nor individual should ever forget their divine mission. How interesting it would be to see a graph of our country's booms and recessions, marking its political, financial, and religious upswings and downdrafts. How would we like to know where we stand on God's altimeter, and see his projection of our future success? Even with such exalted titles as "the Holy Roman Empire," or "Great Britain," or the "United States of America," or "God's Chosen People," a nation can still sink into oblivion if it forgets those righteous principles on which its greatness was predicated and attained. The Tetrarch of Judea was not saved from death by his high title of Herod the Great. And the fact that we give people such exalted labels as Grand Duke, Lord Mayor, President, Kaiser, Czar, Emperor, or Sultan doesn't seem to prevent us from toppling when we do the wrong things.

Someone has said that it is easy to become a captain, but it is hard to stay one. It is particularly hard to remain a captain while we are violating those laws by which our greatness was attained. If we had a graph representing the performance of our individual lives, we might find some very sharp angles where the lines representing our success would zigzag sharply up and down. Some lives are subject to such violent fluctuations that any small disturbance may touch off a precipitous decline and wipe out all of its equity in greatness. Or a life may suffer a more gradual decline by each succeeding episode being a little bit inferior to the one that preceded it. When we start losing our faith, or our sense of identity, or our quality of excellence, then we soon begin getting sick. And often without knowing it, we go into a series of declines resembling the business indicators of a deepening depression.

One of the greatest challenges of our lives is to try to bring about a series of sequels on an ever increasing level of accomplishment. This means that every occasion in life should be a great occasion. The bank letter says that in spite of Canada's substantial progress, she still promises much more than she has ever delivered. Certainly our own accomplishments are not equal to our potentialities. This means that to that extent we are wasting our resources. Think what a happy position the United States would be in if all Americans maintained themselves at their maximums. No one needs to throw away his own chances because someone else does. And by properly regulating our individual sequels, the small acorns of our present accomplishment may become the mighty oaks of our potentiality.

The most desirable sequel for our mortality will come about as we honor that great Being in whose image we were created. Then as a sequel to this important existence, we will all qualify for eternal life in God's highest kingdom.

Father's Day

We have an interesting custom among us of setting aside special days to think about special things. We set aside the second Sunday in May as Mother's Day, and on that day we let our minds reach up and try to understand the purpose for which this day was set apart. We set apart the 30th day of May as Memorial Day in which we remember the departed. We set apart the second Sunday in June as Children's Day, for some very good reasons. We also have Armed Forces Day, Flag Day, Independence Day, United Nations Day, and Veterans Day. We have days on which we celebrate the birth of Washington, Lincoln and Columbus. We have Labor Day, Thanksgiving, Easter and Christmas. God himself has set apart one-seventh of all the days to serve as our Heavenly Father's days. From the top of Mount Sinai, God said: "Remember the sabbath day, to keep it holy. Six days shalt thou labour, and do all thy work: but the seventh day is the sabbath of the Lord thy God: in it thou shalt not do any work, thou, nor thy son, nor thy daughter, thy manservant nor thy maidservant, nor thy cattle, nor the stranger that is within thy gates. For in six days the Lord made heaven and earth, the sea, and all that in them is, and rested the seventh day: wherefore the Lord blessed the sabbath day and hallowed it." (Exod. 20:8-11.)

Someone has said that the human mind has some of the qualities of the tendrils of a climbing vine. It tends to attach itself, and draw itself upward by what it is put in contact with. On these fifty-two special Father's Days we put our minds in contact with God and the program that he expects us to follow in working out our eternal exaltation before him. Then on the third Sunday in June we set aside a lesser kind of Father's Day for the purpose of honoring our earthly fathers, and even though no day should be compared with the Sabbath, our earthly Father's Day is still very important. On the sixth day of creation as the crowning scene in this great drama of the universe man made his appearance upon the world stage. The scripture says:

"So God created man in his own image; in the image of God created he him; male and female created he them." And then God gave the first and probably the most important command ever given. The record says: "And God blessed them and God said unto them, Be fruitful, and multiply, and replenish the earth, and subdue it and have dominion over . . . every living thing that moveth upon the earth." (Gen. 1:27-28.) This was man's great commission providing for his fatherhood. God himself organized the family and he decreed that everyone should be trained in righteousness to the highest point of capability. And yet from one point of view the begetting of offspring, when taken by itself, is an ordinary office, as it is one that is held by all forms of life from the top to the bottom of the scale. However, the lives of animals are governed by predetermined instinctive laws from which they may not deviate. It was only to man that God said, "Thou mayest choose for thyself."

The dictionary has some interesting ideas about fathers. It says that, "A father is a male parent." But this father's title has some broader definitions. One may also earn this title of father by forming ties of marriage or adoption, or he may become a father by his attitudes and abilities in doing the things that fathers do. Father is a designation given to a step-father, or a father-in-law, or a father of his country, or a father of ideas and ideals. When Alexander the Great was twelve years old, his father King Philip arranged for Aristotle, the great Macedonian philosopher and orator, to become his companion and tutor. Later Alexander said that he was more grateful to Aristotle for his knowledge than he was to Philip for his life. He said that while Philip was the father of his body, Aristotle was the father of his mind. And if you would like to have a good phrase to think about on Father's Day, there it is.

Physical paternity is one of the greatest of all wonders. It produces this miraculous combination of flesh and blood, bones and tissue, which is the masterpiece of creation. But what about mental paternity and spiritual paternity? This is the way we get our vision, our understanding, our religion, and our personalities. Certainly the functions of fatherhood do not end at conception or at birth. To be successful the begotten must also be endowed with faith, love, and obedience to God.

The dictionary says that a father is an "originator," but he is also an exemplar, a teacher, and a source of inspiration. A good father is one who cares for someone or who properly directs their lives. The dictionary says that fathers are sometimes the leading men of countries or cities or councils. The senators of ancient Rome were referred to as "the fathers." We have our own American founding fathers who were the members of the constitutional convention of 1787, and other early American statesmen. But the most important founding fathers are those who found families and lead children back to God. Attitudes, ambitions, ideas, ideals, and successes all have to have fathers, the same as people do, to get them started. Nothing either good or bad gets very far without a father.

Shakespeare says, "Cowards father cowards." Swift says, "Men of wit have fathered what they writ." And Jesus referred to Satan as the father of lies. (See John 8:44.) He is the instigator and fosterer of falsehoods. All good comes from God. And among the greatest of a father's duties is to father success and happiness in the lives of his offspring. Fatherhood is the process by which our own inheritance is passed on to others.

Abraham was designated by God himself as the father of the faithful. Hippocrates was the father of medicine. Wilbur and Orville Wright were the fathers of aviation. George Washington was the father of his country. And a father of a good family is the one who passes virtues, abilities, and good attitudes on to his children. Elbert Hubbard once said, "I am looking out through the library window into the apple orchard, and I see millions of blossoms that will never materialize or become fruit for lack of vitalization." The proper destiny of an apple blossom is that it should become an apple. But before that can happen, a bee or some other instrument of vitalization must plant the fertilizing pollen in the blossom's heart to give it its opportunity to reach its destiny. And if human beings are to reach the place that God has ordained for them, it is also necessary that their minds and spirits shall be impregnated with good attitudes and helpful ideas.

A story is told about a situation where it was necessary for a young man to be lowered down over a cliff on a rope to perform a hazardous mission. He was the only one of those available who in weight was light enough to do the job successfully. When he was asked if he would accept the assignment with its accompanying danger, he said, "I will if you will let my father hold the rope." This young man may have had great confidence in the other men around him. They may have been more skilled for this work than was his father, but you need a special kind of confidence in people when you are going to place your life in their hands. Many fathers have been complimented and thrilled when danger or trouble threatened their children, to hear them instinctively call their father's name. What our world needs more than most other things is more people who qualify to hold the rope, and to have someone that we can trust and in whom we can believe without reservation.

Many years ago when I was very young I had what to me was a very serious accident. My face was badly cut, which resulted in considerable bleeding. While we were waiting for the doctor, my mother sat by the bed and held my hand. My injuries may have done just as well if she had gone about her duties and let me wait alone. But at that young age, it helped me to know that my mother had nothing else as important to do as to hold my hand and soothe my fearful spirit in my emergency. By this process she performed more healing in my soul than would have been possible for any medicine. Now after these many years have passed, I have no recollection of the pain I suffered, but I can clearly recall the feeling of assurance that I had because of my mother's presence. She was not only with me physically, but I was healed by the ministration of her spirit. And I felt no fear of harm while my mother was sitting at my bedside. But even if some harm should come, I could bear it far more easily because of the sustaining love of my mother, which not only lessened my pain but also reduced my fear.

Once as Jesus was making his way through the crowd a woman who had been ill for twelve years approached him from behind and touched the hem of his garment. She had thought that if she could but touch his clothing, she should be made whole. And as she touched him, she immediately felt her body acquire the needed healing and strength. Jesus also knew that some healing virtue had gone out of him and he turned around and said, "Who touched my clothes?" His disciples said unto him, "Thou seest the multitude thronging thee, and sayest thou, who touched me?" But the woman knew what he meant, and

she fell down before him and confessed what she had done. And
Jesus said unto her, "Daughter, thy faith hath made thee whole;
go in peace." (Mark 5:27-34.) On another occasion the scripture
says, "And the whole multitude sought to touch him: for there
went virtue out of him, and healed them all." (Luke 6:19.)

On many occasions I have been on the receiving end of this
healing process. I have felt the healing virtue pass into me from
my mother and my father to cure my many infirmities. Virtue
can pass between people in many forms. A mother's kiss can
cure a bump on the head. And a few kind words can change the
direction of one's entire life. The virtues, love and faith, that
radiate from a mother can cure a multitude of troubles. And so
can a father's courage, and a father's example, and even a
father's correction.

Some time ago a father thought it necessary for him to
correct a son with a spanking. Afterward as the son got
undressed and into bed, the father talked to the sobbing boy
about the seriousness of what he had done. Then as the father
left the son's room to go back downstairs, the son stopped his
sobbing long enough to say to his father, "Good night, daddy."
The son had felt badly about what he had done wrong, but he
knew that his father was doing what was right and in the son's
interests. The son knew that the father loved him very much,
and he also knew that the father would not fail his son even
though the spanking hurt his father more than it did him. Even
in the spanking, the son felt virtue pass into him from his
father. It may have been some similar experience that made
Solomon say, "A wise son maketh a glad father." (Prov. 10:1.)

What a great thrill it is to feel absolute confidence in
someone else, especially when you yourself are permitted to
draw on his supply. On the night of Benedict Arnold's betrayal
everything was in commotion. No one knew how widespread the
treason was, or what might happen to the Colonials' cause before
dawn. In appointing the father of Daniel Webster to stand guard
throughout the night at the headquarters of the colonies, General
Washington said, "Captain Webster, I can trust you." Captain
Webster was not only faithful to General Washington, but he was
also able to transmit his own virtue on to his son. Most men
take great joy in becoming a father. What joy there also should

be in developing these godly traits. When the Lord sent Moses down into Egypt to deliver the captive Israelites, he sent Aaron along to be the mouthpiece for Moses. Then God said to Moses, "And Aaron shall be to thee instead of a mouth, and thou shalt be to him instead of God." (Exod. 4:16.) Aaron might have said, as so many grateful people do, "He seemed to me like a father." And one of the duties of fathers is to represent God with his children. Fathers are supposed to have a good firm hold on the rope. There is a popular song entitled, "I'll Get By As Long As I Have You." And that furnishes a wonderful sentiment that we might sing to two of the greatest people in our lives both of whom are our fathers, and the third Sunday in June is dedicated to them both. And we ourselves can learn to be more capable fathers to our own children if we are faithful sons of God.

Andrew Gillies wrote some lines entitled "Two Prayers:"

> Last night my little boy confessed to me
> Some childish wrong;
> And kneeling at my knee,
> He prayed with tears—
> "Dear God, make me a man
> Like Daddy—wise and strong;
> I know you can."
>
> Then while he slept
> I knelt beside his bed,
> Confessed my sins,
> And prayed with low-bowed head,—
> "O God, make me a child
> Like my child here—
> Pure, guileless, and
> Trusting Thee with faith sincere."

Focusing

In providing film strips or moving pictures to be shown by amateurs, the manufacturers often have the first frame made up with the word "focus." Before any beginning, the camera should be adjusted to light, distance, timing, etc., so that the pictures can be clearly and easily seen. Nothing makes us quite as miserable as to have fuzzy pictures, blurred words, and an unsynchronized sound track. Without a good focus, the listeners must strain over garbled, half-understandable sights and sounds, and still get only a fraction of the message. The dictionary says that a focus is a place where the rays of light, heat or sound converge.

This idea of starting off with an accurate adjustment is a good one in any program. But one of the most difficult places to avoid distortions is in human beings. Frequently, our communications even with ourselves are very indistinct. However, like the picture machine, we are also adjustable. Our eyes can adjust to light, darkness, and distance. Sometimes, we wear spectacles to improve our focus. With the right amount of work and discipline our muscles will adjust to the most difficult labor. Our bodies can learn to accommodate themselves to summer and winter, fatigue and hunger. We know that our stomachs shrink when they are empty, and so do our minds. Our conscience is capable of being made more accurate. But when we get too much evil and error operating in our lives, then the images that are flashed upon our mental screens come out all mixed up. It doesn't take very much sin in our machinery to give a garbled sound track, a blurred meaning, and an unsatisfactory emotional outlook.

Without the ability to adjust, all marriage partners and everyone else would be in trouble. Everyone must also make some adjustments to maturity and reason. These wonderful, though complicated, human adjusting devices make it possible for us to tune out selfishness and focus our minds on the best interests of each other. Our accomplishments immediately improve and become more worthwhile when our minds and spirits are adjusted to greater industry, firmer faith, deeper love, and a more fruitful righteousness.

Sometimes a person may get physically cross-eyed, or his eyes lose their coordination, or a double vision may destroy his focus. The story is told of a prize fighter who was rather badly beaten in the fight ring. In commiserating with him after the match one of his friends said, "You really did get a bad licking didn't you?" The fighter said, "I certainly did. But, I know now where I made my mistake." He said, "I should have knocked him out in the first round when he was alone." When one gets a hard enough bump on the head to put some imaginary prize fighters into the ring, his problems become more highly complicated. We also get some spiritual, mental, and financial bumps that occasionally tend to throw us out of focus.

Recently, a little four-year-old boy went to the optometrist. He had one good eye and one that the doctor described as a "lazy eye." Then for a long period the doctor had the boy wear a patch over his good eye in order to force the lazy eye to strengthen itself with twice as much work. This is also a pretty good way to increase the ambition and enlarge those successes that we desire for ourselves.

Jesus spoke of lazy eyes, and he also mentioned lazy ears and hearts. Some people are so unadjusted to the gospel that they don't see, hear, or understand it. Our lazy eyes should learn to see more worthwhile objectives, our lazy ears should hear more of the right kind of sounds, and our lazy souls should take a firmer hold on ambition and develop a stronger grip on righteousness. A firmer faith and a more intense devotion will also give us a better focus on what we want to become. There are some bats and other animals that are blind in the daylight. Their eyes are so adjusted that they can only see at night. But many people also have this unfortunate adjustment to darkness.

Jesus had our bat inclinations in mind when he said, "They have sinned a very grievous sin, in that they are walking in darkness at noon day." (D&C 95:6.) Concerning some of those who are blind to the light, the Lord said, "And their hearts are corrupt, and full of wickedness and abominations; and they love darkness rather than light." (D&C 10:21.) So many people are presently making an adjustment to evil by cultivating an appetite for the wrong things. When people build bars in their homes instead of altars, they are making an adjustment to booze. And by misdirecting our attention we can become more interested in a horse race or in a prize fight than in the celestial kingdom. It doesn't require a great heart or a profound mind to learn to love profanity, nicotine, dope, immorality, selfishness, and disobedience.

More than anything else, we need to adjust our lives to God. We need to understand that to do right is pleasant, and to have faith gives us power. Success always comes when we effectively focus our abilities on doing those things that God has prescribed to bring about our eternal exaltation, and we can avoid stumbling in the darkness only as we center our attention on those things that are right.

An interesting examination in observation and remembering must be passed by all Boy Scouts before they can be advanced to second class rank. They are asked to look into some store window for a few minutes and then report as many as possible of the specific things that they saw. Many Scouts fail this simple examination. Some don't see those things that are right before their eyes, and others soon forget even those objects that they did see. But this only indicates that important human weakness pointed out by Jesus about eyes that see not. Recently, I talked with a man whose problems came because he makes himself blind to reason, and where his wife and children are concerned he can't understand fairness or decency. It is also very difficult for him to see his responsibilities or remember his duties. The scriptures are filled with advice about remembering. They say: "Remember the Sabbath day, remember thy Creator, remember faith, hope, charity, and love." They say we are to remember to keep an eye single to the glory of God. Unfortunately, we fail in many parts of life's observation and memory tests. After many years of looking into our own store windows, we may yet forget the purpose of life and be unable to remember what we need to do to gain eternal success.

God has given us a detailed set of holy scriptures to teach

us life's purposes and help us to remember to do them. But even the scriptures are of little value, if we fail to adjust ourselves to them. Some can't even adjust to the voice of their own conscience, or to the righteous testimony of other people, or to the dictates of their own reason. When these important adjustments are not made, life may appear mostly as a spiritual blur which we don't understand. And what is worse, we never find out what it's about because we don't make the necessary adjustments.

When a baby is born he has eyes, but they can't discern objects. He has ears, but they are unable to distinguish sounds. His legs are as perfectly fashioned as yours and mine, but they are unable to bear even his childish weight. He has hands and arms, but they lack coordination and usefulness. This makes life little more than an unexciting, uninteresting, unmeaningful blur. But if a group of babies effectively work at the controls for a few years, they can change themselves into an equal number of doctors, generals, presidents, and workers. By similar processes, we can change ourselves from weaklings and sinners into doers of righteousness, deserving God's greatest blessings.

Jesus spoke of another important adjustment in order to reach the highest goals. He said that we must be "born again." If we can make this adjustment effectively, we are pretty well on our way. For then we will be able to repent of our sins, be baptized, and start over with a better focus on those virtues in which we were previously deficient. No one needs more than one physical birth, and one water baptism will last a lifetime. But we can be reborn every day, and we can give birth to as many new abilities as we like. We can also make any other adjustments necessary to bring about the fullest measure of success.

Of course, we should be careful not to focus on the wrong things. And when pleasure, crime, and sin get too much of a pull on our attention, we may have some real problems. The great psychologist, William James, said, "That which holds our attention determines our action." People have negative minds because they focus on negative things. We create depraved minds when we keep them filled with depraved, unhappy thoughts. Think what is happening in our America because of the attention that is being given to the vast amount of pornographic literature, and the large number of degrading movies. All of the civilizations of the past have fallen because they have set their attention on those things that the Lord has forbidden. One important instrument to improve our focus is a good set of eye blinders, so that we can block out from our attention all of those things that will do us harm. Then when one's life is properly directed with his mind focused on the right things, and his personality sufficiently motivated, he can reach the greatest accomplishments.

I know of a man who once decided that he would like to become a salesman. He carefully considered all of the facts. He definitely made up his mind that this was what he wanted to do. He then set up a solid unmoving mental focus. He allowed none of the usual distractions to draw him from his course. There was no thinking about the greener grass growing on the other side of the fence. Then he powerized his will with some good promotion books on selling. In every possible way he built up a whole-souled interest, thereby strengthening his determination. He increased his driving ability by making a written list of all of the advantages of his new business, and holding the spotlight of his interest solidly upon them. He studied the laws of successful salesmanship, and made each of them a part of himself. The focus in his attention, the moving power of his conviction, and the actual skill developed in his follow-through was soon working miracles for his success.

When Columbus discovered America, the Indians told him of an herb that took away fatigue. That herb is still growing in America, and it can also be made to blossom in one's own life. This herb is the motivation that comes when one is getting a sufficient volume of actual accomplishment. We never get tired while we are winning. We are not usually thinking of becoming a dropout while we are ahead. Almost from the first day, this salesman was a real sales leader. And each month, each week, and each day, he concentrates on those things that make the greatest possible contribution in materializing his objectives. It has been said that "nothing succeeds like success," but neither is there anything that is more helpful in building up winning techniques, or the champion spirit. Doctors sometimes use stimulants to bring about helpful responses in their patients. But the greatest stimulants are designed for the spirit.

The dictionary says that to stimulate is:

to increase incentives,
to raise objectives,
to invigorate,
to provoke thought,
to incite activity.

Success might be compared to making a run in baseball. When we get our attention effectively centered, we are on first base; when a real interest is aroused, we are on second base; when a firm desire is created, we are on third base; and when we are able to motivate a continual, successful performance, we have crossed home plate.

Therefore, suppose that we decide what it is that we want in life. We have many things to choose from that are more important than being a good baseball player, or a good doctor, or a good salesman. Jesus talked about the thrilling idea of being a good man. He said, "Be ye therefore perfect, even as your Father which is in heaven is perfect." That's not a goal for a weakling with no objective or power of discipline. There are many ways in which we can be perfect, right now. We can be perfectly honest, and perfectly faithful. We can be perfect in Church attendance, and perfect in abstaining from dope, liquor, nicotine and caffeine. We can be perfect in paying our tithing, and perfect in refraining from profanity, vulgarity and immorality. We can be perfectly fair, we can be perfect in our attitudes, and perfect in our industry.

The scriptures tell of God's three general "degrees" or "kingdoms" of glory. The highest one is called the celestial. This is such a magnificent place that Paul says, "Eye hath not seen, nor ear heard, neither have entered into the heart of man, the things which God hath prepared for them that love him." (1 Cor. 2:9.) The celestial kingdom is a perfect goal for near-perfect people with some near-perfect focuses. The procedures for good focus are:

1. Get the objective clearly in mind.
2. Understand the laws on which the desired blessings are predicated.

3. Solidly make up our minds to achieve.
4. Put on our side blinders to eliminate distractions.
5. Get a good set of "thou shalt nots," and develop enough self-discipline to eliminate all guilt and inferiority complexes.
6. Live life at our best so that no boredoms or depressions will blur the picture.
7. Get the spirit of the actual accomplishment into our souls.
8. Add zest by memorizing the greatest scriptures, singing the greatest songs, reading the most inspiring books, thinking the best thoughts, and doing the best deeds.
9. Remember that we can be "born again" as many times as necessary.
10. With a strong hand, hold our mind on the focus and our foot on the accelerator.

Giving Yourself Away

M any years ago I read a book entitled, *Try Giving Yourself Away*. I don't remember very much about what it said, but I was very impressed with its possibilities as a way of life. Of course, the most important values in the world are always found in people. The earth is God's handiwork, but we are his children. God hid the treasures of the metals, the oils, and the precious gems in the earth, but he put his own attributes and potentialities into his children. And what is probably even more important, he made these great gifts negotiable. As Oscar Hammerstein once pointed out, "A heart can inspire other hearts with its fire." To make a gift of some part of one's better self is usually far more important than to give away anything that might come out of the earth. There is another advantage in giving ourselves away, and that is that the more we give, the more we have left. When we try giving ourselves away, we become like the atomic breeders which always produce more fuel than they consume. When we give away our courage or our faith, the remainder is always multiplied; and in the meantime, we have a lot of fun in the giving.

This philosophy was more than ordinarily impressive to me, because at that particular time I had a close occupational association with a man who had given me many things from his own magnificent store of integrity, wisdom, determination, self-confidence, job satisfaction, and occupational know-how.

The human personality, the human ambition, is always more important than mere wealth. John D. Rockefeller was the world's first billionaire. He used to start out each day with his pockets full of shiny new dimes. As he went about, he would distribute these silver coins to children and other people that he met. In building up his great financial empire, he made many other people millionaires. I think that if I had met John D. Rockefeller, and if he had taken the trouble to give me a dime, I would have kept the money to symbolize the ability, ambition, and other virtues of the famous person who made the gift.

One of the greatest of the divine gifts is the power for motivating others. Someone has expressed this idea by saying:

I gave a beggar of my store of wealth some gold.
He spent the shining ore and came again and yet again,
Still cold and hungry as before.
I gave a thought, and through that thought of mine
He found himself the man supreme—divine.
Fed, clothed, and crowned with blessings manifold.
And now he begs no more.

It is interesting that this attitude of giving oneself away usually benefits the one who gives more than the one who takes. Jesus said, "It is more blessed to give than to receive." Our own abilities multiply fastest when we are sharing them with others. The teacher always learns more than the student. Someone said that he once learned a particular lesson, and then he gave it away so many times that it soon became an inseparable part of himself. A spring usually furnishes a better water supply than a storage tank. But there is another angle to this idea of giving, and it is: only that which we give are we allowed to keep, while that which we keep, we lose.

I know of a young twelve-year-old deacon who gave one hundred and fifty dollars toward the building of the Los Angeles Temple, and because of his gift he will always have one hundred and fifty dollars securely invested. It will continue benefiting him and thousands of people throughout and beyond his lifetime. On the other hand, if he had kept the money it might soon have been lost.

Giving of oneself is like the manna that the Lord sent from heaven to the Israelites in the desert. That which was not used, spoiled. Similarly when we fail to use our abilities, they also spoil; we are allowed to keep only those that we give away. I know a man who goes around with his pockets full of himself and, like John D. Rockefeller, he makes it a practice of giving something to everyone that he meets. See what happens when you try to give away a helpful idea, or a little courage, or some needed faith; or when you try to ignite a spark of happiness in someone else—see if your own supply is not made greater after each gift. This is a kind of perpetual motion, plus. Even if you expend your physical strength in hard labor, you always get the accomplishment as a reward; but in addition you get a stronger set of muscles and some added ability thrown in with which you may more effectively perform your future labors.

There are hundreds of exciting applications for this great idea. We remember Bruce Barton's famous story about the two seas of Palestine. He says:

There are two seas in Palestine.
One is fresh and fish are in it.
Splashes of green adorn its banks.
Trees spread their branches over it, and stretch
Out their thirsty roots to sip of its healing waters.
Along its shores, the children play—as children played
    when He was there.
He loved it, He could look across its silver surface
    when He spoke His parables,
And on a rolling plain not far away, he fed five
    thousand people.

The river Jordan feeds this sea with sparkling
    water from the hills.
It laughs in the sunshine.
There are men who are wont to build their houses
    near it, and birds their nests.
And every kind of life is happier because it is there.

The River Jordan flows on south into another sea.
Here there is no splash of fish, no fluttering leaf,
No song of birds, no children's laughter.
Travelers choose another route, unless on urgent
    business.
The air hangs heavy above the waters of this other sea,
And neither man, nor beast, nor fowl will drink of it.

What makes this mighty difference in those neighboring seas?
Not the river Jordan. It empties the same good water
    into both.
Not the soil in which they lie; not the country
    round about—

This is the difference:

The Sea of Galilee receives, but does not keep the
    Jordan.
For every drop that flows into it, another drop
    flows out,
The giving and receiving go on in equal measure.
The other sea is shrewder, hoarding its income jealously.
It will not be tempted into any generous impulses.
Every drop it gets it keeps.
The Sea of Galilee gives and lives.
This other sea gives nothing. It is named the
    Dead Sea.
There are two kinds of people in the world—
Just as there are two kinds of seas in Palestine.

What an important opportunity we have to form some good
habits around this great idea! Of course, we first need to have
something to give, and then we need to be able to dispense it
effectively. Before John D. Rockefeller could give his dimes
away, he himself had to get possession of them. And like
everyone else, John D. Rockefeller gave away the thing that he
had the most of. As Jesus said, "Out of the abundance of the
heart the mouth speaketh." (Matt. 12:34.) If we first get a lot
of God's great blessings into our own hearts, then it becomes a
lot easier to follow him in being a good giver.

I know of a man who loves the great literature. He has
extracted many interesting stories and helpful lessons from the
best books. The holy scriptures are nearly as familiar to him as
though he himself had written them, and he also has an
impromptu command of many great experiences from the lives
of others. All of these he has made negotiable, and he uses them
to enrich his conversation with interesting illustrations of how to
have more fun and live more effectively. Great literature is filled
with the dimes of courage, humor, love and inspiring examples
of how to best solve our problems. There are interesting parables
filled with wisdom that can be transferred to others. We may
drink from a great reservoir of human interest, and make our
own lives more exciting and productive so that we will have
more to give. Everyone can use some of the wealth of friendship, cheer, faith, and enthusiasm that is so easily available in

the great literature. And we can also use a little more beauty, music, color and harmony in our own lives, even though it has been generated by others.

When God was giving us our world, he made it beautiful by putting color into the sunrise, inspiration into the landscape, and fragrance into the flowers. He gave a happy song to the birds, but he put the most inspiring music into human hearts. And he intended that we should pass these melodies on to someone else. When God designed our food, he not only gave it power to keep us alive, but also made it delightful to the taste. And when he gave us the ability to dream dreams of accomplishment, sing songs of joy, see visions of beauty, and feel the uplift of happiness, he made them all contagious.

Of course, everyone who aspires to be a giver should make sure that his gifts are worth having. It is not worthwhile to allow our hearts to be loaded down with dirty stories or degrading ideas. And no real lasting satisfaction can come from trafficking in gossip or hate. There are some people who make a business of dealing in criticism and depression. This is a counterfeit technique devised by Satan to hurt, instead of help, both the giver and the receiver.

Some people feel that they have nothing to give anyone else. But that makes giving all the more necessary, because it compels us to be a getter in order to be a giver. Many of us have some similarities with the Dead Sea, but as soon as we start giving ourselves away, our waters begin to sweeten. Then the grass starts to grow along the banks of our lives, and it is not long before we are able to attract a few song birds, and start the flowers growing so that many happy people will want to come our way.

George Washington Carver lived in the days of the southern sharecroppers when it was customary to move onto the soil, drain from it as much fertility as possible, and then move on and repeat the process in some other location. Some people remember George Washington Carver because of his educational effort among southern negroes. Some remember George Washington Carver because he made some three hundred commercial products from the common peanut. But *I* remember George

Washington Carver because he was a giver. He said, "Every human being owes it to himself to leave the soil a little richer than when he found it." This attitude makes one a Sea of Galilee.

On the other hand, I recently talked with a Dead Sea woman. She complained about her mental depressions. Several times she mentioned how her extreme timidity had seriously downgraded her life. But instead of doing something about it, she seemed to take a kind of pride in her weaknesses. She drew within herself and hoarded and multiplied her inferiority and guilt complexes. An unfortunate marriage had left some scars upon her soul, and although she had been divorced for twenty years, she was keeping all of her wounds green and open. The memories of her husband's bad temper and immorality, as well as his physical and mental cruelty, had grown more painful to her and showed no sign of any letup with the passage of time.

The places that they had visited together are still contaminated cities in her mind. She continues to identify with the ancient sins of her husband in such a way that they are still generating complexes in her. She continues to hold on to these brackish Dead Sea thoughts by remembering them and feeling sorry for herself as well as blaming herself. One of her Dead Sea characteristics is that she stores up her fears, dreads, and darkened memories to become more and more brackish. The negative thinking that she can't get rid of is producing a serious mental and physical illness on top of a continuing spiritual depression. Everyone sympathizes with her because of the brutality and unkindness of her husband. But like the Dead Sea she has never learned to get the poison out of her soul, regardless of how it got in. We all need that wonderful Sea of Galilee ability to transform every experience into a great experience and then to give it away. Then we can soon learn to overcome every evil with good. Like the bee, we need to learn to get honey out of the flowers from which the spider can extract only poison.

Jesus came into contact with every kind of evil, but from each one he drew a good lesson. He made good from such experiences as the Prodigal Son, the woman taken in sin, and the traveler from Jericho who fell among thieves. Jesus also had the superb ability to increase the good in himself by giving it away.

He gave us the principles of the gospel. He redeemed us from
death by giving his life upon the cross. He also gave himself as
our example and we must learn to follow him. Like the Sea of
Galilee, we need to learn to be good receivers and then to be
good givers. And we should not only learn to give of ourselves,
but make sure that our gifts are worth having.

Home

Recently I saw an interesting calendar on which was shown the many holidays, holy days, and commemorative days that are celebrated each year by various people. We have Election Day, Labor Day and United Nations Day. We have Mother's Day and Father's Day and Resurrection Day. And the second Sunday in June has now been designated as Children's Day. And this might well be the idea around which everything else revolves. If there were no children there would never be anyone else.

Of the children Jesus said, "Of such is the kingdom of heaven." Our society has many political groups, occupational groups, social and cultural groups where people may work together in the interests of each other. Governments were instituted by God for the benefit of man. Christ also organized his Church for our good. But before any of these, he instituted marriage and gave directions for adding children to constitute a family with a home as the base of operations. There is an ancient law of the sea applying to rescue work that says "women and children first." And a dramatic voice was given to this idea when on February 12, 1912, on the decks of the ill-fated Titanic, a great man shouted to his fellow passengers, "Let's save the kiddies." That is certainly our greatest present opportunity.

God said, "It is not good that the man should be alone." But neither is it good for women to be alone, and certainly it is not good for children to be alone. So God established the family to train the children, and he established the home to be the most important part of our society, both here and hereafter. Nations appear and disappear. All earthly governments will finally be replaced when Christ comes to reign upon the earth. Business and occupations come and go, but the family continues throughout eternity. The family is the basis for our education, our religion, our culture, our love, and our comfort. It constitutes the greatest welfare program and is the greatest of "the great societies."

God himself has a family. Jesus was the first begotten son of God in the spirit, and the Only Begotten Son in the flesh. We cannot imagine that this relationship would be discontinued after mortality.

To increase our success possibilities for time and for eternity, God has given some special gifts to family members. He has provided that each person should possess an extra amount of love for other family members. A mother's love, or a wife's love, or a father's love, or the love of children for parents can come next to the love of God among the wonders of our universe. The greatest of God's religious commandments have to do with love.

Then God established the home as a place where the family could live together in the closest kind of relationship with mutual helpfulness and satisfaction. At its best the home is a kind of combination school, church, control center and training ground. It is a place of rest, peace, love and joy. Through the home one obtains his food, his clothing, his rest and his education. This is also a place where we say our prayers, celebrate Christmas, enjoy Thanksgiving and commemorate Easter. About this important place John Howard Payne says, "A charm from the sky seems to hallow us there." The home is a kind of city of refuge, a counseling clinic, and a motivation institute. It is a place where inspiration is nourished, kindness is expanded, meditation is fostered, religion is developed, and life is lived. It is where new births are sponsored and deaths are mourned. But in addition, a whole group of family sciences grows out of the home. The dictionary says that "home rule" is that principle which favors self-government with the governing power vested in the people being governed. Family home rule requires training in self-discipline, unselfishness, and a firm belief in the laws of God.

Good "family management" has to do with effective use of the family income, and the direction of family activities, looking forward to the greatest accomplishment both here and hereafter. Non-family institutions are limited to specialized fields, and have restricted areas for their operations. The school is concerned with the mind, the church works with the spirit, the gymnasium attempts to develop the body, the law tries to improve the conduct. But the home has the responsibility for elevating the whole person to his highest point of possibility. At a family's best it has family home teaching, family home evening, family prayers, family mealtime, family worship, family discipline, family love, and family solidarity with all members working together for the good of each other.

However, there are some negative influences that sometimes break into this family picture. In the dictionary is the word "homicide." It describes the act of one human being destroying another. We might add something to the meaning of this word to produce an idea explaining what happens when the good influence of the home itself is destroyed. This new word might describe those unhappy people, bankrupt families, and distorted lives that are the result of home failure. Homes sometimes malfunction, or family members may be guilty of a serious malfeasance in their office. And all homes break down when they are too heavily loaded with wrong. I thought of this the other night as I listened to a television commercial designed to increase the consumption of liquor. By its misleading advertisement, this company was putting some extra temptations before the people in order to increase its sales. Increased consumption of liquor increases family expenses, and deprives the members of other needed things. It was pointed out on television that 70 percent of all of the liquor drinking is done in the home. This is so because of a breakdown in proper home functioning. Family members do not acquire the liquor habit while participating in family worship or conducting a family home evening.

Where liquor is used, it can cause any important organization to misfunction. Certainly a different kind of society results when people build bars in their homes instead of altars. Children will be different where they are taught alcoholism instead of family prayer. These two activities are so antagonistic that there can be no peaceful co-existence between them. The same set of parents cannot effectively teach both right and wrong to their children at the same time. The number of families where more of the family's income is spent for beer than it is for books, is increasing. And in some places more importance is given to

booze than to bread. Of course the most serious liquor costs are
not involved in buying it, but in drinking it.

An interesting anti-family word that is used many times in
the scriptures is "snare." The dictionary says that a snare is a
noose or some other contrivance in which an animal or a person
may be entangled. A snare is a trap or an ambush by which the
quarry is taken by surprise and made a prisoner. Paul tells of the
many people who are taken captive by the snares of the devil.
The Psalmist says that the transgression of one evil man becomes
a snare to others. The bad example of one transgressor sets the
trap in which his friends are caught.

It is probable that liquor is the most destructive snare ever
devised, even by Satan himself. One of the most common ways
to destroy the values in a human being is to entrap him with
the thirst, expense, delusion, and other evil consequences of
alcohol. Then the crime rate, the immorality, the disobedience to
God begin a rapid rise. Not the least of the evils of alcohol is
the serious conflicts that it causes between right and wrong in
the minds of people. It is a natural law that evil in any form
always repels good. Jesus said, "Men love darkness rather than
light because their deeds are evil." What a tragedy when any
institution uses its abilities to increase the use of alcohol, ensnare
individual lives, and help break up homes!

We cannot hope to escape the terrible consequences of any
evil as long as we foster the evil itself. And the punishment may
be even worse if *we* serve as the traps in which the members of
our own families are ensnared. It was Jesus himself who said,
"Whoso shall offend one of these little ones which believe in me,
it were better for him that a millstone were hanged about his
neck and that he were drowned in the depths of the sea." (Matt.
18:6.) Our malfeasance is increased when we disbelieve in God,
or believe that he doesn't care anymore, or that he has lost his
interest in us. To many people practicing evil, God becomes
unreal. The eternal world itself is often thought of as a misty,
dreamy place with unreal people living under unreal conditions.
There are many people who also have considerable vagueness
about the importance of life itself. We sometimes absorb the
feeling that nothing matters very much, and that anyway we are
not responsible.

Anyone who takes time to think about the God of the
scriptures would certainly not suppose that he was neutral on
the great issues of life or on the consequences of violating his
laws. Of ourselves we must find out that life is real. The flood
in Noah's day was a real flood. And those who disobeyed God
were drowned in real water. When fire and brimstone was rained
down on the wicked cities of Sodom and Gomorrah their pains
were real. Hell is real. Sin and degradation are real. Regret is
real, and suffering is real, both in this life and the next. The
world has frequently been confused by so many arguments
favoring destructive things. There is no lack of arguments in
favor of selling dope, encouraging prostitution, and giving a more
or less free reign to such groups known as Hell's Angels, the
Devil's Disciples, and hippies with their evil love-ins, smelly
bodies, uncut hair, ungodly philosophies, and drunken minds.
Many can make wonderful arguments for creating more semi-
saloons, thereby setting up thousands of additional snares where
men and women and television stations are paid to promote the
increased use of booze.

We conduct many opinion polls to get the preferences of
people on important issues. Suppose that we tried to imagine
how God would vote on any idea designed to increase the sale
of liquor, in either large or small amounts. God has said that he
cannot look upon sin with the least degree of allowance. We
might think of dispensing liquor as being merely a great number
of little friendly, sociable drinks. But when you put the whole
American liquor picture together, you get a result of several
million alcoholics, with other millions well on their way toward
that objective with untold misery still ahead of them. Everything
starts small, and while alcohol may seem to be little and friendly
in the beginning, it frequently ends in death and misery. It may
be that those who take part in fostering this evil of entangling
their fellow men, haven't thought about it adequately. And
maybe we should give more thought to the possibility of our
children becoming alcohol, nicotine or marijuana addicts.

Your children love you with a special kind of confidence.
You are the greatest person in their lives, and whether you are
right or wrong in what you do, the chances are that they will
follow your lead. And they will not have a very good chance to
escape the snares of that evil in which you yourself indulge.

Certainly we should carefully weigh the many disadvantages of mistraining those loving, trusting souls given into the custody of that family of which we are the heads. Our greatest trusteeship will have failed if they become more interested in sensual enjoyments than in worshipping God. It is very interesting that our free agency is not free. God insists that we must shoulder the full responsibility of whatever privileges we accept. And maybe we are not prepared to be a part of the snare for any of God's children. There is nothing very noble about contributing to the delinquencies even of those adult strangers who come within our gates. As the Lord has said, "Woe unto him that giveth his neighbor drink, that puttest thy bottle to him, and makest him drunken." (Hab. 2:15.) And to no one has God ever given any *right* to do wrong. Above almost everything else, we need to learn to manage our homes effectively in our number one assignment of building great human beings.

The House of Delusions

One of our interesting words is the word "house." The dictionary says that a house is a structure intended for the habitation of people. It is a human dwelling place. Some dwelling places are called tents, teepees, and wigwams. We have some public houses that serve as inns, hotels, boarding houses, and movie houses. There are houses of correction, gambling houses and publishing houses. Governments have a House of Commons, a House of Lords, and a House of Representatives. The Bible speaks of the house of God. The physical body is referred to as the house of the spirit. But a "condition" is also frequently spoken of as a house.

The Lord brought Israel out of the house of Egyptian bondage. The writer of Proverbs says that "wisdom hath builded her house." (Prov. 9:1.) There are houses of faith and houses of sin. Some houses are divided against themselves. (See Mark 3:25.) The most important houses are built by God in heaven as our reward for faithfulness. Jesus said, "In my father's house are many mansions." In one of his great parables, Jesus advised us to build our houses on a solid foundation. A house built on the sand is probably all right as long as the good weather lasts. However, we might try to imagine what it would be like to live in a house built upon the sand while the rains were descending, the winds blowing and the floods beating upon it. After a few nights of actual exposure we might be in a better position to understand the suffering that results when one is wet, cold, frightened, hungry, and unable to provide for himself.

As we prepare to build our own spiritual and mental houses it might be very helpful to make up the specifications during an actual siege of bad weather. And because we usually build to satisfy needs, an intimate understanding of a few bad storms might inspire us to make our house strong, strong enough to withstand all kinds of troubles. During good weather, even the most flimsy kind of construction carelessly erected on the sand

may seem to serve our interests quite as well as would a house
of concrete and reinforced steel built on the solid rock.

It must have seemed very silly to the people of Noah's day
to see the old patriarch actually building an ark in the very
middle of a summer drought. It could have been a lot easier to
get these people interested in a flood if they could have had an
actual experience with some wild roaring flood waters swirling
around their ears.

One problem that makes life itself so difficult is that if we
are to get any worthwhile benefit we must start building our
own arks while the sky is clear before it even begins to sprinkle.
We must also make our selection from among God's many
eternal mansions before our house built on the sands of sin
begins to collapse. While the enchantment of glue-sniffing and
cocktail parties is still available is the very time when we should
be learning to live like God.

During the course of our lives, we are required to build
houses to serve many different wants. If one were going to be
the President of the United States, he would likely need a
different kind of a house than if he planned to spend the rest of
his life on government relief. Our present mortal house will not
always be available, and we had better prepare for something
now to take its place *then*

If we are planning to build "wisdom's house" or "honor's
house" or a "house of faith," or a "house of success," it ought
first to have a good foundation under it. Sometimes we build
our lives like a house of cards, where the slightest disturbance
can bring on an immediate collapse. It might be smart for a
movie star to plan to "bring down the house," but that is not a
very good idea for our eternal house. In eternity we will need a
house of righteousness, and a house of happiness that is built
upon the rock. In building our house of life we never reach a
place where we can lay down our tools, because we always have
the forces of disintegration at work. If we neglect the upkeep,
our house may be weakened by the termites of sin and the
decay caused by weakness and lack of discipline. Then when
some crisis strikes, it may be so difficult to get our houses in
order that we will have a fallen house on our hands during the
worst season of bad weather.

The story is told of a farmer questioning a prospective hired hand. When asked for his qualifications, the man said, "I can sleep during a storm." The farmer didn't quite understand what he meant. But the man seemed to know what he was doing and so he was hired.

A few weeks later the farmer was awakened by the loud noise of a storm outside. He hurriedly dressed and ran out to help the hired man tie down the hay, and get the animals into the safety of the barn. He found everything in perfect order and nothing to do but to go back to bed. However he woke up the hired man and asked him if there wasn't something that should be done. The hired man told him that everything had already been fully taken care of. Then the farmer knew what the hired man meant about being able to sleep through the storm.

We too need to be at peace with ourselves and the world during the storms of life. Many people wait until they are going to die to pay their debts and get their financial houses in order, and many follow the same pattern of being delinquent in their spiritual affairs until the settling-up day. We need to do our life's housecleaning before the periods of emergency and stress arrive. The best way to keep our spiritual houses in order is to repent of our sins every night before we go to sleep. Then we will be able to sleep while it storms, and keep our behavior on its proper level besides.

Solomon said that wisdom was building her house, but our problems arise because the opposition is also doing some building. Atheism is building her house, Immorality is building her house, and Negative Thinking is also building its house. While Noah was building the ark, disobedience and disbelief were building their houses in the minds of the people. Therefore, Noah and his family were the only ones who could sleep during the storm.

There is another house that we often build as a place of human habitation which has been called "The House of Delusions." To be deluded is to be seriously deceived. When our minds are misled or our judgment is distorted, we believe a lot of things that aren't so. The mind is sometimes defrauded with tranquilizer drugs and dope addiction. Then we send our thoughts into a make-believe land that does not exist. We accomplish the same thing when we put ourselves under the influence of atheism, or expect to live by the efforts of someone else. Hurt feelings may change our attitudes enough to warp our judgment. When we get a little hate or a little jealousy into our minds, or when we try justifying our evil, we can make ourselves believe all kinds of things that have no relation to the facts.

The dictionary says that to be deluded is to be led away from the truth. Other meanings of delusion are to mislead the reason, to make a fool of the mind or to upset the judgment. Certainly we make fools of our minds when we derange them with alcohol, enslave them with nicotine or feed them on immorality and atheism. Those suffering from delusions usually think that their house is built upon a rock, and only when the floods and the winds reduce their houses to ruins do they discover how serious their errors were.

In the dictionary immediately following the word "delude" is the word "deluge," which means an overflowing. A deluge means an inundation caused by a flood. We might have a deluge of mail or a deluge of trouble, or a deluge of misery.

The delusions of dope addicts, alcoholics, and atheists always bring troubles. One unfortunate thing about deluding our minds is that they sometimes become so accustomed to error that they want to continue the opiate that caused it.

What a horrible thought it would be to think of God getting his pleasures by deliberately deranging his mind and making himself into a temporary madman, not subject to reason, responsibility, or righteousness! The ordained destiny of every child of God is that he may eventually become like his eternal parent. In bringing this condition about, we must beware of delusions that would draw us off the track. And of course this does not mean merely the delusions of dope. We need to be aware of the delusions of sin, the delusions of irresponsibility, the delusions of atheism. To deliberately disbelieve all of the revelations of God and the evidence of his power that constantly stares us in the face is to build our houses on the sand.

We inundate ourselves with delusions by ignoring the benefits of righteousness. We say that we are creatures of our environment, and that we are not personally responsible for the wrong things that we do. False doctrines in religion and the condoning of our own misconduct are like doping the spirit, which causes us to lose control of ourselves. Looking forward to our day, a great prophet of ancient America said: "For behold, at that day the devil shall rage in the hearts of the children of men, and stir them up to anger against that which is good. And others he will pacify, and lull them away into carnal security, that they will say: All is well in Zion; yea, Zion prospereth, all is well—and thus the devil cheateth their souls, and leadeth them away carefully down to hell. And behold, others he flattereth away, and telleth them there is no hell; and he saith unto them: I am no devil, for there is none—and thus he whispereth in their ears, until he grasps them with his awful chains, from whence there is no deliverance." (2 Ne. 28:20, 22.) We should appreciate the prophet cautioning us, as these are soul-destroying delusions.

In his letter to the Thessalonians, the Apostle Paul speaks of the "deceivableness" of iniquity that brings destruction upon the people. He mentions those "strong delusions" where people believe lies and take pleasure in unrighteousness. (See 2 Thess. 2:7-12.)

When we get pleasure from unrighteousness, it becomes an easy step for those undisciplined in good to turn more and more to wickedness. Many of our problems begin when we start building a house of delusions by believing merely those things that we want to believe, whether they are true or not. Some people try to relieve themselves of responsibility merely by saying that "God is dead" or that he is no longer interested in us. A few doubts and a little negative thinking can soon neutralize the faith on which our house is built. When we disbelieve in God and don't understand the kind of being that he is, or what he expects of us, we make ourselves liable to every error.

The Apostle Paul said, "Let no man deceive you by any means." Certainly we ought not to deceive ourselves, and the best way to keep from being deceived is to follow the Lord's directions. Jesus said, "If any man will do [God's] will, he shall know of the doctrine." Very few people are deceived when they have their own houses in order and are making a real effort in learning the truth with a willingness to follow it. We have the Holy Bible as our guide in matters of faith and practice. But very largely we have closed up our Bibles; whereas if we lived by his word, we would be able to clear out all of our delusions.

Jesus looked forward to our day and said, "Take heed that no man deceive you." The Apostle Paul said, "Let no man deceive himself." To the Galatians, Paul said: "Be not deceived; God is not mocked: for whatsoever a man soweth, that shall he also reap. For he that soweth to his flesh shall of the flesh reap corruption; but he that soweth to the Spirit shall of the Spirit reap life everlasting." (Gal. 6:7-8.)

Nothing could be more unprofitable than to live in a house of delusions that will certainly crash when the storm arrives. A. E. Housman has observed that "the house of delusions may be cheap to build, but it is drafty to live in."

Two men were once standing on the deck of a ship far out to sea with water all around them. It was their first voyage and they were discussing the vastness of the ocean. One man remarked "This is the first time that I ever saw so much of anything." To which the other replied, "And you are only looking at the top of it."

It might help us to appreciate the magnitude of the ocean by understanding what lies underneath the surface. Paul says that we now see life through a glass darkly and know only in part, but when that which is perfect is come, that which is in part shall be done away. (See 1 Cor. 13:9-12.) Then we shall know what is underneath, and on top of, and behind life. But in the meantime we should build a firm house of faith founded upon that sure rock which is obedience to God.

Ice on the Windshield

A number of years ago Paul Speicher told a provocative human interest story about driving to work in a sleet storm. It was during the early morning rush hour, and as the storm reached its maximum, the sleet began freezing on the automobile windows until soon hundreds of cars were forced to a standstill. Because Mr. Speicher was only a few blocks from his office, he parked his car and went the rest of the way on foot. He thought he could get some work done and then come back for his car after the weather had cleared.

As Mr. Speicher made his way past the stalled automobiles, he thought about the people who were inside of them. He was strongly attracted to people, and it had always been a pleasant experience for him to feel their spirit and exchange ideas and smiles with them. But this morning he was very close to them physically, yet they were invisible and beyond the range of all his other senses. Some of the cars still had their engines running, but the ice on their windows made it almost seem as though they were buried in the earth or marooned on some uninhabited island a thousand miles away. Then Mr. Speicher meditated about how unpleasant it would be to be permanently isolated from people where no association or warm friendly human interchange would ever be possible.

"Man" is what the dictionary calls a gregarious animal. Some of God's creatures feel more at home and better off when living in swarms, herds, families, communities, and nations. One of our most important human instincts is the "flock instinct." And many of our most important pleasures would be meaningless if we lived as the only inhabitants of some far distant mountain top. Even the Garden of Eden would not be a very exciting place if we lived there all alone. We might try to imagine what it would be like to have no one to eat breakfast with, or smile our good mornings to, or share our hopes with.

Then Mr. Speicher made a comparison with some of those who get caught in the sleet storms of life. These may be real people with real talents, interesting personality traits, and great souls. But some of them occasionally get their feelings hurt, or have other problems arise that they cannot solve effectively. This situation would not be too serious if we had some kind of defrosting system that would prevent any permanent defects from being formed. But sometimes our inferiority and guilt complexes can cause a permanent damage to our souls. As a result of some of our injuries, we frequently put on our midget suits, think like pygmies, and perform like weaklings and delinquents. It is a part of life's program that everyone should have some real problems to solve for his own good. But when we allow the sleet of prejudice and hate to freeze on our windows, then we may withdraw within ourselves and become virtual prisoners in that narrow little vehicle in which we are making the journey of life. With too much ice on our windshields we bring upon ourselves a kind of solitary confinement which prevents us from seeing out, and then no one can give us a friendly wave or wish us well. Then even though our engines are still running, we usually aren't going any place.

One early morning last winter while walking to work, I was picked up by a friend. I have discovered that if I get a little bit enthusiastic about jogging on a cold winter morning, I can generate a fairly good head of steam in a couple of miles. I had not been inside my friend's car very long before his windshield began fogging up. I could tell that unless something was done the driver's visibility would soon be at zero. I apologetically mentioned the distressing changes that I was causing in the atmosphere of my host's automobile. But with a disarming attitude of complete confidence he said, "We can soon fix that." He turned the cold air on his windshield for a few seconds, and it was soon perfectly clear. Then again we could see the beautiful early morning landscape with its delightful covering of snow. Then we had a warm, comfortable, friendly visit the rest of the way to town.

However, the defogging apparatus in human beings is not always as efficient as in automobiles. Frequently husbands and wives generate fog. And, if their personal defrosters are not in good working order, it may freeze on their windshields, cut off their views, and bring their progress to a standstill. Sometimes a little marital sleet forms an impenetrable barrier between people, which makes further communications or satisfactions impossible. Then instead of being warmed and cheered at the heart-fires of each other, they both suffer from a miserable kind of cold and loneliness. Some marriage partners living together are about as isolated from each other as though one lived at the north pole and the other at the south pole. And they are also about as chilly. Ice on some parental windshields grows so thick that it becomes a year-round glacier. Then they never see the wonderful qualities that could give them so many delights and successes. It is astonishing what terrible things can happen in human relations when just a little selfishness, or pride, or hate, or evil is allowed to fog up our windows. As the ice gets thicker, the tensions become greater, the frigidity grows more unpleasant, and the misunderstandings are more heartbreaking. While this ice may only be on the windows to begin with, if it is not removed it will start getting into their minds and hearts, forming the icebergs of death. Many parents are unable to break out of this destructive unpleasant imprisonment because of economic restraints and the pitiful cries of their children. And as the sleet of pride, the winds of bitter emotions, and the cold of selfishness continue, the beautiful flowers intended to perfume and decorate our lives are withered by the frost and turn stiff and black in death. When children remain huddled together in this icy climate, their personality growth is stunted and the spiritual heritage to which they have a right is destroyed.

The records of mental hospitals and penal institutions list "broken homes" as being the chief offense in our society. And no home can long survive after these deadly sleet storms put out the fires of love and cause selfishness, prejudice, hate, and sin to make us prisoners. One of the greatest opportunities for our inventive genius is to develop within ourselves something comparable to the defrosting mechanism with which automobile manufacturers equip their cars. Such an ability assures us of a clear vision, a good communication, and a comfortable, invigorating success.

Someone once wrote a song about keeping our windows clean. He said:

If I knew you and you knew me;
If both of us could plainly see
And understand with sight divine
The meaning of your heart and mine,
I'm sure that we would differ less
And clasp our hands in friendliness.
Our thoughts would pleasantly agree,
If I knew you and you knew me.

Then, contemplating a defrosting failure, he said:

I can't know you; You can't know me,
For the best in each we never see:
The kindly thought, the hidden word,
The melody that's never heard.
But loving acts and deeds divine
From human hearts must freely shine.
Through them if we can only see—
Then I'll know you and you'll know me.

There are a lot of wonderful people in the world who never allow anyone or anything to fog up their vision. Everyone is required to go through an occasional sleet storm, and everyone has to get along with some overheated pedestrian once in a while. But when some offense arises, instead of letting it develop into a crisis they turn on their de-icers and blow the steam away before the ice has time to form. Jesus was speaking of this defrosting procedure, when he said, "Blessed is he who is not offended."

And when Jesus suggested that we love our enemies, he still had this human de-icing device in mind. Every modern, up-to-date automobile is now also equipped with a windshield washer and wiper. And as a comparable aid to us, the great laws of repentance were given to help us get rid of the mud that gets splattered on our windshields. There are a large number of troubled people who let too many mental, spiritual, social, and physical problems accumulate in their lives. Probably the biggest one of them all takes place when our communications are cut off because of dirty windshields.

It doesn't take much mud smeared on our windows before

we begin having difficulty in getting through to others. Then
even our prayers to God seem to flatten out against a blank
wall. No one ever goes very far in life before he starts making
some mistakes, or someone steps on his toes, or he gets a few
unpleasant bumps on his ego. But instead of cutting off our
exposure to life by drawing inside of our own shells or abandon-
ing our life's vehicles by the roadside, we need to learn how to
use the windshield washer to clean up our attitudes, and we
should always have on hand a sufficient supply of cold air to
blow away the fogs of irritation and bitterness with which we
may get splattered.

The proper association with other human beings and a good
friendly relationship with God gives us some of our most
pleasant experiences, as well as our most productive successes;
whereas to be isolated from life, and love, and joy by a little
dirt and ice causes our most miserable failures. The most
devastating of all human emotions is that sense of being alone,
of being unworthy, of being inferior, of being unwanted. All
through life some people suffer from intolerable feelings of
loneliness and long periods of depression. Even in the midst of a
crowd, some people are always terribly and irretrievably alone.

We think it strange that the women in some foreign
countries veil their faces so that they cannot be seen by others.
But our procedures of hiding our love from our families and
from God and keeping our friendliness and helpfulness to others
a secret, is even more ridiculous. The book of Genesis tells of a
characteristic response made when Adam and Eve, our first
parents, got some mud on their windshields. The record says,
"And Adam and his wife hid themselves from the presence of
the Lord God among the trees of the garden." (Gen. 3:8.) But
since that early day, this ancient Edenic scene has been re-
enacted several million times by us. After a few sleet storms or
some splashes of mud, we tend to park our automobiles and run
and hide in the bushes of life. Too many of us live as hermits
with our families and put great distances between ourselves and
God.

We often hear someone say, "I have never been able to get
very close to so-and-so." It is quite likely that God, himself, has
used that phrase many times. Many of us are noted for our

coldness and aloofness. A few bad habits and some negative
attitudes can soon isolate us even from those we are nearest to.
God's influence is always very close, yet we handicap ourselves
by putting great spiritual and social barriers between us. Even in
the midst of wonderful people we frequently cut ourselves off as
completely as though we put ourselves in steel cells through
which we cannot see, hear, feel, breathe, or think. Under these
conditions we might actually be only a quarter of an inch from
someone that we love, and yet be a million miles away.

Suppose you knew that someone you loved more than
anyone else in the world was very close to you physically, but a
dirty windshield or bad attitude or a lack of faith was cutting
off all sight, sound, light and possible communication. Our
families and friends are close by, yet they may be so far away.
God, himself, is very near to us. He loves us far more than we
can possibly understand; he stands ready to inspire and help us
to direct our lives in the most effective way. He is our Father
and he desires that we will develop the greatest possible capaci-
ties for feeling love and understanding righteousness. But the
contact often fails, the messages don't go through, and our
efforts come to a standstill because of impenetrable self-imposed
barriers, or because of the great weight of ice that has formed
on our wings during our life's flight.

Emerson once painted a picture of our situation when he
said: "On the brink of an ocean of life and truth we are
miserably dying. Sometimes we are furthest away when we are
closest by. We stand on the shore of an ocean of power but
each must take the steps that would bring him there." So
frequently that is true. Think how near they were who lived
contemporaneously with Jesus. He lived among them, they saw
him walk down the street, they heard him speak, they knew of
his miracles, yet they were so far away that they said, "His
blood be upon us and our children," and so it has been, and so
it may be with us. In our journey of life, we are so near yet we
may be so far away. We are so near to God, happiness, and
success and then we allow a little prejudice, a little lethargy, a
little hate, and a little sin to get splashed on our windshields and
destroy our vision. Then the heavy ice formations on our wings
may drop us into the distant isolation of oblivion. No one is
ever permitted to make all of life's journey driving in the bright,

warm sunshine down a paved street with perfect visibility. Sooner or later we are going to run into some splashing mud and a few foggy passengers. But if we have a good understanding of windshield washers, and wing de-icers, and if we have some good up-to-date defrosting equipment with an ample cold air supply, then we may be able to keep a clear vision, a faithful heart, a vigorous industry, and a devoted love of God and our families. And then God will bless our life's passage and bring us safely to our destination.

Identity

A s a soldier enters military service, he is given a small metal tag. This is to be worn on a chain around his neck as a means of identification should he be killed or wounded. But whether one is in or out of the army, or whether he is alive or dead, one of his most important possessions is his identity. Sometimes a brain injury or a mental illness may cause a person to forget who he is, or to believe that he is someone else. One's moral image is sometimes damaged so that his spiritual identity is destroyed. But to everyone in good health, our identity is one of our most important assets. When we are buried, we want our graves to be marked. And even the immortality of our souls would be meaningless without the immortality of our identities.

We would not like to resemble a raindrop and be merged with a trillion other raindrops in a big ocean without individuality, memory, or personal importance. It has been said that in this great free land of America "anybody can be somebody." And one of the most attractive things about heaven is that you will be yourself and I will be myself throughout eternity, with quickened senses, amplified powers of perception, and vastly increased capacity for love, understanding, and happiness. In the celestial kingdom "everybody will be somebody," with these great identifying qualities of righteousness, ability and beauty developed to their uppermost limits. We will also be identified with God our eternal Heavenly Father. No one wants to lose his family, his privileges, or his possessions. No one wants to be a nobody, or a nothing. We don't relish the idea of going to prison and having our names changed to numbers. A uniform with circular stripes making us look like everyone else does not excite our pleasure. Many women are horrified even to see some other woman wearing the same kind of a dress. This trend toward uniformity is a kind of sin against her identity.

God was very careful to give each of us his own distinctive

body, mind, and personality. And everyone has some identifying papers to prove who he is. If we can't identify ourselves, we may cut ourselves off from our privileges, our property, our family, our church, and our citizenship. If one loses his identity he may also lose his right to his credit, or to be trusted, or to his claim for prestige and rank. When a manufacturer puts out some product, he usually marks it with the most distinctive identification and then builds up for it the most favorable reputations. But no one ever gets very far along life's way before he starts putting those marks upon himself that will most favorably distinguish him as a person.

In the beginning God created us in his own image and endowed each one of us with a set of his own attributes and potentialities. With this original capital he turns over to us the job of completing our identity according to our own pleasure. He said, "Thou mayest choose for thyself." Every one of us has two creators—one is God and the other is man himself. And the image that we finally end up with will depend on what modifications we ourselves make. If one becomes a Democrat he immediately begins gravitating toward a certain image. If one chooses to be a prize fighter, he thereby selects a different set of identifying marks. The scriptures identify some people by such names as Simon the Sorcerer, Matthew the Tax Collector, Joseph the Carpenter, Judas the Betrayer, John the Beloved, Solomon the Wise Man, and Moses the Lawgiver.

We remember the story about the lion cub that strayed into a flock of sheep. He ran with the sheep, behaved like a sheep, and identified with the sheep. Then one day on the distant skyline there appeared the silhouette of a great lion. His head was thrown back and his tail was lashing wildly about. With a great roar, the lion on the hillside sent his voice booming across the fields. Then the lion playing with the sheep stopped his playing. Something was stirring within him. Like was calling to like, and the lion playing with the sheep discovered that he was not a sheep but a lion. With an answering roar that sent the timid sheep scattering before him, the lion with the sheep ran to join the lion on the hillside.

We too can make ourselves great or small according to what we identify with. If we allow the lion to sleep within us too long while we play with the sheep, we may never realize that our lot in life is not to play in the meadows, but to hunt on the mountainside with the lions. Many of us attract to ourselves the effect of a belittling curse when we identify with that destructive myth about the average man. We are sometimes a little bit embarrassed when the lion within us begins to show. Frequently we don't want to attract attention by standing out from the sheep. It is sometimes so comfortable just to be average where nothing extraordinary is expected of us. However, it is interesting to remember that average is halfway between something and nothing. The average man is as close to the bottom as he is to the top. To be average is just as bad as it is good. Average is midway between God and Satan. Then we are as susceptible to the influence from below as we are to that from above. No one likes to see this mediocre trait in other people. When we go to a baseball game, we would rather see a Babe Ruth at bat than someone who is just average. We would not like to have a brain operation by a doctor who was just average. And there is not much challenge going through life like Christopher Robin on the stairs just halfway up and just halfway down.

We become not only what we eat but also what we identify with. The little boys who play at being gangsters may eat the same food, but they will be a different kind of men than those who play at being statesmen and patriots. Twenty-one-year-old Nathan Hale was able to look down the musket barrels of the British firing squad and say, "I regret that I have but one life to give for my country," because he had previously identified with those great souls who loved freedom. When one identifies with booze, immorality, guilt, and inferiority he soon becomes their servants. Some deliberately join themselves with the tares instead of the wheat, and some choose to be located on God's left hand among the goats, rather than on the right hand with those who have won his approval. Consciously, unconsciously, or subconsciously, too many people continually identify with drunkards, lawbreakers, atheists, sinners, and ne'er-do-wells.

Recently I talked with a man who had always told himself that he wanted to do right. But for many years he had associated with the wrong people and thought the wrong thoughts. When he was very young, he was jealous of his brother and did him a serious injustice. As these two boys grew older a kind of Cain and Abel relationship developed between them. It was only natural for him to hate his younger brother whom he had injured. Like Abel, the younger brother was offering a more acceptable offering to the Lord. The younger brother identified himself with the Church and the things for which it stood. As the older brother's problems developed, he became more and more jealous, and his own hate pushed him further away from those very things that could have made him happy. He did many wrong things because he wanted to prove that he was different from his brother. As his reason told him he was wrong, his evil activities started as a conflict that developed in him a kind of Dr. Jekyll and Mr. Hyde personality. It soon happened with him as it did in Mr. Stevenson's famous story: it became much easier to remain an evil Mr. Hyde than to change himself back into a respectable Dr. Jekyll. And his evil soon became strong enough to push his good aside at will.

He himself said that he often felt he fitted Mr. Stevenson's description of Mr. Hyde as that of being "pure evil." He had tried to justify his wrongdoing for so long that he said he frequently felt like the devil himself. To some extent he was proud of being evil, and bragged about it. He said, "I've done everything in the book." There are many people who have gone so far that they actually take pleasure in drunkenness, vandalism, rebellion, immorality, and even murder. Many murders have been committed for the thrill. And many young people begin a life of subversion by deliberately going against the teachings of their parents in order to satisfy some false pride or some false desire to be independent of good people and good deeds.

The man mentioned above had rejected his own race and had identified himself with a minority group. The more serious problems and lesser abilities possessed by his new associates made him feel like a kind of superman by comparison. He justified being unfaithful to his wife on the grounds that he was unworthy of her, and he ought to act accordingly so that he would be punished and sent to hell where he belonged. Besides, he reasoned that he would be more at ease in hell with other goats like himself. When such serious defects get into one's reasoning processes causing unhappy emotional attitudes and mental illness, it also wreaks its havoc upon members of his family and his friends.

The counseling of psychiatrists, social workers, or religious leaders is of little help because he rejects everyone who disapproves of his evil. And with these two opposing forces working in his life he is largely incapable by himself of knowing right from wrong. Even at his best his margin of power in matters of good and bad are very slim, and he makes such excuses as "I'm all mixed up," or "I don't know what I am supposed to do." When one gives to evil as much authority in his life as he gives to good, then it is difficult to get any majority vote on the right side, and he will always be "all mixed up." Anyone can get himself unmixed and unconfused if we will cease doing wrong. Someone has said that if you want to break a bad habit just drop it. That is also the only good way to handle any kind of evil.

For generations some of the backward peoples have lived under the caste system. When one is born an untouchable, it becomes very difficult for him to be anything else but an untouchable. Likewise when one identifies with sin and mediocrity, he just feels dirty and inferior. On the other hand it is one of life's most productive abilities to understand his lion powers and be able to release himself from his inferiority and learn to identify on a higher level.

A husband and wife are supposed to become "one flesh"; and when because of this mutual identity they live together agreeably and happily for a long period, they frequently grow to look like each other. But mentally, spiritually, morally, and financially we all grow to look like those people with whom we identify.

George Washington died nine years before Abraham Lincoln was born. But Lincoln's feeling for Washington was intense. Lincoln said, "Washington is the mightiest name on earth, long since the mightiest in the cause of civil liberty, still mightiest in moral reformation. On that name a eulogy is expected that cannot be. To add brightness to the sun or glory to the name of Washington is impossible. Let none attempt it. In solemn awe pronounce the name and in its naked deathless splendor leave it shining on." Lincoln created himself in Washington's image by identifying with him. And the greatest idea of our lives is to identify with God our eternal Heavenly Father. Lincoln once

said, "It is difficult for a man to be miserable while he feels
that he is worthy of himself and claims a kinship with the great
God who made him."

One of the most thrilling parts of the scriptures has to do
with Jesus identifying with his Father. Before his mortal birth
Jesus had been a part of the Presidency of heaven and he said,
"Not my will but thine be done." Again he said, "The Father
and I are one." Neither of them ever gets mixed up. They are
always one in purpose, one in righteousness, one in their love for
each other. When Philip said, "Show us the Father," Jesus said,
"He that hath seen me hath seen the Father." (John 14:9.)
Because of complete righteousness they also had grown to look
like each other. Paul said that Jesus was in the express image of
his Father's person. And Jesus gave that thrilling expression of
unity when he said, "The Father is in me, and I in him." (John
10:38.) Then in turn he prayed one of his greatest prayers for
us in which he said, "Neither pray I for these alone, but for
them also which shall believe on me through their word; that
they all may be one; as thou Father art in me, and I in thee,
that they also may be one in us." (John 17:20-21.) Jesus was
speaking of identification when he said, "Be ye therefore perfect,
even as your Father which is in heaven is perfect." (Matt. 5:48.)
We were created in God's image and belong to his lineage. What
a thrilling idea that we can be constantly reaffirming our destiny
by thinking his thoughts, and keeping his commandments. Then
he will be in us and we will be in him, and God will abundantly
bless us.

Life's Library

One of the finest institutions in our world is the library. This is a place where we do study and research from books. There are many important books in the library about science, fiction, history, literature, humor, and religion. We also have some good dictionaries, encyclopedias, and other reference books giving us access to most of the useful ideas that have been discovered since time began. Some of our greatest men have carefully written down the results of their lifetimes of study, and made it possible that we, their beneficiaries, may absorb all of the good from their years of investigation and experimentation in just a few hours.

Even a small home library may be a treasury of wisdom and know-how from the wittiest men in all countries and ages. These men themselves may have kept so hidden from view as to be inaccessible during their lifetime; or their solitary nature, or the rushed spirit of their lives, may have made them impatient of interruption. They may have been fenced in by etiquette or other considerations. But the thoughts that they did not reveal to their bosom friends are clearly written out for us in impelling words, even though we may be strangers living in a far country and another age.

A library containing a wise collection of books is the diary of the human race. It is a consulting room where we meet with the wisest men. It is the greatest university of our times. Our books are our tools, and the greater their variety and perfection the more they help us to live effectively. We have many kinds of libraries. There are home libraries, public libraries, university libraries, medical libraries, religious libraries, and a Library of Congress. The books they contain may be used to build up our faith, develop our job competence, supply us with entertainment, or furnish us with the most satisfactory personal pleasures at a minimum of cost. While we occupy this solemn library chamber to take council with all of the wisest, greatest, best, and glorious

among men for our own good, there is no danger that our
preferences will cause any jealousies, nor is there any fear of
giving them offense. In perfect safety we may question the most
illustrious men as long as we please and then leave them as
abruptly as we choose. Each of the great men in our books may
stand before us to speak, or he may remain silent according to
our own pleasure. We alone may convene or adjourn these
meetings and be the sole judge in deciding the issues according
to our own pleasure.

There is another kind of library that may be even more
important. This we might call "our life's library." The most
important commodity in the world and the one that contains the
greatest of all values is life. Life is our endowment from that
mysterious and most important element that is known only to
God. Life is the base on which all other values rest, and it is the
source from which all good things come.

To help us produce a life's library we are given an
important piece of equipment called a brain with which we may
do some of our own printing. The brain itself is made up of 14
billion cells and it can contain more information than could be
found in a dozen libraries. A prominent neurophysicist recently
said that you could not build an electronic computer equivalent
to the human brain for three billion dollars. Each of us is
designed to be the self-recording instrument of his own life, and
there are many books that have been printed in our hearts and
engraved upon our souls. These special volumes may be prepared
by us according to our own need.

Robert Louis Stevenson once said that everyone should
always carry with him two books—one to read from and the
other to write in. We may have books to read from that contain
the distilled essence of the greatest lives. There are books of
information, books of inspiration, and books of instruction in
almost limitless variety. Someone has pointed out that we can
live without reading, but not very well. That is, life itself would
lose much of its value without books to read from.

We also need some books to write in. However, before we
write our ideas down they should be thought through and made
definite. Then by writing them down either in our hearts or on

paper we can make them rememberable and useful. One of the important books that we should have to write in is a Book of Dreams. People are equipped to have some wonderful dreams, but if we don't do something about them they will soon evaporate and disappear. In a single night the future of the entire world was unfolded to the mind of King Nebuchadnezzar. But its meaning and even its memory was soon lost from his mind. In his book *Research Magnificent,* H. G. Wells tells of a young man who lost the righteous dreams of his youth, and these were the most precious possessions of his life. We can make more of our dreams come true if we carefully write them down and take care of them. The poet had our book of dreams in mind when he said, "Dream, oh youth, dream nobly and manfully, and thy dreams shall be thy prophets."

Everyone should also have a special Book of Memories. There are many wonderful things to remember. In a book of memories one may record those beautiful, wonderful, high-point experiences of life. Then these may be rerun as his life needs strength and enrichment.

Then there is a Book of Decisions. For many years, Rudger Clawson served as the President of the Quorum of the Twelve Apostles. Every Thursday this quorum meets in an upper room of the temple to discuss important questions and plan for the welfare of the Church. It is reported that President Clawson always kept a large notebook containing a written record of official actions taken as each problem was solved and the program of the Church decided upon. This Book of Decisions soon became a rather complete set of rules and regulations to guide future action. It also made it unnecessary to spend any time on those matters that had already been settled. What a great idea to serve as the foundation of our individual success! More than almost anything else we need to get some definite decisions on such great issues as: Do we really believe in God? What kind of life do we want to lead? What kind of moral standards are we prepared to maintain?

Certainly each of us should have an up-to-date Book of Decisions in his life's library where a firm ruling has been made on every issue. It is interesting to remember that a great many of life's most important decisions have already been made by an authority that is much higher and more dependable than our own. Henry C. Link once said that nothing puts so much order into one's life as to live by a set of sound principles. And the most sound principles are the principles of the gospel of Jesus Christ as found in the holy scriptures. How profitable it would be for us to officially adopt each of them as part of our own Book of Decisions!

As early in life as possible, everyone should get on an intimate basis with the word of the Lord and then govern himself accordingly. One of the prominent books of the New Testament is the Book of the Acts of the Apostles. This might suggest that there is another "book of acts" that God keeps for each of us. In his vision John the Revelator saw many of these books that we write in that God will read from in the final judgment. He said, "And the books were opened: and another book was opened, which is the book of life: and the dead were judged out of the things which were written in the books, according to their works." (Rev. 20:12.) Each of us should keep a kind of diary in his life's library in which he might record the same information that God will put down as he keeps score on us.

Benjamin Franklin used to keep a book to write in which he called his Book of Virtues. In analyzing himself he discovered thirteen main faults that were causing most of his problems. He decided that the best way to eliminate his faults was to replace them with an equal number of virtues. He said, "I wished to live without committing any fault at any time, and I conceived a bold and arduous project for arriving at moral perfection." He said, "I made a little book in which I allotted one page for each desired virtue. I ruled each page with red ink, then at the end of each day I made a black check for every fault that I had committed during the day against that virtue. By means of this constant attention and daily practice it was not long before these rules became a permanent part of my character."

Of course, one of the most important things about these books is that they should become a part of us. It has been said that some people are only Bible Christians. This is a condition where the Christianity remains in the Bible and not very much gets into us. Even the religion of Christ has little value as long as it remains only in the book. But one of the greatest of techniques for spiritual success is to actually get into us some ideas out of good books.

Another important book for our life's library should be a Book of Plans. Every successful architect has a book of plans. These ready-made drawings give him a greater range for his personal choices. Everyone is an architect. Whether we like it or not, each of us is working on the greatest of all construction jobs: building his own eternal life. And it can be very helpful if each of us has some good blueprints from which we may take suggestions as to how to improve our own program. It has been said that planning is the place where man shows himself most like God. What can you think of that is more godlike than an effective planner! The planner is the one who draws the blueprints for success. He is the one who builds the roadway on which accomplishments can travel.

One successful businessman has a very constructive system for developing effectiveness in himself. Each morning he writes down in his diary his objectives and makes an outline of what he expects to do about each of them that day. Then before going to bed at night he analyzes what he has done. If he has succeeded, he writes down the reasons for his success, and tries to identify and further refine those factors that have been responsible. By this process he makes his good ideas even more effective and ready for the next opportunity to use them. In the places where he has fallen down, he tries to determine the reasons for his failure so that he can avoid making these same mistakes again. When he finds that any technique works, he quickly perfects and enlarges upon it; and when a principle proves unsound, he quickly discards it.

If we actually kept this kind of a programming book we could always know where we were going. And we might not be quite as surprised on judgment day if we kept a running score as we went along. One of the most important elements of any defeat is surprise; and if we make every day a judgment day, the effectiveness of our lives will take an immediate and sharp upturn. Any game loses much of its interest, as well as its motivation, when we fail to keep score. Think what would happen at a baseball game if they failed to keep track of the

balls, and the strikes, and the hits, runs, and errors. In football
the kicks, passes, runs, and downs are measured, timed, counted,
and put into the record. Any Boy Scout will have a better
record of daily good turns if he himself keeps the score.

It wouldn't be very wise to drive an automobile without a
fuel gauge, and a speedometer. Neither should we do an extensive banking business without a record of deposits and withdraw-
als. Many lives fail because we have no idea about the condition
of our own spiritual solvency. Judgment day will be a day of
great triumph if we have kept a good Book of Acts, based on
sound intelligent planning.

We also need some books of inspiration and some books of
motivation. Motivation transcends every other thing in importance. I know a man who has some 8½- x 11-inch looseleaf
binders in which he keeps his literary treasures. He accumulates
the motivating poems, inspiring scriptures, gems of wisdom, and
quotable philosophies that make an especially strong appeal to
him. Many of these he memorizes and stores away in his
notebooks, much as a squirrel stores his acorns away for the
winter. If someone gave us a hundred-dollar bill every day, we
would put it in the bank and see that a record was kept of it.
However, a motivating thought or the acquisition of an inspiring
idea may be worth much more than a hundred dollars. If we
accumulate the right kind of ideas that are effectively loved,
used, and lived with, we will soon be wealthy. The items in this
treasury can then be used to stir up our industry, and give us
courage, power and faith. They can mold our attitudes and put
us in the frame of mind for any desired accomplishment.

People can develop a love for ideas just as they can develop
a love for people or things. And the right kind of ideas can have
great power in giving us a healthy forward thrust. We might also
have in our life's library a book of friendships that need to be
developed and a book of the accomplishments that need to be
materialized. Among the most important books in our life's
library should be some worthwhile biographies, and one of the
most important of these should be our own. If we write it down
as we go along we will surely be inspired to make it better. But
certainly our total success both here and hereafter will be greatly
improved by a first class life's library with some good books to
read from and some good books to write in.

Life's Tapestry

The most important responsibility that has ever been laid upon the shoulders of any human being is that of building his own life. Socrates had an interesting way of carrying out this undertaking, by a kind of split personality arrangement where he regarded himself as two people. One part of him was General Socrates and the other part of him was Private Socrates. The general was the thinker, the organizer, the motivator who had a commission to command. The private was the worker; his talent was to follow directions with an obligation to accept discipline and obey orders. This success technique might be related to the prerogative of royalty, where the sovereign refers to himself with the plural pronoun "we," instead of the less impressive singular pronoun "I."

We do have some grounds for thinking of ourselves as a plurality. Plato referred to the upper and lower soul. We speak of our better self and our poorer self. Jesus called this duality "the spirit and the flesh." The poet said, "Within my earthly temple, there's a crowd." This may be related to the interesting old fable about a cat having nine lives. But in one way that also becomes a kind of necessity for us if we are ever to realize a complete fulfillment of ourselves. We need a strong physical life, a keen mental life, a healthy spiritual life, a pleasant social life, a well-disciplined moral life—all combined into a vigorous active life.

But no one can get along very well without a happy family life, a successful occupational life, a stimulating cultural life, a satisfying emotional life, and a secure and adequate financial life. To accomplish all of this we need a strong general to command, and some good privates that are obligated to obey. One of the factors determining the number and quality of our lives is the preparation we make for them, and the kind of discipline that the general is able to develop in the private under his direction. We prepare for school, we prepare for family responsibilities, we prepare for citizenship, we prepare for our life's work, we prepare for death. In our antemortal existence we prepared for this life; in this life, we prepare for the next life.

All of the occupations are primarily about ourselves. Agriculture is how we feed ourselves. Sociology is how we live together effectively. Law is how we keep ourselves out of trouble. Then we have the great science of religion to teach us how we keep ourselves well spiritually. To be successful in this responsibility of making the best and the most of our lives, we must be effective on all fronts and in all periods of life, including the one extending beyond the boundaries of mortality.

Certainly one of the greatest of all of our human concepts is the one having to do with the immortality of the personality and the eternal glory of the human soul. Man is God's greatest masterpiece, fashioned in his own image and designed to be everlasting. Under the right conditons the family organization, which God established, will be the basic unit throughout eternity. When God performed the first marriage and said, "It is not good that the man should be alone," death had not yet entered the world.

The family is the base on which almost everything else depends. To the apostle commissioned to carry the divine program forward, Jesus said, "Whatsoever thou shalt bind on earth shall be bound in heaven." And upon our immature shoulders here and now rests the tremendous responsibility of laying a foundation of character and accomplishment that will support the weight of our eternal lives. Because we cannot live nine lives or even two lives, all of the facets of our existence must be integrated and coordinated into one, and motivated toward the single goal of perfection.

The primary tools with which we work are represented by that big combination word "personality." Like an automobile, a human being is not made up of just one part, it is a collection of many parts all working together. All of the creations in Nature itself are actually combinations. The scientists have identified 104 elements in Nature. We know some of them as nitrogen, oxygen, hydrogen, carbon, and iron. These with the ninety-nine others make up Nature's building blocks. Out of these elements in the right combinations and proportions, Nature fashions all of the material things of the world. A sack of sugar, or a bag of salt, or an ocean, can each be represented by a chemical formula. Then someone has said that in human person- ality there are fifty-one elements, such as kindness, faith, cour- age, industry, ambition, righteousness, love and devotion. These are the attributes of God himself. And when we put these elements together in the right combinations and proportions in ourselves, we have what someone has called a "magnificent human being."

✓ God not only created man in his own image, but he also endowed him with a set of his own attributes and potentialities, the effective development and utilization of which makes us heirs to his glory. In the physical areas of life, man has many things in common with the animals. But in the field of the personality and the spirit, our only companion in the universe is God our eternal Heavenly Father. In all creation only man can smile and plan and aspire. It was only to God's own offspring that he said, "Thou mayest choose for thyself." Man has built pyramids, skyscrapers, and temples. He has painted pictures, carved images and filled the air with music. But the greatest of all his scientific and artistic possibilities is the ability to develop himself and become like God by following God's personal specifications. ✓

The most spectacular values are always in people, never in things. All wealth, all happiness, and all glory is in people. Jesus said, "The kingdom of God is within you." Every man carries within himself the very things that he seeks. If we seek faith, we need only develop those seeds of faith that God has already planted within ourselves. If we seek courage, we need only search our own souls. And God has given us his word that he will grant unto every man according to that man's own desires. Whatever we elect in our hearts, and foster in our ambitions, life will make ours. If we effectively follow God's directions and keep the inharmonies and discords out of the pattern, then life may become a thing of great beauty and value. Life at its best has been compared to a valuable tapestry, with all of the necessary colors and fabrics effectively harmonized.

Probably among all of the products of man's hands, no work is more attractive or has been more highly praised than

that of the finely designed oriental tapestries. And while weaving
is one of the most primitive of the handicrafts, it is one of the
most fundamental. In addition to its utility and beauty, one of
its most inspiring uses has been to serve as a symbol of life
itself. Over the ages, the prophets, poets, and wise men have
referred to what we do in life by saying that we were "weaving
our own fate," or that we were bringing about our own eternal
destiny.

Many years ago, Anson G. Chester wrote some very constructive lines emphasizing this symbolism. His poem is entitled,
"The Ways of the Tapestry Weavers." The finest quality tapestry
was woven on high-warp vertical looms. The long warp threads
were hung on movable cylinder rollers supported by uprights of
wood or iron. The weaver first sketched his design on the warp
threads and then worked at the back of the loom. With
painstaking care he wrought out the beautiful woven design. The
complete pattern in colors was placed above or immediately
before the workman so that he might be guided in weaving the
exact design with perfectly matched threads and harmoniously
blended colors. If he wished to see his real work he had to step
to the front of the loom or wait until the web was "loosed and
turned." The poet saw in the patient, faithful, and skillful
weaver the symbol of one who effectively designs and works out
the most attractive and useful patterns of life. Mr. Chester
wrote:

THE WAYS OF THE TAPESTRY WEAVERS

Let us take to our hearts a lesson, no braver lesson
  can be,
From the ways of the tapestry weavers on the other
  side of the sea.
Above their heads the pattern hangs, they study it with
  care,
And as to and fro the shuttle leaps, their eyes are
  fastened there.
They tell this curious thing besides, of the patient,
  plodding weaver;
He works on the wrong side evermore, but works for
  the right side ever.
It is only when the weaving stops, and the web is
  loosed and turned,

That he sees his real handiwork, that his marvelous
    skill is learned.

Ah, the sight of its delicate beauty! It pays him
    for all its cost.
No rarer, daintier work than his was ever done by
    the frost!
Then the Master bringeth him golden hire and giveth
    him praise as well,
And how happy the heart of the weaver is, no tongue
    but his own can tell.
The years of man are the looms of God, let down from
    the place of the sun,
Wherein we are always weaving, till the mystic web
    is done.
Weaving blindly but weaving surely, each for himself
    his fate;
We may not see how the right side looks, we can only
    weave and wait.

But, looking above for the pattern, no weaver hath need
    to fear;
Only let him look clear into Heaven—the perfect
    Pattern is there.
If he keeps the face of our Savior forever and always
    in sight,
His toil shall be sweeter than honey, and his weaving
    is sure to be right.
And when his task is ended, and the web is turned and
    shown,
He shall hear the voice of the Master; it shall say to
    him, "Well done!"
And the white-robed angels of Heaven, to bear him
    thence, shall come down,
And God shall give him for his hire—not coin, but a
    golden crown.

Next in importance to the saving of one's own soul is this
thrilling opportunity of designing his own personality and weaving the fabric of his own eternal fate. We may have complete
freedom in the selection of our materials and in the determination of life's quality. And we have the perfect honesty, perfect

fairness, and perfect righteousness of the Master's own life as the pattern to follow. How unfortunate it is when we shift our eyes even temporarily to those patterns where immorality, drunkenness, idleness, falsehood, and profanity are permitted in the design! No matter how hard we try to justify our evil, the discord still becomes a part of the fabric to mar the beauty of our masterpiece with the unsightly blotches of sin. We may argue that a little ugliness will not show, or that it won't matter. But how unhappy any disfigurement will make us when the web is "loosed and turned," and our handiwork is made available for all to see!

In one way, our success in life is like our health. We don't need to suffer from every disease in order to die. One may have a perfectly healthy heart, lungs and kidneys, and yet die with cancer of the liver. In one's life he may be perfectly righteous in almost everything and yet the whole picture may be spoiled if he is immoral, dishonest, disloyal or alcoholic. Martin Luther once said that "one small vice could overcome ten great virtues."

✓ There is a fable about a caterpillar crawling across a magnificent tapestry. The caterpillar stopped on a black spot to inspect the design and try to appreciate the tapestry's beauty. But he could see nothing very attractive about a tapestry so somber, monotonous and lacking in variety. It was only after the caterpillar had become a butterfly and could see the tapestry from a better perspective that he was able to appreciate its thrilling attractiveness. Like the caterpillar, we sometimes get too close to life's weaving to appreciate its design. But when our lives have been completed and our work is put on display, we will be glad if none of the authentic design has been left out and no blotches have been permitted to get in. Certainly we must not leave out the love, or the faith, or the godliness illustrated in the divine pattern on display over our heads. If we are faithful weavers, we will sometime see the beautiful results from our butterfly perspective. Then we will know why there were some black spots included and why the rest of the design was as it was.

A few disciplines are sometimes necessary to make us obedient. We may have some disappointments to make us humble. Some difficult challenges might be included to make us strong, and a lot of faith is necessary to make us godly. And while man has been called the "masterpiece of God," we should remember that each of us will also be his own masterpiece, and our greatest skill must be employed if the final result is to be satisfactory to us and to God.

To do this we must keep our eyes and our hearts centered on the pattern over our heads, while our minds and our hands are faithfully carrying out the work of reproduction.

A Limitless Museum

In his book entitled *The Meaning of Persons*, Paul Tournier says that the intelligence registers everything and turns every person into a kind of limitless museum. This process has been going on for a long time and makes us what we are. Each individual was given a magnificent original endowment when he was created in God's image. We registered some valuable experiences during the long antemortal existence, when we lived with God and walked by sight. Although this knowledge is being temporarily withheld while we learn to walk a little way by faith, it will all be given back to us some day and become a part of our limitless museum.

The dictionary says that a museum is a temple of the muses. It is also a place where valuable art and science treasures are displayed. It is an institution equipped to foster all that is best in life. In the ancient Egyptian city of Alexandria, Ptolemy I built a great museum which served essentially as a university, as well as the world's scientific and cultural center of that day. The museum also contributed to the magnificence of the Golden Age of Greece. There are many museums of art, nature and history still effectively serving our society.

Anciently the muses to whom the museum was sacred were known as the sister goddesses. Aoede sponsored song, Melete, meditation, and Mneme, memory. Later this responsibility was taken over by the nine daughters of Zeus and Mnemosyne. Each presided over her particular art. Calliope—epic poetry, Clio—history, Erato—lyric poetry, Enterpe—music, Melpomene—tragedy, Polyhymnia—religious music, Terpsichore—dance, Thalia—joy, and Urania—astronomy. These great supermortals motivated artists and inspired patrons to make the most of their artistic work and its appreciation. One of the most pleasing expressions of the muses is music. This divine art fosters melody, harmony, rhythm and all of the delights of creating, writing, or rendering colorful musical compositions.

Music in one's own soul makes his spirit responsive to the highest forms of harmony. We sometimes speak of the music of the spheres that was supposed to be produced by the movement of the heavenly bodies, although it was inaudible to human ears. The limitless museum of our souls also has other delights stored away that are as yet unknown to us. And in addition, each soul is capable of producing a kind of music of its own. There is great accomplishment indicated in the song wherein we sing:

There is sunshine in my soul today,
More glorious and bright
Than glows in any earthly sky,
For Jesus is my light.

There is music in my soul today,
A carol to my king,
And Jesus listening can hear
The songs I cannot sing.

There is springtime in my soul today,
For when the Lord is near,
The dove of peace sings in my heart,
The flowers of grace appear.

There is gladness in my soul today,
And hope and praise and love
For blessings that he gives me now,
For joys "laid up" above.

Oh there's sunshine, blessed sunshine,
When the peaceful happy moments roll;
When Jesus shows his smiling face
There is sunshine in the soul.

We can get more beauty into our lives when in the temple of our souls there is more musing about God and faith and righteousness. Our spiritual meditations and ponderings make our lives more pleasant but they also bring us closer to the glory of God.

The word *mathematics* is also associated with the temple of the muses. It infers a disposition toward learning that has a

scientific exactness and precision, leading toward a more accurate
logic and wisdom. There are some other great words that we get
from the muses. One of these is "mosaic." A mosaic is a
beautiful picture or artistic decoration made up of small pieces
of inlaid stone, glass, or jewels. A literary composition may also
be called a mosaic. It too is made up of many diverse elements
producing a picture beauty. Some literary essays are made up of
borrowed thoughts, worked into pleasing, helpful patterns for our
inspiration.

However, the greatest mosaic is that which belongs to life
itself. If we could see our own lives laid out in picture form, we
would probably recognize the various sources from which each
portion came. Some of these inlaid traits and abilities came from
our parents, some from our friends, and some were developed by
our own musings. Many parts of life's mosaic came from God
himself. And some were brought with us from our antemortal
experiences.

Our success in life depends on the amount of skill we use
in putting these various and diverse elements together. A great
ability in the construction of the mosaic of life is the finest of
fine arts. With some good spiritual jewels, some fine moral
ambitions, some excellent social ideals, and some outstanding
mental experiences, we can form some beautiful patterns to
adorn the temple of our lives. This concept of ourselves as a
limitless museum means that we must be experts in museology.
This is the science of collecting only those things that will
upgrade the quality of our museum. The museologist is the one
responsible for the museum. He understands how the selection,
arrangement, and proper care of the things belonging to the
temple should be handled. If the wrong things get into the
temple of our lives, then we may have to get a psychiatrist to
search through our mental rooms and ferret out those inhar-
monious experiences and emotions that are causing us trouble.

Sometimes even a forgotten sin can cause severe spiritual
inharmony. And a discord can grow so that it soon poisons the
atmosphere of the entire temple. Even one guilt or inferiority
complex, when allowed to go untreated, can bring on a kind of
unpleasant malignancy that may destroy ambition and paralyze
the will to achieve. If we have serious personality problems that

remain unsolved, they will often fester, canker, and inflame the tissues, thereby causing serious mental and emotional illness.

Everyone knows the harmful experience that can come from having an uncared-for sliver in the flesh. It may not be visible and the time and place of the injury may have been forgotten, but one foreign element can cause an intolerable inharmony and make the entire body sick. Other foreign elements may have that same effect in the department of our spirits. In either case a good doctor may be able to cut into the infected areas, remove the foreign matter, drain out the poison, kill the infection, and thus help to restore the health.

Certainly it is difficult to live pleasantly while pockets of poison are scattering weakness and soreness through our systems. But in effect this is what happens when we fail to keep our spiritual lives free from the corrosion or attrition of evil.

Sometimes the infections of hate, fear, or misunderstanding can get so deeply embedded in our lives that the personality is made comparatively useless. A broken-hearted wife was recently trying to find some miraculous cure for the liquor addiction that was threatening to ruin the life of her husband and their family. The wife herself has a great love of righteousness. She has high ideals, fine attitudes and the best habits of spiritual success. But her husband has allowed some wrong things to be stored away in the back rooms of his limitless museum which are causing the inharmony that is now threatening to destroy their marriage. Because of his problems, life has become almost unbearable for her. It has been said that "there can be no greater suffering than to love someone purely and perfectly who is bent upon evil and self-destruction." However, she has little chance to escape her suffering, as she knows that if she leaves him the liquor disease will get worse, the immorality will increase, and the immortal welfare of his soul itself may go down the drain, so to speak.

Socrates said, "Know thyself." Because the husband has not followed this instruction, he does not realize the awful ruin that he is causing in himself and in others. However, all of us could improve our situation if we would follow Socrates a little more closely and make an accurate catalogue of those things which make up the mosaic of our lives. Any slivers in our fingers should be attended to, and those skeletons in our closets should be gotten rid of. If we cleaned out a few of our unsightly back rooms, we might then very profitably upgrade our life's collection. We can know ourselves better if we will get a little more truth into our meditations, a little more music into our minds, and some more religious harmony into our souls. We should also make sure that some cultural shortage is not throwing our lives out of balance too far. If we desire a more beautiful mosaic for our temple, we should give a greater attention to the expertness of our museology.

Even without Mr. Tournier reminding us, we should find out more about some of the deeper meanings of our own persons. We have known for a long time that everything that we think and everything that we do is being recorded and stored away in our lives, and each of us is furnishing the temple in which he will live forever. We should build such a pleasant environment that the Divine Spirit will be pleased to dwell with us. The Apostle Paul said, "Know ye not that your body is the temple of the Holy Ghost which is in you." (1 Cor. 6:19.) The Holy Ghost has a specific assignment for teaching us truth and righteousness. His function is to help direct our meditations and increase the amount of the music and harmony in our souls. The body, mind, personality, and spirit which make up that limitless museum where these things are being recorded have a tremendous value. If the worth of a soul is greater than the wealth of the whole earth, then certainly it surpasses the value of the Louvre, or the Metropolitan Museum of Art, or the Smithsonian Institute. In the various departments of our limitless museum, there should be sufficient amounts of love, truth, devotion to right, and faith in God. We should have good attitudes in our minds, integrity in our hearts, joy and color in our personalities, and harmony in our souls.

It seems that this conception of ourselves as a limitless museum where everything is registered and everything is limitless is a very helpful one. We know that all human beings are self-registering instruments of everything that they do. Every one of us is limitless. We know that God is limitless, and if as his children we obey his laws we will be limitless also. Our destiny to become like God means that we have limitless possibilities. The eternal duration of our lives makes us limitless as to time.

The divine proclamation that "men are that they might have joy" indicates that we are limitless in our happiness potential. Certainly we are limitless in our opportunity to do good. We are limitless in the harmony, love, and music that may be generated in our souls. Our individual mosaic may include as much beauty, righteousness, and faith as we have the ability to put into it. And we are not required to include in our lives anything that is not beautiful, useful, and entirely agreeable with us. God gave us a kind of unlimited museologist authority when he said, "Thou mayest choose for thyself," and we may make our limitless museum a storehouse of faith, a treasury of righteousness, and a mosaic that will include every ability.

The museum that Ptolemy built in Alexandria has long since returned to the dust; the ancient temple presided over by the daughters of Zeus and Mnemosyne has also passed away; but the temple of the soul will last forever. It was built in the very image of God. It is constructed to receive the inspiration of the Holy Ghost and it was intended that we should do our full part to make it the most worthwhile of all of God's creations. He will help us to constantly reaffirm this eternal destiny in our lives by our good deeds.

Living Waters

E merson once said, "There is a great deal more kindness than is ever spoken. The whole human family is bathed in an element of love like a fine ether." The whole human family is also bathed in a universal success and happiness. The world is filled with courage, initiative, industry and understanding. But while the greatest success possibilities are all about us, they often go unused because we fail to internalize them. Every success is an inside job. And it is pretty difficult for us to utilize the available education or to be effectively motivated by the great virtues as long as they remain external to ourselves. For this reason the children of ambitious parents do not always reach the objectives that their fathers hope they will. This is also the reason why the children of God usually fall so far below the destiny that he has marked for them.

Thirty-four centuries ago God came down to the top of Mount Sinai and, to the accompaniment of the lightnings and thunders of that sacred mountain, gave those important success laws called the Ten Commandments. But only as the Israelites got these laws inside themselves were their goals realized. All of the successes, even as God has outlined them, would be easy to accomplish if God's Spirit activated us as it does him. Someone has accounted for our failure as followers of the Master by explaining that mostly we are only Bible Christians. This is a condition where the Christianity remains in the Bible and not very much of it gets into us. As has been pointed out, it doesn't do us very much good to go through college unless the college goes through us. No matter how great the possibilities are that surround us, there is usually no significant accomplishment until they are internalized.

As I left my home a few mornings ago I stepped on a black walnut. I held it in my hand as I walked to work, and I thought about it as a symbol of life. Its outside is covered with a shell as hard as stone. And if you could see into its insides you would discover a great network of stony reinforcements. But in the labyrinths in between, there is an unimpressive substance that has a gigantic power. If this seed is planted under the right circumstances, heat is developed on its inside. You might turn a blowtorch on the outside of a walnut with little effect, but when heat begins to form on the inside of a man *or* a walnut, important things begin to happen. In the case of the walnut, this great internal power breaks the stony external shell as though it were paper, and a little shoot is started up on an important mission toward the sun. Within this walnut God has placed an ability with sufficient power to attract, out of the elements in the soil, the water, and the air, all of the ingredients necessary to make a great walnut tree, producing wood, foliage, blossoms, fragrance and fruit, and multiplying by a million times the original investment.

But God did not put his greatest gifts inside of walnuts. Every human soul was created in the image of God and he has been endowed with a set of the attributes and potentialities of Deity, the development of which is one of the purposes for which we live. The greatest idea that I know of in the world is that by living the principles of the gospel of Jesus Christ we can acquire a far more miraculous power whereby we may attract out of our environment all of the elements necessary to become "even as God is."

Sometimes we err because we attempt to accumulate our success as we do our material wealth, by piling up around us a lot of external things. In illustrating his instructions for accomplishment, Jesus referred to water as the primary success ingredient. The comparison is a good one, as water is the universal element, and it also serves as a symbol of life. However, much of the earth's water is either salty, stagnant, or otherwise unfit to serve our human needs. Therefore in his illustration Jesus spoke of living water—that is, water that has life and power. The biggest material problem of mankind has always been the sources, supply, purification, and distribution of good water. Pure living water is the best means we have for making the earth itself a beautiful, pleasant, and productive place to live. Even in the wastelands of the desert, some of the richest treasures of the earth can be brought forth when the right kind of water is applied to thirsty soil; whereas without water everything fails,

including our agriculture, our commerce, our manufacturing, and
life itself. We need water to cool our engines, beautify our
landscapes, wash our faces, and maintain our health. But even so,
our success is not like pouring water into a cistern; rather it is
like opening a spring. And the fact that every living thing must
drink in order to live applies as much to the spirit as it does to
the body. People die when they remain too long in the desert
without water. But there is a more serious kind of spiritual
death, which takes place when our sources of truth and righteousness are cut off.

The Lord effectively pointed out this danger to the ancient
Israelites through the Prophet Jeremiah. He said, "for my people
have committed two evils; they have forsaken me, the fountain
of living waters, and hewed them out cisterns, broken cisterns,
that can hold no water." (Jer. 2:13.) Jesus amplified this success
procedure a little further as he was passing through Samaria on
his way to Jerusalem. He stopped to rest at Jacob's well near
the ancient sity of Shechem, and requested a drink from the
woman of Sychar. During their conversation he said to her, "If
thou knewest the gift of God, and who it is that saith unto
thee, Give me a drink; thou wouldest have asked of him, and he
would have given thee living water." He said, "Whosoever drinketh of the water that I shall give him shall never thirst; but the
water that I shall give him shall be in him a well of water
springing up into everlasting life." (John 4:10, 14.)

A spring of living water can transform a barren desert into
a beautiful and productive oasis. And the spiritual counterpart of
this operation can work an equal miracle in human lives. The
Samaritan woman seemed to be greatly impressed with this idea.
And we should all get excited with the possibility of having this
living water springing up within ourselves to bring about our
eternal life. Pure water will be one of the secrets of the
regeneration of the earth as it is being prepared for its millennium of a thousand years of peace and happiness. The Lord said,
"And in the barren deserts there shall come forth pools of living
water; and the parched ground shall no longer be a thirsty land."
(D&C 133:29.) But the richest of life's treasures do not come
about as a result of water breaking forth in the wastelands of
the desert. The greatest enrichment comes when this refreshing
spiritual influence washes up through our lives to purify them
and make them productive in godliness.

Dr. Henry C. Link once said that nothing puts so much order into life as to live by a set of sound principles, and the most sound principles are the principles of the gospel of Jesus Christ. Living God's law is the process by which eternal life is brought about. The scriptures say, "For as the Father hath life in himself; so hath he given to the Son to have life in himself." (John 5:26.) If we are properly obedient to the principles of the gospel, our lives will be made self-sustaining with a supply of their own. The Lord has said, "Unto him that keepeth my commandments I will give the mysteries of my kingdom, and the same shall be in him a well of living water, springing up unto eternal life." (D&C 63:23.)

As water is the symbol of life, so it is also the symbol of cleanliness. We can keep our bodies clean by thoroughly washing them with soap and water. We can also cleanse our souls by the effective use of the soap and water of repentance. And then in the waters of baptism, we may have our sins washed away by the Savior's atoning sacrifice. In describing the long black night of apostasy that would settle upon the world following the crucifixion, the Prophet Amos told of a time when this water would not be available. He said, "Behold, the days come, saith the Lord God, that I will send a famine in the land, not a famine of bread, nor a thirst for water, but of hearing the words of the Lord: and they shall wander from sea to sea, and from the north even to the east, they shall run to and fro to seek the word of the Lord, and shall not find it." We might imagine the tragedy of such a disaster, for Amos said, "In that day shall [they] . . . faint for thirst." (Amos 8:11-13.)

God always provides the remedy before the plague. On the Tuesday before his crucifixion on Friday, the Lord sat on the Mount of Olives and foretold the wars and troubles that would immediately precede his second coming to the earth. He said, "And this gospel of the kingdom shall be preached in all the world as a witness to all nations; and then shall the end come." (Matt. 24:14.) At the Feast of the Passover, Jesus stood up and cried, "If any man thirst, let him come unto me and drink." (John 7:37.)

In spite of the fact that the gospel of Jesus Christ has now been restored to the earth in the fullness never before known, and in spite of the fact that the old invitation to drink of the waters of life freely (see D&C 10:66) has been extended to us anew, there are many in our world who still faint from thirst.

Travelers to that ancient city of Shechem near the site of Jacob's well tell us that there are rivers of water flowing beneath the streets. During the daylight hours they cannot be heard, but when evening comes and the clamor dies out of the streets, and kindly sleep rests upon the city, then quite audibly in the hush of the night you can hear the music of these buried streams. In a similar way in the quiet obedience of faithful lives, God touches those hidden abilities implanted in the depths of our own souls and releases that great source of spiritual strength to vitalize our souls and bring about our eternal exaltation.

As God has provided our earth with its many underground reservoirs and its rivers that can be brought to the surface and used to keep our earth productive and beautiful, so our own great hidden reservoirs of life may be tapped to make us become like God our Eternal Father. As already stated, Jesus said to the woman of Sychar, "If thou knewest the gift of God, and who it is that saith unto thee, Give me a drink; thou wouldest have asked of him, and he would have given thee living water." He said, "Whosoever drinketh of the water that I shall give him shall never thirst; but the water that I shall give him shall be in him a well of water springing up into everlasting life." (John 4:10, 14.) And God has promised that when this underground source is tapped and made into flowing wells these life-giving waters can turn our human wastelands into beautiful, fruitful gardens.

While John the Revelator was serving out his banishment in solitude and loneliness on the island of Patmos, he received a visit from the resurrected Jesus. John says that he was in the spirit on the Lord's day when he heard behind him a great voice, as of a trumpet, saying, "I am Alpha and Omega, the first and the last." John turned to see who had spoken to him and he saw "one like unto the Son of man, clothed with a garment down to the foot" and girded about with a golden girdle. Then in trying to describe this great resurrected, glorified, indescribable being, John said, "His head and his hairs were white like wool, as white as snow; and his eyes were as a flame of fire." We sometimes try to describe a certain trait of someone's personality by saying his eyes twinkle, or there is a light in his eyes, or his face glows. We might try to imagine how many hundreds of times that trait must have been magnified to have prompted John to say that "his eyes were as a flame of fire." (See Rev. 1:10, 13-14.)

In continuing the comparison, John said, "And his voice [was] as the sound of many waters." (Rev. 1:15.) I do not know exactly what prompted him to make this comparison, but I like to think of this function of the Redeemer which he expressed in his own terms as being like a great fountain of living waters bringing life to all mankind. Then as his voice touches the depths of our own souls with power we can feel living water bubbling up in us, invigorating our minds and making our lives beautiful, productive and happy.

Water is still the universal element. It is still the symbol of life and a sign of our success. It was also designated by the Master to be one of the emblems of his sacrament to remind us to always remember him. And my prayer is that God will bless us, that living water will spring up in us unto our eternal lives.

Marasmus

Some time ago, it was reported that the babies in a certain South American foundling home were getting sick from an unknown cause. Some of them were even dying from a mysterious malady that no one could diagnose. The children showed no physical signs of disease, and the local doctors were baffled in trying to determine the cause of their trouble. In spite of all that could be done, the children continued to get worse. They lost interest in their food, their toys, and even in their surroundings. It just happened that a team of United Nations doctors were working in this particular country at that time and they were invited to make an investigation.

After studying the situation for a few days, these doctors wrote out an interesting prescription. They directed that for ten minutes out of every waking hour, each child should be picked up by one of the nurses and hugged, kissed, fondled, and made a substantial fuss over. After a period of this treatment, an interesting thing happened. The children began to brighten and were soon eating again. Within a fairly short time they were also back playing with their toys, and it was not long until the strange epidemic had disappeared altogether.

The United Nations doctors identified this fatal lethargy as marasmus. This disease is a mysterious and gradual wasting away of the body, which seems to strike at the very young and the very old when there is not enough love in their diet. It is a kind of progressive emaciation that takes place in the body and the mind when the constitution has been enfeebled by a lack of the greatest of all health requirements—love. William James, the great Harvard psychologist, once said that "the deepest hunger in human beings is the desire to be appreciated," and when this hunger is not satisfied, serious problems develop.

Some of the most primary human needs are centered in

loving and in being loved; both are important. Someone once asked a distinguished churchman what the religious commandment was that ranked next to love in importance. He said he didn't know that there was one. When love is absent, this enfeebling, disabling, miserable sickness known as marasmus usually sets in, in some form. It has no organic cause; yet, in some variety, there is probably more marasmus in the world that any other kind of disease. All too frequently, to our own detriment, we ignore or trample on that great command wherein Jesus said, "love one another."

Presently, there is a serious marasmus epidemic in the world because, either consciously or unconsciously, too many people have gone too far in this process of withholding their love. Many children as well as older people have contracted serious mental and emotional disorders because they feel that they are unwanted and unloved. Among the most serious sins committed within the marriage relationship is either a withholding of love or a withholding of its expression.

I know a number of high ranking Churchmen and some other officials who cause a lot of marasmus because, as they take themselves a little too seriously, they tend to draw within themselves and deny their followers of the natural right to feel the warm, friendly interest that should come from leadership. Everyone should occasionally examine himself for his friendliness. Someone has said that the butcher's boy couldn't make a mistake because he loved everybody. When anyone has the right kind of love in his heart, even his cat and his dog are better off as a consequence. All animals do better when they are highly regarded and treated with kindness.

The story is told of a little dog that served as a mascot in a hospital. The nurses all played with him and the doctors patted him. As the little dog was stimulated by the kindness of many people, he frolicked about and leaped for joy. He always smiled happy, little puppy-dog smiles and wagged his tail with great enthusiasm. His coat was shiny, and he had excellent health in every way because he had happiness on his insides.

Then the people involved decided to perform an experiment on the puppy by withholding their affection. Instead of cheerfully greeting him, everyone scolded him and made threatening motions when he got in their way. The little dog soon felt that he didn't have a friend in the world. Under this new treatment of being ignored, scorned, and abused, the happy twinkle soon disappeared from his eyes. His tail lost its enthusiasm, his food no longer had any appeal, and the poor little dog became terribly sick with a miserable case of marasmus. His coat lost its glossy sheen and he probably would have died if the experiment had not been discontinued.

When the little dog's friends returned to their natural attitudes of admiration and love, he soon became his old self again. His tail got back its enthusiasm, his coat recovered its luster, and his health and vigor fully returned. One of the characteristics of the millennium will be the decrease in marasmus because the enmity now existing between man and man and man and beast will cease.

But marasmus is now one of the most common and most serious of all diseases among people. When one lacks friends, he is much more likely to get physically, mentally, or morally sick. When a salesman leaves his home in the morning feeling like a harassed puppy-dog, he usually doesn't do very well in his work. And many wives actually die or lose their mental balance because of the marasmus caused by their husbands. It is a well-known fact that many people die soon after retiring from their work because they feel that they are no longer needed. Many mothers die or get sick soon after their children have moved away and can get along without them. The morbidity rate is much higher than it need be among the general population because so many people think that they get too much of the unloved-puppy-dog treatment. Certainly the most devastating of all human emotions is this sense of being alone, of being unloved or being not wanted, of being unworthy, of feeling that one's own self is not worthwhile. I know of a frail, delicate, timid-looking little wife who has almost beaten her husband to death, emotionally, by committing the capital sin of belittling him.

Anyone who has to do with counseling people about their family problems knows of the terrible toll that is taken each year by marasmus. Someone had a great idea when he said there should be an eleventh commandment saying, "Thou shalt not be unkind." Many wives are laid low by nervous diseases and mental illnesses because of the criticism and unkind treatment they receive. One husband tries to cover up his own shortcomings with a daily ritual of telling his wife how much he hates her. This is in spite of the fact that she is already a marasmus invalid. The suffering forced upon others by our unkindness will probably constitute a bigger percentage of our total sins than many of our other crimes put together.

Centuries ago, it was foretold that hate and scorn would be one of the primary problems of the latter days. Speaking of our time, Jesus said: "Then shall many be offended, and shall betray one another, and shall hate one another. . . . And because iniquity shall abound, the love of many shall wax cold." (Matt. 24:10, 12.) The Apostle Paul said: "In the last days perilous times shall come. For men shall be lovers of their own selves, covetous, boasters, proud, blasphemers, unthankful, unholy." He mentioned one of our most serious problems when he said that we would be "without natural affection." He said that we would not only be disobedient to parents but we would also be "haters of God." (See 2 Tim. 3:1-3, Rom. 1:30-31.)

Our newspapers bear their testimonies that all of these prophecies are now being fulfilled. The body of our civilization itself is now bloated with the pus of hate. Our wars, our race riots, our divorces, our rebellious children, and our disobedience to God are all manifestations of this awful disease.

How fortunate one is who is equipped with a strong "natural affection," having an abundance of love and good feelings in his heart for others! And how grateful one should be if his wife, his children, his employer, and his employees are kind, considerate, and loving as human beings! "Love is a beautiful necessity of the soul."

Plato says that "all loves should be merely stepping stones to the love of God." Everyone wants to be loved and everyone needs a good supply of love in his own heart. No one will ever be really successful in his own life until he knows how to feel, live, give and express this most noble emotion. There are so many who fail in this accomplishment merely because they don't know how. For some, these laws of love are as difficult to master as the laws of electricity.

I once heard a daughter complain that her father was not very friendly to her boyfriend. But I know that her father wanted to be friendly more than almost any other thing; he just didn't know how. Sometimes we see someone trying so hard to be a good conversationalist, or a good public speaker, or just a good person, only to fall on his face because he doesn't know how. We need to learn how to love good people, good ideas, and worthwhile accomplishments. Jesus said that it is our duty to love even our enemies and do good to those who injure us, and probably the best way to develop this ability is by a more effective practice. Jesus said, "Give, and it shall be given unto you; good measure, pressed down, and shaken together, and running over." (Luke 6:38.) Of course, we should be careful not to let any perversions get into our love by loving the wrong things. Some people develop a great love of liquor, immorality, and dope. The scriptures tell us of people who loved Satan more than God, and these evil loves have a terrifying ability to take their devotees captive, whereas a righteous love leaves us free.

When the freedom-loving United States captured Cuba, the Philippines, West Germany, and Japan, they educated their subjects in the responsibility of liberty and then set them free. However, when Russia captured Eastern Germany, Hungary, and Czechoslovakia, the people were made slaves. Slavery has always been the course followed by evildoers. And force and dictatorship have always been the practices promoted by Satan. This idea has an interesting parallel in that if one falls in love with any evil thing, such as dope, booze, nicotine, immorality, crime, or sin, he is always taken captive by it. For when the habits of evil are well enough established, they become almost impossible to change. This is not the case with good habits. That is, one may fall in love with telling the truth, being righteous, loving beauty, or going to Church, and still maintain his freedom so that he may change his program at any time he desires. God is the God of freedom and he has said that if we will serve him, he will make us free. However, if we serve Satan we are soon lost, inasmuch as everything that Satan does is connected with force and slavery. In the council in heaven Satan said that he wanted to save all mankind, but he wanted to do it by compulsion. Wouldn't it be interesting if it had been made a part of our natures to become "addicted" to "study" and to "prayer" and to "righteousness" and to "paying our tithing"? But this is not God's way of doing things. In the council of heaven, Lucifer proposed that all men should be saved by compulsion; and when God held out for freedom, Satan rebelled, and he and his followers were expelled from heaven.

However, it seems that Satan was able to get some kind of slavemaking properties into all of these evil practices. Jesus himself said, "Whosoever committeth sin is the servant of sin." (John 8:34.) But where righteousness is concerned, we are free. And it is possible for us to get a great thrill of satisfaction from doing great and good things merely because they are right. And we may be as righteous as we desire to be, merely because we want to. We may learn to love God with the greatest possible love. Jesus said, "A new commandment I give unto you, That ye love one another; as I have loved you, that ye also love one another." (John 13:34.) That would be wonderful. If we are capable, we may love our fellowmen as much as we love God. What a great ability it would be if we could love life, love our work, love our families, and love God with a genuine affection!

In the Church, we speak a great deal about the advantages of Christian fellowship; and yet we don't always do very much about it on an extended scale. There are a great many inactive Church members. Some may be inactive because they do not believe in the doctrines of the Church. However, most of the inactivity in the Church is because the one afflicted with it has developed some guilt complex, or because someone has offended him, or because he has been made to feel inferior or not wanted. Consequently, he has turned away from Church activity, and because of the religious marasmus that has developed, even his soul may sicken and die. Of course, we should keep in mind the fact that the reason some people may not love us is primarily our own fault. And just suppose that because we follow Satan we may cause God to withhold his love from us. Then, like the orphans in the South American foundling home, we may wither and die spiritually, which may be the most dreadful kind of marasmus.

Jesus was trying to prevent the spread of this disease by getting us to practice righteousness, and he prescribed that love instead of force should be the dominating emotion in our lives. As Goethe pointed out, "We are shaped and fashioned by what

we love." If we love the right things, our lives will be good. And
if we remember what happened to the little puppy-dog, we may
be able to give more importance to that great commandment of
Jesus: "A new commandment I give unto you, that you love one
another as I have loved you." Obedience to this law requires
that we must really understand and learn to practice one of the
greatest of all skills having to do with love. We must not
withhold our love or distort this great emotion in violation of
God's command. If we do our best, God will help us to be
successful in keeping the two greatest commandments.

The Mask

There is an interesting custom in our society where we sometimes wear masks. Robbers may occasionally wish to disguise their appearance, and some welders, deep sea divers, athletes, or those engaged in warfare with poisonous gas, may want to give their faces a protecting cover. In the ancient Grecian and Roman theaters, the actors always wore masks. This was not to conceal their identity, but to enlarge upon it. They painted the appropriate characters upon the actor's mask so that his theater personality would fit the part he had been cast to play.

Because our present-day actors do not wear masks, we are often unable to distinguish the hero from the villain even by the end of the play, whereas the ancients knew what each actor was from the beginning. We still put masks on clowns so that we can know in advance what to expect. In the past, masquerade balls have been held where everyone comes in costume and wears a mask. Then no one knows who he is dancing with until he is asked to remove his mask during the last dance. There are some real life situations where we have difficulty finding out who we are dancing with. Some of life's masks are made of selfishness, some are of pride, some of prejudice, some of deception, some of fear, and some of sin. But consciously, unconsciously, or subconsciously, in one way or another, we frequently conceal our real identities even from those who are closest to us.

Many men never really get to know their wives, and there are many husbands who keep their own identity a secret. There are many great souls living in our society whose greatness remains forever unknown to us. Sometimes we never appreciate or understand people because we are not able to see into the depths of their minds where the real person is, or we are never able to feel the ambitions that are burning in their souls. We can understand why a criminal sometimes has an urge to hide behind a mask, but other people have many different reasons for hiding behind falsehoods, excuses, pretexts, subterfuges, promises, inferiority and guilt complexes. Even when we go to borrow money, seek employment, or do our courting, we put on the camouflage of a new suit, or a red necktie, or the false front of some assumed behavior to distract attention and prevent others from knowing us as we know ourselves.

We hide our skeletons in a closet and put on our poker faces to make sure that our secrets will not be given away. With a certain amount of bluffing and deception we keep the facts away from as many people as possible, including ourselves. Those make-up men who used to try to hide the theater villain behind a set of false whiskers weren't much ahead of certain female members of our species who hide themselves behind a set of false eyelashes, green eyeshadow, pink cheeks, multicolored wigs, padded figures, and lifted faces.

Our society itself runs the kind of a general masquerade that led John Milton to refer to "The World's Vain Mask." For centuries, nations at war have tried to camouflage their armies and have given out a great deal of misleading information to deceive the enemy. As individuals, we more or less follow that same pattern, and the most common place to begin any disguise is to cover up the face. The face is not only the most identifying part of the person, but it is also the most important part. In this very small area, located on the front part of the head, the Creator has assembled most of the keys of our personal power. The face is the general agent of our public relations, as well as the producer of our general success. We have had a great furor going on recently as to how many inches above the knees a female's pedestal limbs should be exposed. In some of the eastern countries, women not only keep their knees completely covered but they also wear heavy veils over their faces.

As far as all practical purposes are concerned, when one's face is covered his entire personality is pretty well hidden. A picture of one's face is usually required when he is making an application for a job, or securing a passport, or trying to preserve his identity for posterity. It is not necessary to photograph the whole body, or to show a likeness of the knees, or to include a picture of the backbone. A picture of one's face can usually represent and identify the whole personality to everyone's satisfaction. Certainly the human face is one of the greatest of all of God's creations.

Some time ago while I was in Western Canada, the Canadian Pacific Railroad brought to the hotel a colored film of the beautiful Canadian Rockies. If you want scenery at its best, here it is. The photographers had gathered together the most impressive landscapes from thousands of square miles. They had included the most famous mountain peaks, giant forests, spectacular waterfalls, colored flowers, and other striking scenic attractions. But where could you find any glacier, or tree, or sunset, as beautiful as the face of your wife, your mother, or your daughter? The great Creator did not put nearly as much human interest into a thousand square miles of his greatest natural wonders as he did in the few square inches of a smiling, righteous, loving, radiant, happy, human face.

Those parts of the face called the eyes serve as our instruments of vision. But they play other important roles. They are also the windows of the soul. They are the registrars of a person's inner joys and sorrows. Even more than the voice, the eyes speak the approval or disapproval of the person. They also express our loves, hates, and fears. We sing a song saying, "Drink to me only with thine eyes." In the eyes we may see thoughts and emotions. There we recognize the eagerness, scorn, guilt, or ambition that activates the personality. Through the eyes we can estimate mental ability, measure enthusiasm, or feel the depth of some despair that may be torturing the soul. The eyes are also one of our most important inlets for light and understanding. God did not fashion the eyes only for their utility, he also made them for their beauty. He was very generous in putting color, sparkle, and interest into the eyes. He decorated the eyes with graceful eyebrows, covered them with automatic protecting eyelids, and ornamented them with smart-looking eyelashes. The eyes have a most remarkable ability for expression, and they are among our chief instruments for teaching, selling, and inspiring.

Another prominent member of this important facial team is the mouth, and while there is sometimes a good reason to keep it closed and covered up, it serves as the port of entry for our physical nourishment. It is also equipped to produce oratory,

music, logic, and words of faith. It is one of the chief
instruments used in education, motivation, and communication.
But in building usefulness into the human face, God also kept its
general landscaping in mind. In its center he placed a set of
pearly teeth in an attractive framework of red lips, and under-
girded by a strong chin.

The nose is another facial wonder. While it is an important
part of the general decoration, it also serves as our oxygen inlet
and carries the responsibility for our magic sense of smell.
Through the nose God fills our lives with the fragrance of the
lilacs, the roses, the violets, and the honeysuckle. Through this
source he also gives us the wonderful exhilaration that can come
from breathing his own creation of fresh, clean, invigorating air.
A good nose also contributes its full share to the delight of a
savory Sunday dinner. The impressiveness of the face is also
increased by the color of the cheeks, the dimple in the chin, and
those two useful ears that protrude at right angles out of the
semi-background. The ears also have great utility. They bring to
us the harmony of music and the inspiration and beauty of a
great variety of sounds. This entire facial team is dominated by a
broad forehead that houses the master intelligence called the
brain. The brain was created to be the presiding officer of the
personality. Most of our satisfactions in life come from the way
that we ourselves think. And whatever thought may occupy the
brain, it is soon pictured in the face.

As a crowning glory for the face, the head was adorned
with a colorful and useful covering of hair which, when properly
cut, arranged, and cared for, puts some beautiful finishing
touches on the whole picture. The entire person of a human
individual is the functional wonder, as well as the artistic
masterpiece, of the universe. Where would you look for any
form more noble than a great human being with its many
godlike relationships? The human form, the human personality,
the human mind, and the human spirit, combine to make the
most beautiful, the most inspiring, the most valuable creation in
the world. Even the knees have a great value in addition to that
which comes from exposure. They are among our most effective
instruments of locomotion. They elevate and lower the person
and regulate the posture. And the grandeur of the entire body is
greatly increased when the soul is on its knees.

However, the face stands for the whole person. It is the chief agent of the intelligence; it is our greatest social asset; it is the gateway to learning; and it is the foundation for the success of our souls. Every human being was created in God's image with a destiny to become like his eternal parent. We need to be constantly reaffirming our inheritance. And this can best be done by taking off our masks so that we can at least get a good look at ourselves as we actually are. We cannot bring about our greatest accomplishments while we ourselves are hiding behind our delusions and errors.

The apostle Paul says, "Now we see through a glass, darkly; but then face to face: now I know in part; but when that which is perfect is come, then that which is in part shall be done away." (See 1 Cor. 13:12, 10.) Long before the last dance of life arrives, everyone ought to know who he is dancing with. C. S. Lewis says that there are no ordinary people. Not once in our lifetime have we ever talked with any mere mortal. Nations are mortal. Our culture, arts, and civilization are mortal, but all human souls are eternal and will live forever. The Apostle Paul says, "Be not forgetful to entertain strangers: for thereby some have entertained angels unawares." (Heb. 13:1.) Mr. Lewis says that when the veils of our mortality are drawn aside, then the dullest and most uninteresting person with whom we have ever talked may be the kind of being that we feel like worshipping. What a challenging idea—that we are now preparing for unlimited privileges in a society of gods and goddesses!

In the light of our overwhelming possibilities it is not too early to start conducting all of our dealings on the highest possible plane. Certainly the most godly standards should apply to all of our friendships, our loves, our social activities, our religion, and even our politics. And when we are asked to unmask for the last dance, we will all want to be at our best and be on good terms with ourselves. We will then want to be in harmony with that most magnificent company of which we will then be an important part. In the courting process, a future companion is supposed to have an opportunity to get acquainted with his prospective mate. But we sometimes put on our false whiskers, make unrealistic promises, are untruthful in our philosophies, and attempt to hide our defects behind some outward show. Then in the living process we pursue a similar course by putting on our masks in the hope of covering up our bad habits, our personality shortcomings, and our ridiculous sins. When the last dance arrives we may be seriously humiliated if we are still counting on being able to keep our weaknesses and bad judgments out of sight.

It is an interesting fact that all people do not go to a masquerade ball dressed as princes, kings, and wise men. For some mysterious reason some of us seem to prefer to dress ourselves as clowns, weaklings, hippies, beggars, sinners, and ne'er-do-wells. One of our most destructive human weaknesses is our strong tendency to want to play those parts that are beneath us. No one goes to the masquerade dressed as a clown and then goes around thinking, acting, and feeling like a king.

When, for too long a period, we disguise ourselves as drunkards, delinquents, and sinners, we may have difficulty in changing those characteristics when the last dance is called. What a shock it may be to some of us when we come to stand before God, if we then find that we have lived empty lives! If we have not included a sufficient amount of faith, righteousness, obedience, and the love of God, we may have empty faces.

Many years ago a horror movie serial was going around called "No Face." The climax always came each week when the villain was captured and unmasked. Then everyone was horrified to discover that this poor unfortunate had no face, and without a face he was nobody. We must not tolerate any activity that would tend to produce a "no-face" ending for our eternal lives.

Jesus was not planning for us to play a small or a low part when he referred approvingly to the Psalmist's words: "Ye are gods; and all of you are the children of the most High." (Ps. 82:6; John 10:34.) What a tragedy it would be if we distorted the image of our eternal possibilities by acting as though we were the children of Satan! If we act like the devil now, we may find that his defects will be showing in our faces during the last dance. What we should do is to have some good self-evaluating interviews while we are unmasked. Then with a lot of good works, God may help us to build those great eternal values into our lives that will show up in our faces and qualify us for our high calling as children of God, created and matured in his image.

Mealtime

Some of the most important responsibilities of our lives have to do with our diet. In a physical sense we become what we eat. From our food we get our energies, our abilities, our bodies, and our lives themselves. Eating is the process by which we build our faculties and our senses. This is also how we strengthen our personalities. Our hands, our heads, and our feet are made up of the things that we have eaten. And one of the most important lessons of life is to learn to eat the right things, in the right amounts, in the right ways, and at the right times. While Magellan was making his famous first trip around the world, many of his sailors died of scurvy because of a deficiency of vitamins in their diet. But while this was happening, they had on board a cargo of limes which would have solved their problems if they had only eaten them. By adopting and maintaining a proper diet we can increase not only the length of our lives, but their breadth and meaning as well.

Among the important considerations involved in eating are content, volume, regularity, and pleasantness. For this purpose we set aside three periods during each day that are known as mealtime. The beginning meal is breakfast. It comes the first thing in the morning. After a night of refreshing sleep, we arise to greet a brand-new day. God dispenses our lives to us a day at a time, and it is with the strength derived from our food that we are able to complete our share of the work of the world that has been allotted to us for that day. A good breakfast puts fuel in the tank and gives us the necessary power for the day's accomplishments. But food does much more than provide power. It also increases our interest in life. By its pleasant taste, its appetizing aroma, its stimulating strength, and its general joy, it adds much to a life that might otherwise be dull and drab. Our food is filled with energy, warmth, vision, health, strength, and life itself. It also benefits our senses of pleasure, sociability, and ambition.

Many people add to this sense of well-being by saying a grace before eating in which they express their gratitude and appreciation. What a delight it can be to start off a great day with a morning prayer directed to the Creator and Giver of all good things! At its best we begin the day by breathing some invigorating fresh air into our lungs, getting a good breakfast into our stomachs, and a sense of gratitude to God into our hearts. These generate the energy, strengthen the will, motivate the spirit, and help to solve the challenges of a wonderful new day in the best possible way. Therefore, we might well think of breakfast as our opportunity meal.

The second meal period is scheduled for the noonday. By midday the fuel tank has run a little bit empty, which makes it desirable for us to pause, relax, refuel, and revitalize ourselves with lunch. As with breakfast, the pleasure of this meal can be greatly increased when eaten in the presence of good company. To take a friend to lunch helps to recharge our satisfactions, and it renews our physical and spiritual energy. Then during the afternoon we finish the work that life has prescribed for that day and approach the richest part of the day, which is the evening period. This is the period that has been set aside as dinnertime. Dinner is not just one of our most necessary activities. It can also be one of our most pleasant. This is when we have that stimulating experience of sitting around the table with those who are the most important people in the world to us. These are the members of our own family for whom God has given us a special affection.

John Howard Payne once said about the home, "A charm from the sky seems to hallow us there." A good dinner period builds up the family physically; but when eaten under the right circumstances it also builds up the family members socially, mentally, and spiritually. There can be many reasons for Mr. Payne and for us to sing, "Be it ever so humble, there's no place like home." Sometimes people dress for dinner. They put on formal clothes in order to look, feel, and be at their best. Appearance is a very important part of every mealtime, just as it is also a very important part of life. And in addition to wearing attractive dinner clothes, everyone at mealtime should have his spirits, attitudes, and manners also arrayed in their best apparel. The activities of this important dinnertime function also provide

genuine companionship and great fun for everyone. We should be
particularly careful that no perversions are allowed to get into
our mealtime. The dinner table is no place to read the newspaper, or indulge in accusations, or to cause someone embarrass-
ment, or to foster any kind of bitterness. The woodshed may be
a proper place to settle disagreements, or dispense punishments.
But the period allotted for the evening meal should be a time of
happiness, joy, fraternity, and mental stimulation. It is a time for
bringing about an increase in family unity and cementing family
solidarity. The dining room is that special part of the family
sanctuary where no discords should ever be permitted. Mealtime
should always be a time of great social and spiritual refreshment.

The greatest of all authorities reminds us that "man does
not live by bread alone." And as there are other kinds of food
besides the physical, so there are other kinds of mealtimes.
Physically, we are what we eat; but mentally, we are what we
think; and spiritually, we are what we do. As we need to feed
the body, so we also need to feed the mind and nourish the
spirit. While we are actually eating, it is a pretty good idea to
have some pleasant conversation. It makes the food more palata-
ble, adds to our enjoyment of it, and aids our digestion.
Sometimes we express a common need when we say, "I wish I
had someone to talk to me—someone to give me encouragement;
someone to wind up my enthusiasm, impart of their faith, and
motivate my accomplishment." Sometimes doctors prescribe that
we lie down for a few minutes after our meals, in order to let
our stomachs settle. We might also eat a few after-dinner mints
for that purpose. But we can also help to settle our day's affairs
with a few chapters from a good book. As a post-adjunct to
mealtime, we might treat our mental and spiritual stomachs to
the inspiration of some good ideas. A few chapters from the
holy scriptures will put a sunset-colored glow on a wonderful
day. To add the right kind of finish to the day we might
consider a kind of post-dinner mental vitalization which may
carry with it a social, mental, spiritual, or occupational recharge.

Sometimes at mealtime we overfeed our bodies while our
minds and spirits are becoming emaciated with a kind of actual
starvation. Certainly we should not re-enact the Magellan scene
and allow ourselves to die of a mental or spiritual scurvy in the
presence of the very things that would make us well. Many

people understand the desirability of taking a vitamin pill every day in order to keep the physical body alert and strong, but we sometimes haven't the slightest idea that we also need to keep our minds and spirits in good health.

As the day has its mealtimes, so does the week and the month, and the year. Every day each human being should read some good literature, think some good thoughts, listen to some inspiring music, feel a charge of uplifting happiness, and make some faithful expressions of love. Of course, we should also do some noteworthy deeds enabling us to end the day at a high point. This should also apply to our weekly mealtimes. The Lord himself has set aside one special day out of each week as a kind of spiritual mealtime. On the Sabbath day we are supposed to rest our bodies, exercise our minds, and have the satisfaction of getting some nourishing spiritual vitamins into our souls. On each Sabbath day we go to the house of prayer and let our minds reach up to God, as we try to bring about a vitalization of our spirits. The Master said, "Blessed are all they who do hunger and thirst after righteousness, for they shall be filled with the Holy Ghost." (3 Ne. 12:6.) As a high point of our Sabbath, we partake of the holy sacrament and ponder the significance and blessings of Christ's atoning sacrifice. This is also the time when we may have that thrilling experience of feeding on the holy scripture. A little daily motivation in our faith can cure us of those destructive doubts and depressing fears that cause our fractional devotion, our marginal morals, and our minimum performance. Magellan's sailors suffered weakness, sickness, and death because the right kind of vitamins were not circulating in their bloodstreams. And a little scurvy begins showing up in us when we starve the mind or abuse the spirit by showing up only spasmodically for this mealtime of the spirit.

Our world is presently having many troubles that are diet-related. Consequently there are many people suffering from some kind of spiritual scurvy. This sickness causes many of our ideas and ideals to turn sour. And many of the attitudes that our success depends upon for its life may become leprous or cancerous.

When we finish the day by watching a television horror murder or feed our souls on some movie sex perversion, we are adopting a diet of evil which will fill us with weakness and degradation. There are thousands of good people suffering from a kind of spiritual ptomaine poisoning. When the wrong kind of food putrifies in our attitudes our success can easily be destroyed. With an ineffective kind of spiritual mealtime, the worship of many people loses its savor. Nowadays there are some people who seldom permit God in their thoughts except when they are using his name in a curse or some profane oath. Yet with all of the mental illness in this great country, we have on board, readily available for our use, all of those great principles of life and salvation which if regularly lived would keep us in vigorous, glowing, radiant, good health. Once each week we have another interesting mealtime that is called family home evening. One night each week we gather our family members together to "feast" upon each other and those ambitions and ideas that can have the greatest possible importance to the welfare of all family members. Family home evening is a time for close family association, family affection, real family worship, refreshing family fun and meaningful family activity.

But just as a great amount of physical labor is required to bring home enough physical food to meet our needs, so a lot of time and care is required in preparing for the needs of these mental and spiritual mealtimes. Some people used to believe that God made the world out of nothing, but now we know that that is impossible. And we should not fall into the even greater delusion of thinking that we can make a successful family home evening out of nothing. A great teacher once said that he had never gone before his Sunday School class without spending an average of at least eight hours in preparation. No wonder he was an inspiring, delightful teacher. And each of us can also generate a stimulating, inspiring, uplifting period for our families if we work at it as diligently and as long.

It takes a lot of time and effort to provide either the food or the inspiration to keep us in the best of health. God is not our only Creator. And the creation of man is not something that was finished and done with in the Garden of Eden six thousand years ago. The creation scene has now shifted from the Garden of Eden to the home, where an exciting creation is presently taking place, with us as the creators. Every day we are creating the faith and the enthusiasm and the character that will determine what we will be throughout eternity. We are presently molding, for good or for evil, the soft clay that makes up our human lives. And the shape that our lives receive they will retain forever. We have an interesting monthly mealtime called fast day. This is one special Sabbath day each month when we abstain from physical food while we feed the spirit. Then our souls get on their knees as we express our gratitude, bear our testimonies, and renew our covenants to serve God. We also have some yearly mealtimes. One of these is Christmas time, when we spiritually feed ourselves on the blessings that came surrounding the birth of Christ. We also have Thanksgiving, in which we express our appreciation to God for his material blessings. We commemorate the great Festival of the Dawn that we call Easter. This is when we contemplate our new beginnings and think about the eternal glories of the resurrection. What a thrill to commemorate in our own minds the brilliance of that first Easter morning and have the spiritual joy and feasting contemplated in our anticipation of the holy resurrection!

There is a sacred song wherein we sing, "I Walked Today Where Jesus Walked." Wouldn't it be a thrilling idea to go and stand on that very spot of ground where Jesus stood, while we tried to reabsorb the spirit of his life? Or we might go on into the Garden of Gethsemane and kneel at that place where under the burden of our sins he sweat great drops of blood at every pore. While it may not be practical to walk today where Jesus walked, yet there is something that we can do that is practical, and it is also a lot more important. We can think today what Jesus thought, we can run his ideas through our minds, and we can feed our spirits on the inspiration of the great prophets who spoke as they were moved upon by the Holy Ghost. And we can live by every word that proceeds forth from the mouth of God.

The great psychologist William James said, "The mind is made up by what it feeds upon." And we can feed our souls as well as our minds on the greatest of all ideas and ideals. But we must avoid that spiritual ptomaine poisoning that can cause so much trouble if we allow our spiritual food to be contaminated. Our faith itself may die if we allow our lives to be too seriously oppressed by our ignorance, or harassed by our doubts, or ravished by our indecision, or depressed by our gloom, or horrified by our fears. The best cure for weakness is a good mealtime of truth and inspiration. We can cure our fears by strengthening our hearts with a diet of courage and faith. And we can dissolve our doubts by regularly living the word of the Lord. We can also revitalize our spirits at the end of each day by losing ourselves in the magic spell of some of the great literature, including the great scriptures. What a thrill when we can use our eyes, our ears, our hearts, and our emotions as intakes through which we feed our souls on the word of the Lord! Our minds are capable of absorbing the greatest ambitions, and a good mealtime can also strengthen our souls with the most solid religious convictions. May God give us this day our daily allotment of that bread with which the best in our lives may be fully nourished.

Oratory

When Alexander the Great finished the job of conquering the world, he wanted to be an orator like his teacher Aristotle. Accordingly Aristotle wrote out and published his sixteen laws of oratory. Alexander was very disappointed when he discovered that the secret was out and he said, "Alas! now everyone will become an orator." And that would probably be true if everyone would work on these sixteen laws as conscientiously as did Aristotle. However, what the great Alexander did not know was that even when the greatest men publish their most prized secrets of success, almost no one will make any serious attempt to follow them.

In fact, our generation itself has been accused of actually going backward in some things. It is said that we have lost many of the arts and skills which we once had. And one of these places where we have given up ground is in several of our communication skills, one of which is oratory. The great orators knew how to make ideas memorable and impressive. It has been said that oratory is the process of dressing language up in its best clothes and giving it a maximum of meaning. An oration is an elaborate discourse treating an important subject impressively. An orator is an artist with words. He is an architect of speech. He knows how to measure, color, and weigh language in order to give it its greatest possible firepower.

An orator has been described as one who knows how to think on his feet. He has a passion for expression, a face that thought illuminates, and a voice that is harmonious with the ideals expressed. "He has logic like a column, and poetry like a vine." He transforms the commonplace and dresses his ideas up in purple and fine linen. In a dozen different ways he creates the climate in which the best ambitions of people flourish and burst into full bloom.

An oration is related to an oratorio. An oratorio is a

dramatic text or poem usually founded on a scriptural theme and set to music.

A large number of our present-day problems have come about because so many of our communication skills have been lost. We just don't seem to be able to talk effectively any more. If we try to follow the orators, we may be afraid of becoming more involved with life, and so we drop our more intense feelings and convictions and settle back into the ordinary. However, it may be that a revival of Aristotle's Laws of Oratory would produce in us a more effective general expression, and do us a great deal of good in our other kinds of communication.

One of the great orators of our immediate past was Colonel Robert G. Ingersoll. He was noted for the elegance and power of his expression. He made the following denunciation of booze; which then, as now, is one of our greatest public enemies. Colonel Ingersoll said: "Everyone who touches whiskey is demoralized. It demoralizes those who make it, those who sell it, and those who drink it. From the time it issues from the coiled and poisonous worm of the distillery, until it empties into the hell of crime, dishonor, and death, it demoralizes everyone who comes in contact with it. I do not believe that anyone can contemplate the subject without becoming prejudiced against this liquid crime. Think of the wrecks upon either bank of the stream of death, of the suicides, of the insanity, of the poverty, of the ignorance, of the distress, of the little children tugging at the faded dresses of weeping and despairing wives asking for bread, of the men of genius it has ruined, of the millions struggling with imaginary serpents produced by this devilish thing. And when you think of the jails, of the almshouses, of the asylums, of the prisons, of the scaffolds, I do not wonder that every thoughtful man is prejudiced against the damned stuff called alcohol."

At the national political convention held on June 16, 1876, Colonel Ingersoll was selected to nominate James C. Blaine for President of the United States. The press described his great prestige and the effect that he had upon his audience by saying:

"Ingersoll moved out from an obscure corner and advanced to the central stage. As he walked forward, he was greeted with thundering cheers. As he reached the platform the cheers took on an increased volume, and for ten minutes the surging fury of acclamation, the wild waving of fans, hats and handkerchiefs transformed the scene from one of deliberation to that of a bedlam of rapturous delirium. Ingersoll waited with unimpaired serenity, until he could get a chance to be heard . . . and then he began his impassioned, artful, brilliant, and persuasive appeal. Possessed with a fine figure, and a face of winning cordial frankness, Ingersoll had half won his audience before he spoke a word. And it is the attestation of every man who heard him, that such a brilliant master-stroke had never before been uttered before a political convention. Its effect was indescribable. The coolest heads in the hall were stirred to the wildest expression. The adversaries of Blaine as well as his friends listened with unswerving, absorbed attention. Curtis sat spell-bound; his eyes and mouth were wide open, his figure moving in unison to the tremendous periods that fell in a measured exquisitely-graduated flow from Ingersoll's smiling lips.

"The matchless method and manner of this man can never be understood from any report in type. To realize the prodigious force, the inexpressible power, the irrestrainable fervor of his audience requires actual sight. Words can do but meagre justice to the magic power of this extraordinary man. He swayed and moved and impelled and restrained the mass before him as if he possessed a magic key to that innermost mechanism that moves the human heart. When he finished, his fine, frank face was as calm as when he began, and the overwrought thousands sank back in an exhaustion of unspeakable wonder and delight."

A reporter of the *New York Sun* once asked Colonel Ingersoll, "What advice would you give to a young man who was ambitious to become a successful public speaker or orator?" And under date of April, 1896, the *Sun* published Colonel Ingersoll's reply under the title of "How to Become an Orator," from which everyone might profit, whether he ever expects to make a public speech or not. In substance, Colonel Ingersoll said:

"In the first place I would advise him to have something to say that is worth saying and that people will be glad to hear. Back of the art of speaking must be the power to think. Without thoughts, words are empty purses. Most people imagine that almost any words uttered in a loud voice and accompanied by appropriate gestures, constitute an oration.

"I would advise the young man to study his subject, to find what others had thought, to look at it from all sides. Then I would tell him to write out his thoughts or to arrange them in his mind, so that he would know exactly what he was going to say. Waste no time on the 'how' until you are satisfied with the 'what.' After you know what you are going to say, then you can think about how it should be said. Then you can think about tone, emphasis, and gestures. But if you really understand and believe what you say, emphasis, tone and gesture will more or less take care of themselves. All of these should come from inside so that the thought will be in perfect harmony with the feelings. Voice and gesture should be governed by strong emotions. The orator must be true to his subject, and avoid any references to himself.

"The great column of his argument should go unbroken. He can adorn it with vines and flowers, but not in such profusion that they hide the column. He should give it the variety of episode by illustrations for the purpose of adding strength to the argument. The man who wishes to become an orator should study language. He should know the deeper meanings of words. He should understand the vigor and velocity of verbs and the color of adjectives. He should know how to sketch a scene and so paint a picture with words and feeling that it is given life and action. A perfect picture requires lights and shadows, and now and then a flash of lightning may illuminate the intellectual sky. He should be a poet and a dramatist, a painter and an actor. He should cultivate his imagination. He should become familiar with the great poetry and fiction that is so rich in heroic deeds. He should be a student of Shakespeare. He should read and devour the great plays and should learn the art of expression and compression with all of the secrets of the head and the heart.

"The great orator is full of variety and surprises. His speech is a panorama. The interest does not flag. He does not allow himself to be anticipated. He does not repeat himself. A picture is shown but once. An orator should avoid the commonplace. He should put no cotton with his silk, no common metals with his gold. He should remember that 'gilded dust is not as good as dusted gold.' The great orator is honest, and sincere, he does not pretend. His brain and heart work together. Nothing is forced. And every drop of his blood is convinced. He knows exactly what he wishes to say . . . and stops when he has finished.

"Only a great orator knows when and how to close. Most speakers go on after they are through. They are satisfied with a 'lame and impotent conclusion.' Most speakers lack variety. They travel a dusty road, whereas the great orator convinces and charms by indirection.

"Of course, no one can tell another what to do to become an orator. The great orator has that wonderful thing called presence. He has that strange something known as magnetism. He must have a flexible, musical voice, capable of expressing the pathetic, the humorous, the heroic. His body must move in unison with his thought. He must be a reasoner, a logician with a keen sense of humor. He must have imagination. His wit must be sharp and quick; he must have sympathy, and his smiles should be the neighbors of his tears.

"While I cannot tell a man what to do to become an orator, I can tell him a few things not to do. There should be no introduction to an oration. The orator should commence with his subject. There should be no prelude, no flourish, no apology, no explanation. He should say nothing about himself. Like a sculptor, he stands by his block of stone. Every stroke is for a purpose and its form soon begins to appear. When the statue is finished the workman stops. Nothing is more difficult than a perfect close. Few poems, few pieces of music or novels end well. A good story, a great speech, a perfect poem should all end just at the proper point. Thoughts are not born of chance. They grow, bud, blossom and bear the fruit of perfect form. Genius is the climate but the soil must be cultivated and the harvest does not come immediately after the planting. It takes time and labor to raise a crop from that field called the brain.

"Theodore Parker was an orator. He preached great sermons. His sermons on 'Old Age' and 'Webster' and his address on 'Liberty' were filled with great thoughts, marvelously expressed. When he dealt with human events, with realities, with things he knew, then he was superb. When he spoke of freedom, of duty, of living to the ideal, of mental integrity, he seemed inspired.

"Webster had the great qualities of force, dignity, clearness and grandeur. Clay had a commanding presence, a noble bearing, a heroic voice. He was a natural leader, a wonderful, forcible, persuasive, convincing talker. He was not a poet, nor a master of metaphor, but he was practical. He kept in view the end to be accomplished. He was the opposite of Webster. Clay was the morning, Webster the evening. Clay had large views, and a wide horizon. He was ample, vigorous and a little tyrannical.

"S. S. Prentiss was an orator. He said profound and beautiful things and uttered the most sublime thoughts.

"In my judgment, Corwin was the greatest orator of them all. He had many arrows in his quiver. He had genius. He was full of humor, pathos, wit, and logic. He was an actor, his body talked. His meaning was in his eyes as well as on his lips. Governor Morton of Indiana had the greatest power of statement that I have ever heard. His facts were perfectly sound and his conclusion was a necessity.

"Lincoln had reason, wonderful humor, and wit. But his presence was not good. His voice was poor, his gestures awkward. But his thoughts were profound—his speech at Gettysburg is one of the masterpieces of the world.

"Of course I have heard a great many talkers, but orators are few and far between. They are produced by victorious nations, born in the midst of great events and marvelous achievements. They utter the thoughts, the aspirations of their age. They clothe people in the gorgeous robes of genius. They interpret dreams, and with the poets they prophesy. They fill the future with heroic forms and lofty deeds. They keep their faces toward the dawn of the ever-coming day."

Our day is one of greatest confusion and it may be that we could increase our skill in communication by working a little more on the idea of Alexander, that everyone might greatly improve his abilities to think and to communicate. Certainly everyone should be able to talk as convincingly about righteousness and freedom and law and God as we do of politics, sports, inventories, and the stock market. We live in the most wonderful age in history and our *ability* in expression should match our *opportunities* for expression. May God help us all to have greater thoughts that we are able to express more effectively.

Our World

The other day I visited with a young couple who were making the final plans for building their new home. They had given expert attention to every detail of how many rooms they would have, what their size would be, how they would look, and what function they would serve. They had given careful thought to all of the considerations of light, heat, air conditioning, and furnishings. They had been particular in choosing a home site with a wonderful view and providing for appropriate landscaping.

It occurred to me that building a home must be one of the most exciting experiences in anyone's life. Then I tried to imagine how God must have felt as he was planning this earth to serve as our home. Not only is God very wise but he must have put a lot of thought into planning this earth with all of its countless wonders and its endless fascination. In addition to its utility, our earth has been made beautiful by a great variety of mountains, trees, flowers, and carpets of grass. The oceans, lakes, waterfalls, and gardens make sightseeing one of our earth's chief activities. To make the earth more comfortable and productive, it has been set in motion and given an orbit. By its daily revolutions we are provided with our days and nights. The earth's positions, its movements and tiltings give us our seasons, with their delightful variety in temperature, its changes in the color of the landscape and in our own activity.

Of course, we are not limited to the benefits that are provided just on *our* planet. Our earth is held in its orbit by the attraction of other heavenly bodies. And many of our most important material and spiritual needs are supplied from some great universal storehouses that are located millions of miles away. Emerson said, "We live in the lap of an immense intelligence." We are benefited by God's Spirit that pervades the universe. We get our life itself from him and his "Spirit giveth light to every man that cometh into the world." (D&C 84:46.)

In planning this earth especially for our benefit, God said, "We will go down, for there is space there, and we will take of these materials, and we will make an earth whereupon these may dwell, and we will prove them herewith, to see if they will do all things whatsoever the Lord their God shall command them; and they who keep their first estate shall be added upon; and they who keep not their first estate shall not have glory in the same kingdom with those who keep their first estate; and they who keep their second estate shall have glory added upon their heads forever and ever." (Abraham 3:24-26.) That is, if we make the most of our present situation our condition will be made even better.

What a great piece of engineering it must have been to put the earth into its orbit with all of the details of light, heat, and air conditioning so carefully attended to! God also arranged for many benefits to come to us from outside of our own sphere. For example, at this very instant God is sending us energy, light, heat, vitamins, and millions of tons of daily food from the sun. He also ordained and established the great universal laws of electricity, locomotion, and food production to promote our welfare and happiness.

The information and inspiration provided by him for our recent knowledge explosion were mostly foretold hundreds of years ago. By utilizing this knowledge we are now able to fly through space at a speed faster than sound. We are presently testing our space wings in flying to the moon. In perfect comfort we can now sail under the polar ice cap or live for months on the bottom of the sea. With miraculous results we are using the treasures of gold, oil, uranium and coal that God has stored up in the earth for our benefit. The earth has also been covered with sixteen inches of a miraculous substance called topsoil from which we may bring forth almost every conceivable kind of food, clothing, fuel and housing.

Thoughtfully, God has filled the sixteen miles of space immediately over our heads with a magic, life-giving substance called atmosphere, which keeps the plants and animals as well as ourselves alive. And at the same time our atmosphere supports the wings of our airplanes as they carry us through the skies. Recent scientific developments have greatly added to the length, wonder, beauty, interest, and productivity of our lives and of the world around us.

However, as important as our relationship may be with the sun, the earth, and the other planets, by far our most important relationship is with God and with each other. How effectively we develop these relationships will determine every other success and happiness. In one of God's most important laws, he has granted us the great privilege of free agency. However, this blessing was not given to operate automatically by itself. With it there is always a full and complete responsibility attached. It is interesting that none of God's other creations are free. Neither electricity, nor gravity, nor light, nor heat, nor growth, nor the animal creations can do as they please. It was only to man that God said, "Thou mayest choose for thyself." However, because we don't always understand freedom's companion law of responsibility, we sometimes bring a considerable amount of conflict and confusion into our lives. When we abuse the privileges of our free agency by going contrary to the order of God, an important foreign element called sin is introduced into our program. The Apostle John describes sin as the transgression of the law. Sin is a violation of the important laws on which our blessings are all predicated. For example, when we violate the laws of health, the blessings are withheld. God has said, "I, the Lord, am bound when ye do what I say; but when ye do not what I say, ye have no promise." (D&C 82:10.) He said, "I command and men obey not; I revoke and they receive not the blessing." (D&C 58:32.) Therefore when we break the Ten Commandments or fail to follow the Sermon on the Mount we lose the corresponding blessings.

While our lives upon this earth were being planned in the antemortal council in heaven, Lucifer, who was then a personage of great influence and authority, proposed that some serious restrictions should be placed upon our freedom. According to his plan we were all to be saved by compulsion. That is, we would not be allowed to vary from the pattern that would be set for us. This idea seems to have drawn a considerable number of followers and caused a division in heaven. When Satan's plan was rejected, he rebelled and drew away from God one-third of the hosts of heaven. But God himself has made an irrevocable commitment to man's free agency, even though man may choose to use it as Satan did to fight against God or work against man's own interests. But the law that requires man to shoulder the full responsibility for whatever he does cannot be changed. To protect our interests God has given us the greatest possible incentives for doing right. He has given us what has been called a "God instinct." This is a great natural tendency to develop ourselves so that we, the offspring of God, may someday hope to become like him, the parent. As a kind of compass to show us the way, he has given us a wonderful little instrument called a conscience. He has also given us certain rights to tune in on his inspiration which will always tell us what is right and what is wrong. Also, at various periods God has had prophets here upon the earth through whom he has given the great scriptures to tell us what we should and what we should not do in our own interests. Yet in spite of all of this, many people continue to disobey God's laws, and consequently lose the benefits that otherwise would be available.

God's house is a house of order, and even *he* cannot give us blessings when we violate the laws on which they are predicated. When the people of Noah's day were unrighteous, they were swept from the earth by the flood. When Sodom and Gomorrah turned away from God, a storm of fire and brimstone was rained down upon them. When Babylon became a wicked city, it was destroyed. Because of this same law, the welfare of our own civilization is now trembling in the balance. However, one of the greatest of all possible blessings is the privilege of living here upon this wonderful earth and enjoying the inestimable privileges of mortality. Before our births we lived for a long time with God in heaven. We have all seen God—he is our Father. When we lived with him we walked by sight. But it was necessary that we learn to walk a little way by faith. In our life with God we had come to a place where young people always come, where it is desirable for them to move away from the homes of their parents. It has always seemed a little surprising to me that young people are so anxious to move away from the homes of even wealthy parents to establish a home of their own, even though they may not have the benefits and advantages that they had in the homes of their parents. But it is necessary for young people to learn to stand on their own feet and do some of their own thinking and planning.

God wanted us to live in this world of contrasts where we could be tested and proven and tried, and where we could see good and evil side by side. He wanted us to learn to accept good and reject evil. He wanted us to develop our characters and use our free agency in helping to bring about our own salvation. This life was the place where we would be "added upon" with these beautiful, wonderful bodies without which we could never receive a fullness of joy, either here or hereafter. It is one of our greatest privileges that our bodies will be resurrected so that we can have them throughout eternity. There are some false notions that belittle the importance of the body. But if a body were not a good thing, God never would have created it in the first place. If it were not necessary for eternity, the resurrection never would have been instituted. If a body were not necessary for God the Father, then God the Son never would have been resurrected. Jesus did not lose his body after his resurrection. It did not evaporate or expand to fill the immensity of space. It did not lose its identity by merging with someone else. At the resurrection the spirit and body will be permanently connected so that separation is no longer possible.

One of the punishments of Satan and his followers is that they will never be permitted to have bodies. Of course, we think this earth is a pretty wonderful place just as it is, but since the fall of man this earth has existed in its telestial or fallen state. Before the curse was placed upon the earth by man's disobedience, it was in a paradisiacal state. It was then a terrestrial earth. But we ought to know that this earth has a wonderful future. God has told us that at the time of the glorious second coming of Christ this earth will be cleansed of its sin and wickedness. The curse that has held it bound since the fall of Adam will be removed. The last part of the first resurrection of earth's people will then take place. And Christ will usher in his millennial reign of a thousand years upon our earth. Paul says that he will come with his mighty angels in flaming fire. During the thousand years of peace and righteousness both mortal and immortal people will live upon the earth. For this thousand-year period Satan will be bound and have no power over the lives of people.

Then will come the end of the thousand years and the time for the final judgment. Then the earth will again be changed. This time it will move up in the scale of development and become a celestial sphere and it will be the permanent abode of those who qualify for the celestial kingdom. Concerning this period the Lord has said to us, "He that endureth in faith and doeth my will, the same shall overcome, and shall receive an inheritance upon the earth when the day of transfiguration shall come." (D&C 63:20.) He said: "Therefore the earth must needs be sanctified from all unrighteousness that it may be prepared for celestial glory. For after it hath filled the measure of its creation, it shall be crowned with glory, even with the presence of God the Father; that bodies who are of a celestial kingdom may possess it forever and ever; for, for this intent was it made and created, and for this intent are they sanctified." (D&C 88:18-20.) The people who live here will then all be members of the celestial order which is the order to which God himself belongs. Those who do not qualify as celestial beings must be cast out and live elsewhere. As the Lord says, "For he who is not able to abide the law of a celestial kingdom cannot abide a celestial glory." But he said, "Verily I say unto you, the earth abideth the law of a celestial kingdom, for it filleth the measure of its creation, and transgresseth not the law—wherefore, it shall be sanctified; yea, notwithstanding it shall die, it shall be quickened again, and shall abide the power by which it is quickened, and the righteous shall inherit it." (D&C 88:22, 25-26.)

Much of what we know about the future glory of this earth is by comparison. Paul compared God's three degrees of glory to the sun, moon, and stars in the firmament. And the celestial surpasses the telestial as the blaze of the noonday sun surpasses the twinkle of a tiny star. When our earth becomes a celestial orb, it will be a place that will be even more glorious and far more pleasant than it now is. This will then be our heaven where we will live with our families and friends. A modern-day revelation says that even the telestial glory of God will have a magnificence which surpasses all understanding. Then what will the celestial be like? Paul said to the Corinthians, "Eye hath not seen, nor ear heard, neither have entered into the heart of man, the things which God hath prepared for them that love him." (1 Cor. 2:9.) Now is the time when we may earn an everlasting inheritance to be enjoyed upon our wonderful earth when it shall have become celestialized.

The Parables

One of the most important functions of human beings is to get good ideas and motivations over to other people. Helping someone else is the greatest responsibility of everyone, including parents, teachers, orators, musicians, lecturers, and friends. One of the most effective ways of giving something to someone is by the use of parables. The word *parable* comes from a Greek word meaning, "placing beside." It means to make one subject understandable by comparing it with something else. If we want to more clearly see whether or not a stick is straight, we just lay another straight stick down beside it. In giving his parable of the prodigal son, Jesus placed on exhibit the mistakes of a wasteful, unwise, unprofitable life, in order that we would not have to make all of these same mistakes personally. Think of the great library of wisdom that may be had in the parables of the New Testament, the Old Testament and those that we ourselves develop. As synonyms for the word *parable*, the dictionary gives such words as *symbol, emblem, allegory*, and *fable*.

A fable is a brief narrative intended to reinforce some useful truth. It is a precept that may be presented by animal actors. An allegory is a description of one thing under the image of another. It is a veiled presentation, a figurative story, or a narrative with an implied meaning that is not expressly stated. Bunyan's *The Pilgrim's Progress* gives some celebrated examples of famous allegories. A few of these symbols can greatly increase the effectiveness and power of our human communications.

The Old Testament prophets used parables to make a deeper impression and give more force to scriptural ideas. Of course, the master in the use of the parable was Jesus himself. It is interesting to recall the subjects that this greatest of all religious leaders discussed. He didn't talk very much about religion as such. He discussed the simple everyday things that his hearers fully understood, and he then made religious principles out of

them. By his skillful comparisons, Jesus helped people understand
those things that were more difficult. Jesus told of a farmer
planting his grain by the laborious processes of those days. He
said: "Behold, a sower went forth to sow . . . and some seeds fell
by the wayside, and the fowls came and devoured them up.
Some fell in stony places, where they had not much earth: and
forthwith they sprung up . . . and when the sun was up, they
were scorched; and because they had no root, they withered
away. And some fell among thorns; and the thorns sprung up
and choked them: But others fell into good ground, and brought
forth fruit, some an hundredfold, some sixtyfold, and some
thirtyfold." (Matt. 13:3-8.) Then in explaining, he said: "When
any one heareth the word of the kingdom, and understandeth it
not, then cometh the wicked one, and catcheth away that which
was sown in his heart. This is he that received seed by the
wayside. But he that received the seed into stony places, the
same is he that heareth the word, and anon with joy receiveth
it. Yet hath he not root in himself, but dureth for a while: for
when tribulation or persecution ariseth because of the word, by
and by he is offended. He also that received the seed among the
thorns is he that heareth the word; and the care of this world,
and the deceitfulness of riches, choke the word, and he becometh unfruitful. But he that received seed into the good ground is
he that heareth the word, and understandeth it; which also
beareth fruit, and bringeth forth, some an hundredfold, some
sixty, and some thirty." (Matt. 13:19-23.)

One of the great teachings of Jesus had to do with people
actually doing things. He was not very enthusiastic about those
having strong professions with little performance. He used the
word *hypocrite* rather freely and frequently. One of his greatest
lines gave us a means of comparison when he said, "By their
fruits ye shall know them." He said: "Do men gather grapes of
thorns, or figs of thistles. Even so every good tree bringeth forth
good fruit; but a corrupt tree bringeth forth evil fruit. . . . Every
tree that bringeth not forth good fruit is hewn down, and cast
into the fire." (Matt. 7:17, 19.)

One day he came to a fig tree and searched it for food but
found nothing but leaves. Then he said: "Let no fruit grow on
thee henceforward forever. And presently the fig tree withered
away." (Matt. 21:19.) The Lord made it clear that fig trees were

created to produce something useful, and by this comparison he emphasized what was expected of us also.

The other day at an Aaronic Priesthood dinner, I sat by a young man who was telling me that the bishop had just asked him to take a certain job in the Church, and he was telling me all of the reasons that he could not do it. After ten or fifteen minutes of recital, he said, "What would you do if you were in my place?" I told him that would be very easy. I would merely tell the bishop that I wouldn't do it. He seemed a little disturbed and thought this was not a very good answer. He said, "I have always been taught that I should do what I am asked to do in the Church." I said to him: "But that was not what you asked me; you asked me what I would do if I were in *your* place. For over ten minutes you have been telling me of all the reasons why you can't do it, and that is what I would tell the bishop." Then I told him Jesus' story of the vinedresser's sons. The vinedresser said to his two sons, "Go and work in the vineyard." In substance, one of them said, "I won't do it." Disobedience might be a very minor sin in comparison with some others. I said to my friend: "If you tell the bishop you won't do it, I can tell you what the bishop will do. He will find someone who *will* do it, and the only one that will be hurt will be you."

I continued, "But you are planning to do what the vine- dresser's second son did. The vinedresser's second son said, 'I go, sir,' but went not. Now I can tell you what will happen if you follow the example of the vinedresser's second son. If you tell the bishop that you are going to do it, he will set you apart for the job. Then it will be *your* job. Then no one else will have a right to do it, and because *you* are not going to do it the job will not be done. Then not just one person but many people will be hurt as a consequence."

You may remember that the Lord said to those who had the attitude of the vinedresser's second son, "The publicans and harlots go into the kingdom of God before you!" (Matt. 21:31.) By promising to do something that he didn't do, the vine- dresser's second son put himself back in the line behind the publicans and harlots, and that is a long way back.

It is an interesting fact that most people fail in life not because they want to be sinful, but because they don't use good judgment. There are probably as many references made in the scriptures to fools as to sinners. Jesus told the story of a foolish rich man. He said: "The ground of a certain rich man brought forth plentifully: and he thought within himself, saying, what shall I do, because I have no room where to bestow my fruits? And he said, this will I do: I will pull down my barns and build greater; and there will I bestow all my fruits and my goods. And I will say to my soul, Soul thou hast much goods laid up for many years; take thine ease, eat, drink and be merry. But God said unto him, Thou fool, this night thy soul shall be required of thee: then whose shall those things be, which thou hast provided? So is he that layeth up treasure for himself, and is not rich toward God." (Luke 12:16-21.)

This parable indicates the most severe kind of poverty, which is to be poor toward God. This rich man must have been a very industrious man. The record does not say that he was dishonest, or immoral, or drunken. He was a very good provider and apparently he was a hard worker. He had done well in his occupation, but he had been foolish in his objectives and had not made himself rich toward God. Therefore, when his score is added up and he is judged from the perspective of eternity he is a very poor man. Even if he had done many times as well in his occupation, he would still have been a failure if he had failed in the things of God.

Jesus said, "What shall it profit a man, if he shall gain the whole world and lose his own soul." (Mark 8:36.) Jesus puts your eternal soul in a side-by-side comparison with the wealth of the entire earth with all of its real estate, natural resources, and man-made improvements. Then he asks you to compare values. There are a lot of people who have not spent much time thinking about this question, and consequently they have not made many decisions as to what they should do about it. They also run a great risk of having the "foolish" label placed upon them.

How regrettable it would be to have such a great value as that of the entire world within our easy grasp, and then let it slip through our fingers because of our own foolishness! There are a lot of real sins that would not hurt us as much as this sin of foolishness. We might even make a parable of our own about the bee that extracts honey from the same flowers that the spider gets poison from. It has often been suggested that we might well use the bee as a pattern for our own lives in other ways. As we analyze the great parables, get the wisdom from their blossoms, and learn to match the bee industry, we may be well on our way to building some great honeycombs filled with eternal successes for ourselves.

Every single one of the parables of Jesus contains an important message; and some of his listeners will receive a hundredfold, some sixty, and some thirty, according to what we do about them. We must not miss the point of just how the prodigal son came to end up in the swine pasture. Jesus painted us a picture of the wheat and tares, the lilies of the field, and that little mustard seed which became a great tree. He talked about the laborers in the vineyard, the wicked husbandman, the tax money, the tribute money, the ten talents, and the lost coin; and each of these stories is loaded with honey. He told about a man building his house on the rock, the city that was set upon the hill, the unmerciful servant, the pearl of great price, the new wine in the old bottles, the debtors and creditors, the mote and the beam, the wedding feast, the unprofitable servant, the lost sheep, the good shepherd, and the sheep and the goats.

He talked about agriculture, horticulture, architecture, business, and how to catch fish. He discussed human relations, marriage customs, the home, proper etiquette, and the advantage of a good mental attitude. In other words, in a language that everyone understood, he taught people how to live effectively; and yet he wasn't talking about religion at all as such. He was talking about people, their work, their surroundings, and the things that they understood. The Master used these ordinary ideas to inspire religious doctrines, industry, fairness, truth, mercy, love, and success in people. In telling of a carpenter turning out a yoke to comfortably fit the neck of two oxen, Jesus was practicing his religion. And in our daily lives we may also practice our religion by doing those ordinary things that should be done. Jesus discounted the value of faith without works. And someone has added to this idea by saying that "the hands that help are holier than the lips that pray." Douglas

Mallock put a part of this idea in verse when he said:

> What does it matter what duty
> Falls to the part of a man?
> All have a share in the building,
> All have a part in the plan.
>
> All have a part in the building,
> No one buildeth alone,
> Whether the cross he is gilding,
> Or whether he carries the stone.

Of course not all of religion is centered in physical effort. There is also an important part involved in worship, prayer, testimony, and teaching the great religious doctrines of Christ. To add to our effectiveness we should probably make some parables of our own. No other person in the world has a set of circumstances that is exactly like ours. No one's abilities and needs are the same as ours. We ought to compare our own values of good and bad and make our own judgments of the important and unimportant, and of the successes and failures in our own opportunities. God has given us some great gifts and abilities that no one else has, and we should make sure that we make the most of them. The scriptures say: "Another parable put he forth unto them saying, The kingdom of heaven is like to a grain of mustard seed, which a man took, and sowed in his field. Which indeed is the least of all seeds but when it is grown, it is the greatest among herbs, and becometh a tree, so that the birds of the air come and lodge in the branches thereof." (Matt. 13:31-32.)

We may presently think that the mustard seed of our faith and ability is very small; but if it is properly nourished by us, it may become one of the greatest of the trees. The life of each of us is like a great library, and on the wall where we can see them clearly we might hang a framed picture of each of the great parables of Jesus. These we should understand, memorize, love, and practice until each one produces a hundredfold for us. Jesus said, "Follow me," and we might make the greatest of all comparisons of putting our lives side by side with his. Only then can we see how well we are doing.

A Pile of Rocks

Recently a newspaper cartoonist pictured one of our forefathers sitting on a pile of rocks. The cartoon identified some of these rocks as being coal, iron, uranium, and some were precious metals. However, because their potential power and great value were not understood, they were completely useless. In the beginning God gave man dominion over everything upon the earth, yet for thousands of years we have allowed this tremendous energy to lie about us unused, while the world's work has been performed by the feeble muscle power of man and the few dumb animals that he has been able to press into his service. But this picture also has some other interesting implications. The greatest power represented in this cartoon is not in the rocks, but in the man sitting on top of them. The greatest source of either power or wealth is never in things, but always in people. And while we have greatly developed the uses of our rocks, we have not done very much about the man sitting on top of them.

Man's projected history upon this earth was divided into seven one-thousand-year periods, corresponding to the seven days of creation. The seventh of these periods is to be the earth's Sabbath. We call it the millennium. As shown on our calendar, we are now in the late Saturday evening of time; yet even seventy years ago there were still no automobiles, no radios, no television, no airplanes, and no atomic bombs. In the few years since then, we have accomplished wonders with the heat, steam, electricity, and firepower of our rocks. But what about the man sitting on top of them? How much has his faith been increased since the days of Abraham, or his leadership since the days of Moses? How would present-day men compare with the Apostle Paul in devotion? How much would *our* honesty exceed that of Abraham Lincoln? There is no dispute about the wonders man has performed with his *things*. But what has he done with *himself*? According to the press reports, the chief characteristic of present-day man seems to be his crime waves, his delin-

quencies, his wars and contentions, and the increases in his sins.
Yet, all of the time, we have within ourselves every ability
necessary to make this earth a paradise, and our age the golden
age of time. All we need to do is to fulfill the potential of the
man sitting upon the rocks.

In the first trip ever made around the earth, Magellan left
Seville, Spain, with five ships and 270 men on September 20,
1519. His expedition returned in September 1522, with only one
ship and thirty-one men. Many of his men died of scurvy, yet
they had on board a cargo of limes which, if effectively used,
could have cured their diseases. This might furnish an apt
comparison for our day. The present low tide of life in our
world is also showing a lot of unnecessary losses. They are not
only making us miserable and threatening our physical destruction, but they are also causing a serious damage to our eternal
souls. Yet we have aboard our lives a cargo of divine gifts that
could make our lives more nearly resemble him who placed us
upon this earth. We may not be able to do much about the
collective problems in the world, but suppose that we visualize
the development of this great collection of possibilities that God
has stored away in us individually. We might think of our
potentiality for "personal righteousness," "happiness," "personality development," "obedience to God," "reason," "good judgment" and our many other potential virtues. It is interesting that
the greatest of these possibilities is our own happiness. We might
give particular attention to this, inasmuch as it includes the sum
total of all of the others and is a result of them.

Long before the automobile or radio was invented, God set
up happiness as the chief purpose of life. Through an ancient
American prophet, he said, "Men are that they might have joy."
(2 Ne. 2:25.) Our primary purpose in life is not to fly in
airplanes or to set off atomic bombs or even to watch colored
television. "Men are that they might have joy," and yet none of
our new inventions or scientific wonders seems to have increased
our joy very much. Our age is more noted for its crime and sin
than for its joy. We may not be any happier now than if we
had lived in the days of Adam or Enoch. But judging by our
broken homes, our suicides, our psychiatric diseases, and our
nervous breakdowns, we surely are not reaching our full happiness potential. Certainly criminals are not happy, and sin always

destroys joy. Guilt complexes with their consequent feelings of
inferiority and depression do not bring happiness. The confusion
of wrongdoing and the conflicts caused by guilt, upset our
mental and emotional balance and leave us bored, restless,
nervous, unstable, and miserable. Last year in the United States
alone, over twenty thousand people went so far as to commit
suicide, and many others would have followed suit, except for
their lack of courage.

Recently a man came seeking some advice about his own
unpleasant, depressed emotional state. He began by saying that
he thought he was losing his mind. But after hearing a recital of
his long list of moral sins, it was evident that besides losing his
mind, he was also losing his reason and his honor. He bemoaned
the fact that during this transgression period his income had
dropped to less than one-half, his peace of mind had been wiped
out, his faith and optimistic outlook on life had vanished, and
he was wondering if suicide wouldn't be the best way to solve
his problem. He refuses to give up his sins; and yet they have
cost him almost everything he has, and have brought him
nothing but misery. He said that he had shed more tears and
come nearer to a mental collapse in this twelve-month period
than in all of his previous life put together.

His unpleasant situation is the inevitable result of his
violating this natural law. He suffers this miserable existence
because he is living a degrading life. He is dealing in a kind of
dishonor that will probably ruin the lives of many people,
including several children, four of whom are his own. He is
attempting the impossible in seeking happiness in wrongdoing.
The scripture says, "Wickedness never was happiness." Wickedness
always brings loss and misery. I read to this man a statement
made by the ancient American prophet, Samuel the Lamanite. In
speaking to some people in a similar situation, he said, "For ye
have sought all the days of your lives for that which ye could
not obtain; ye have sought for happiness in doing iniquity, which
thing is contrary to the nature of that righteousness which is in
our great and eternal head." (Hel. 13:38.) It is a fundamental
law of life that cannot be changed, that when we go contrary to
the nature of God, we create a state that is contrary to the
nature of happiness. (See Alma 41:10-11.) Happiness is a result
of doing those things that should be done. To do wrong is to go

against God, reason, conscience, wisdom, and our own best interests. Then we start developing conflicts, harmful rationalizings, crooked thinking, and before we know it we are all mixed up. As long as we continue indulging in evil, there isn't very much that anyone else can do to help us. It is pretty hard to clean up a disease while we continue to generate the poison that causes it.

As long as we insist on doing wrong, we will always find our plans being thwarted, our income getting less, our judgment becoming more erratic, our discouragement getting greater, and our souls getting further away from God. The man who said that he was losing his mind was greatly underestimating his situation. He was not only losing his mind—he was also losing many other worthwhile things, including the eternal welfare of his own soul. The greatest cure of all problems is repentance and reformation. Righteousness is the best health tonic. But righteousness is not only hygienic, it is also extremely profitable and the most pleasant of life's experiences.

Suppose that in your imagination you test a few evil experiences for their joy content. Suppose the next time you meet an old lady crippled up with rheumatism you were to knock her down, kick her into the gutter, and hurt her as much and in as many ways as you can. Even though your evil is not discovered, you are not likely to go on your way whistling "Jingle Bells." How you behave yourself toward others will determine how you yourself will feel. How much happiness do you think your children will ever be able to get from dishonesty, or immorality, or drunkenness? Every nicotine addict wishes that he didn't smoke, and every sinner is unhappy, and every moral transgressor wishes he were decent. There is an eternal law controlling our lives that says that we can only feel as our actions entitle us to feel. The prophet has said, "If there be no righteousness there be no happiness." (2 Ne. 2:13.)

The eternal nature of this law was established before the earth itself was created. The Lord himself has stated this law in words that everyone should memorize and say to himself every day. The Lord said: "There is a law, irrevocably decreed in heaven before the foundations of this world, upon which all blessings are predicated—and when we obtain any blessing from

God, it is by obedience to that law upon which it is predicated." (D&C 130:20.) This divine regulation is permanent, it cannot be changed—it cannot be evaded, and no one can escape the natural consequences of violation. There is a great unseen avenger that always stands guard in the universe to see to it that no sin goes unpunished. On the other hand, anyone can multiply his joy as much as he likes, merely by following this governing law. Isn't it strange how tenaciously we cling to the very faults and sins that are causing our pain and misery, threatening the final destruction that we are all trying to avoid? Yet there is no chance of success when we cling to our sins with one hand, and try to catch genuine happiness and peace in the other.

I told this misguided man the story of Frank Buck of "Bring Them Back Alive" fame. Frank Buck used to capture monkeys in Africa without the use of guns, poisons, or harmful traps. Knowing a little bit about monkey psychology, Mr. Buck prepared a sweet-scented rice that the monkeys are very fond of. Then into some coconuts he bored some holes that were just large enough to admit the monkey's empty hand when the fingers were extended. The coconuts were fastened to trees by small chains and the rice was put inside. Then the monkey would reach through the hole in the coconut to get the rice. But as soon as the monkey's fingers were closed on the rice, he could not then get his loaded fist back out through the hole. The monkeys would try every conceivable method of freeing themselves—except that they would not let go of the rice.

This might seem a little stupid to us, but at the same time there are many examples where we behave no more intelligently. What do *we* do when *we* get our own fists full of bad habits, or our minds loaded down with wrong attitudes? We frequently do exactly as the monkeys do and refuse to let go of them even though it may cost us our eternal lives. The monkey has at least one argument in his favor, inasmuch as he is merely trying to provide his daily bread. But it is with much less worthy motives that we grab on to the evil-smelling rice of liquor, and the harmful effects of cigarette addiction; and then in spite of our knowledge of the terrors of alcoholism or the awful possibilities of death from lung cancer, or the foul odors of dishonesty, we still hang on to our sins with all of our might. Then, like the monkeys, many of us become lifetime prisoners of sin because we won't let go of our unworthy ideas or evil ambitions. It may be much more desirable to resemble a monkey in physical appearance than in our unreasonable mental responses.

What should an accurate appraisal of our mental ability be when we allow ourselves to be trapped by the rice of atheism, ignorance, indifference, immorality, or disobedience to God? Certainly our greatest opportunity is that we can earn happiness instead of misery; we can produce rewards instead of penalties; but first we must open our hands and our hearts and our minds to God. God is much wiser than we are, and we can save ourselves a lot of unnecessary trouble and pain, both here and hereafter, by a little simple obedience to his direction. Certainly our own happiness possibility is one of the valuable rocks that we are sitting on without knowing its value. There are some other rocks that we are sitting on that we should find out about.

In a great parable Jesus encouraged everyone to build his house of life upon the rock of obedience, so that it would continue to stand when the rains came and the winds blew to destroy those houses that were built upon the sand. Jesus also declared that *he* would build *his Church* upon the rock of revelation. Certainly that is a rock that we should get a great deal of power from. With this in mind we might well redraw our cartoon and further identify our pile of rocks and what we can do about the man who sits upon them.

Playing Faces

Some time ago there was a movie going around called "The Three Faces of Eve." This was the story of a young woman with such a serious personality split that she became three people instead of one. While her first personality was dominant she was Eve White, solemn, sad, and neurotic, with an introvert tendency to draw within herself. But a kind of automatic gearshift would sometimes cause her to slip out of herself and become Eve Black. Then she was a careless extrovert with loose morals and irresponsible behavior. But on some other occasions she would be enveloped by a third personality that was more realistic and responsible. Then she was identified as Jane. When either one of her three selves was in power, she seemed to have difficulty in recognizing, or even remembering, the other two. Her loosely segregated personality was closely related to Robert Louis Stevenson's story of Dr. Jekyll and Mr. Hyde, where a kindly, capable physician by day became a violent, deadly, immoral criminal by night.

But this idea represents far more than just an interesting plot for a movie. In some degree everyone has a multiple personality, and unless it is properly integrated and controlled, many conflicts and serious problems are likely to arise as a consequence. Jesus cast a multitude of devils out of one person, and sometimes we need to do something similar for ourselves. Sometimes one person becomes a large group of antagonistic traits held loosely together by whatever circumstances may prevail at the time. One person may be kind and considerate while at work, but quarrelsome, irresponsible and unpleasant at home. Some are strictly honest in money matters, and highly dishonest in their personal conduct. Very frequently we try to hide these less desirable identities and have people see us only on one side. Because of our rationalizings and our multiple identities many of us are strangers even to ourselves.

A polaroid picture was recently taken of a native family in

an out-of-the-way section of a primitive land, where cameras were largely unknown. In the group picture each one could recognize everyone but himself. The mother pointed to herself and said, "Who is this woman?" Sometimes we may cling to that identity of ourselves which we call Dr. Jekyll, but refuse to recognize in ourselves the Mr. Hyde who may be closer to being our real self.

Recently I talked to a young woman who identified herself with her moral image as her parents had taught her it should be. But she would not recognize herself in the deceitful role that she was actually playing. The dictionary says that a hypocrite is one who puts on an act in order to make himself look better than he actually is. A hypocrite is a false pretender to virtue and piety in order to promote his own interests. Life has frequently been compared to a drama where each of us has a particular part to play. Many of us imitate the ancient Greeks in the theater where all of the players wore masks on which they had painted the particular facial qualities that they were to play although that might not represent their true characters. We have made an adaptation of this idea of masks by dressing our circus clowns up in ludicrous costumes so that everyone may know in advance how this particular person is expected to behave. For a similar reason we put crowns on the heads of kings and dress our court jesters in caps and bells. We shave the heads of convicts and let the hair grow on the heads of hippies so that no one will be confused about the role that each is supposed to play. However, the most important clue as to what a person is has been painted by life itself into the face of each individual.

The face is the most important part of a person and has been given the best location—on the front part of the head. It is here that God bunched together a great group of important personality members including the eyes, the nose, the mouth, the cheeks, the forehead, the chin, and the countenance, with the ears sticking out in the semi-background. The face also acts as the projection screen where the emotions and ambitions are portrayed for everyone else to see. When extreme rage takes over the control of a person it always shows up in his face. If you snap a man's picture at the instant of his most intense anger, the facial distortion may be permanently captured on the paper. However, after the rage has passed, the face itself tends to go back to its original form except that the restoration is never quite complete. The face, like an overstrained piece of steel or an overstretched elastic band, will never quite recover its original dimensions.

Abraham Lincoln was once in the process of appointing a postmaster. He was giving consideration to one man who had been strongly recommended by a particular Senator. When Lincoln turned the candidate down the sponsoring Senator asked him why. Lincoln said, "I don't like his face." The Senator said, "But you can't hold the poor man responsible for his face." Lincoln said, "After age forty everyone is responsible for his face."

It might be said that what shows in our faces comes about from our particular adaptation of that interesting children's game called "Playing Faces." The idea is for the players to so manipulate their faces that the spectators can guess who they are representing. In an enlargement of this game we sometimes get on the stage with our clothing, our faces, and personalities made up to play the part of Abraham Lincoln or George Washington. Our faces may be made to look grave and solemn, or happy and carefree. One person is made up to act the part of the hero and the other to play the villain. It is also a part of this game of playing faces to use such other personality equipment as our voices, mannerisms, etc., to give the feeling that we are someone else. Some people can so effectively imitate the speech of Winston Churchill, Franklin D. Roosevelt, or Jimmie Durante, that only an expert could tell the difference. Sometimes in life we play the part of the fool, or the wise man.

Each time we participate in our life's game of playing faces, we actually become a little more like the part that we are imitating. Many times we play this interesting game without knowing it or what it is doing to us. Frequently a husband and a wife who love each other over a long period of time actually grow to look like each other. During this game of playing faces there is no way of disconnecting the other parts of our anatomy. Therefore, in every game we also involve our minds, our hearts, and even our souls. In our real-life game of playing faces we also play at expressing the cowardice, alcoholism, nicotine addiction, and immorality of those with whom we identify. Frequently we play the parts of failures, ne'er-do-wells, hippies, and sinners. After each performance is over, our faces or our souls never quite recover their original positions. And sometimes it doesn't take very long before our faces begin filling up with the particular kind of guilt, hate and evil that we get into our game. Then these traits remain with us both on and off the stage. In this game of playing faces, without meaning to do so, we sometimes develop red noses, bodies bloated by booze, eyes that are shifty with guilt, and faces that are bloodshot with sin, merely because we have been playing one of the more foolish versions of our game of playing faces.

Some time ago a press dispatch indicated that the man who had been playing the part of Judas Iscariot in the Bavarian Passion Play had just committed suicide. But it also reported that this was the third Judas who had recently committed suicide. That is, three men had lost their lives merely because they had played an ugly part. There are many other casualties in this deadly game, but fortunately, if we desire we may choose the most ennobling parts for ourselves in our game of playing faces. For example, a little girl playing with her dolls assumes the finest imagined virtues of maturity. And as she cares for these children of her mind, she is actually building the roadway on which her own future success in life will travel. The little boys who play at being patriots and good citizens will be different kind of men than those who play at being robbers and gangsters. As we grow up, if we will play the lives of greatness and righteousness and think the most important thoughts of truth, our lives will fill themselves up with nobility and success. There are certain parts of this game of playing faces that will put a twinkle of happiness in our eyes and a glow of health on our faces. In the right kind of a game one may develop a strong face that shows that it is filled with reassurance, self-confidence, and faith in God. As the face expertly mirrors the many facets and degrees of spiritual power and accomplishment, the right kind of game will help us to pass all of the later face tests that God himself has devised as the basis on which our success and happiness will be determined.

Because every face has an original lie detector built into it, it might be a pretty good idea to occasionally take a good look at ourselves in order to check up on how we are getting along.

Someone once wrote a poem entitled, "The Man in the Glass."
He said:

> When you get what you want in the struggle for self,
> And the world makes you king for a day,
> Just go to the mirror and look at yourself,
> And see what that man has to say.
>
> For it isn't your father or mother or wife,
> Whose judgment upon you must pass;
> The fellow whose judgment counts most in your life
> Is the one staring back from the glass.
>
> You may be like Jack Horner and chisel a plum,
> And think you're a wonderful guy;
> But the man in the glass, he says you're a bum,
> If you can't look him straight in the eye.
>
> He's the fellow to please. Never mind all the rest,
> For he's with you clear to the end,
> And you pass the most dangerous, difficult test,
> If the man in the glass is your friend.
>
> You may follow the world down the pathway of years,
> And get pats on the back as you pass,
> But your final reward will be heartaches and tears,
> If you've cheated the man in the glass.

Every successful gambler tries to develop the kind of
non-committal expression that is often referred to as "a poker
face"—then his opponents will be unable to tell the kind of
cards he holds or whether or not he is bluffing. The Russian
Communist leaders have also tried to develop this kind of a face,
so that they can be as deceitful and unfair as possible without
anyone knowing it. They have become notorious for not honoring their commitments. Every criminal and every sinner also
wants to develop a "poker face," as they also want to keep their
real ambitions and purposes a secret. But sooner or later
everything shows up in the face, and therefore we ought always
to play this game in its most constructive versions.

Recently a man was describing how much fun he had in

playing "patience." In the early part of his life he had been irritable and nervous. Everything seemed to upset him so that he responded in a manner that was far below his best. Then he began taking great joy from the fact that when he made up his mind to have patience he could go through the most irritating situations with perfect composure. He loved to feel his own power of self-control and know that he was stronger than anything that could happen to him. For similar reasons we ought to play the games of virtue, and faith, and righteousness. We can be successful at anything when we fully center our minds on the right things. This idea reminds us of King Philip of ancient Macedonia, who once had a great wild stallion named Bucephalus that no one could ride. Then Philip's young son, Alexander, discovered that the giant wild horse was frightened by his large shadow. Alexander turned the wild stallion's face into the sun so that the shadow fell behind. Then he mounted and easily subdued the famous stallion. At this display of generalship, Philip proudly embraced Alexander and predicted that he would rule a greater kingdom than his father. Alexander was not long in fulfilling his father's prophecy. He had conquered the whole known world by the time he was twenty-six years old. Thereafter men called him "Alexander the Great."

It is an important part of the game of playing faces to know which way our own faces should be turned. At one point the scripture says of Jesus, "His face was set as if he would go up to Jerusalem." Jesus was also talking about pointing our faces in the right direction when he said to people, "Love your enemies." This was also one of the success secrets of Abraham Lincoln. Lincoln kept two of his most bitter enemies in his cabinet in order to get their frank criticism. He wanted them to keep him going in the right direction. At one time one of Lincoln's generals kept him waiting for several hours. One of Lincoln's advisors suggested that the general should be reprimanded for the insult, but Lincoln said, "I would gladly hold his horse if he will only give us victories." Speaking of playing games, there is another Lincoln game that we might profitably play. In his day, Lincoln was considered a very tall man. It is reported that on his way to Washington for the inauguration, many of the tallest men stepped up onto the train platform to stand back-to-back with Lincoln and measure their height against his. Of course, most of them were shorter. But at the Pittsburgh train stop a husky coal-heaver proved to be exactly the same height as Lincoln, and throughout the rest of his days this man told everyone that he was "as tall as Lincoln."

It is a great game when one plays at being as tall as Lincoln. Lincoln was not only tall in stature, he was also tall in character. He stood head and shoulders above the crowd in humility, and he is still our measuring rod for virtue and honesty. What would it be like to be as tall as Lincoln in fairness, and as tall as Lincoln in integrity, and as tall as Lincoln in manhood? What a great victory it would be to be as tall as Lincoln in tolerance and understanding! At the end of the bitter Civil War, Lincoln uttered those immortal words, saying, "with malice toward none, with charity to all, with firmness in the right as God gives us to see the right, let us press on to finish the work we are in, to bind up the nation's wounds, and to care for him who has borne the battle."

Lincoln was tall in mercy. He pardoned many erring soldiers. He once said, "A boy should not be blamed merely because his legs are cowardly." Lincoln was tall in humor. He was big enough to laugh at himself. When it was reported that one of his cabinet members had called him a fool, Lincoln said, "He must be right, for he is a very smart man."

But Deity himself has given us the high mark of the gospel to measure our virtues against. The gospel of Christ is life's greatest standard. And we can measure up to gospel principles only as we set our faces in the right direction. If we turn our faces toward God's sun of truth and away from fear, sin and evil, we will also someday rule a greater kingdom than either King Philip or Alexander the Great. In the meantime may God help us to excel, as we play the best versions of life's great game of faces.

Religion

We have many problems in arriving at our proper destination in life because we fail to understand the laws on which our success is predicated. Our world is filled with failure. Our business bankruptcies are a national disgrace. The waste and blunders made in government certainly leave much to be desired. Over a fourth of all of our marriages come to their end in a disagreeable divorce. And many of the marriages that are still holding together are operating in a state of near bankruptcy. Crime and delinquency run rampant throughout our society. Our bulging mental hospitals, our crowded penal institutions and the bitterness and depression of our own individual lives all testify that either we don't understand the laws of success or that we are unwilling to obey them. Neither are we very effective in maintaining the proper relations with God or with others of our kind. Many wives do not understand their husbands, and most husbands do not understand their wives. Children complain, "My parents don't understand me," and parents say, "I can't talk to my children." There are not very many of us who love our neighbors, or even our families, as we do ourselves.

Recently a very strong mother who has always been devoted to right living and the welfare of her children was seriously upset by being told unexpectedly by her husband that her children were afraid of her. Her husband was far behind her in his degree of righteous excellence, and a kind of unconscious conflict had been going on between the parents for the regard of their children. Although this good woman had spent most of her life working and sacrificing in their interests, they had followed their father's evil example, which had given them a kind of harmony with him. At least his bad example had muddied the water sufficiently that the children were confused and apathetic about what their course in life should be. While they loved their mother, their feelings of guilt had caused a kind of subconscious uncomfortableness with her which the contesting husband had interpreted as fear. This emphasizes the line saying, "United we stand, divided we fall." These family divisions were causing many group and individual problems. The resulting unhappiness testifies to the wisdom of the statement made by the Apostle Paul which says, "Be ye not unequally yoked together. . . ." (2 Cor. 6:14.)

All husbands and wives take a pledge to love, honor, and support each other, and if they are to reach God's objective that "the twain shall become one flesh" then they must make whatever adjustments are necessary in order to bring about this unity, strength, and happiness. One of the most important responsibilities of husbands and wives is to be the official custodians of the happiness and success of each other. For no spouse can be happy unless the mate is happy. And yet there are many husbands and wives who spend more time torturing each other than in trying to make this most important relationship work. Sometimes the misery that we inflict on each other would do credit to one of the torture chambers of the ancients.

Many years ago Dr. Henry C. Link, head of the Psychological Service Center of New York, wrote a great book entitled, *The Return to Religion.* He told of his own early life as a member of a religious household. But as he began to climb the educational ladder, he abandoned his religious attitudes for what he considered to be a more intellectual approach to life and its problems. However, some years later it became his job to discuss with thousands of troubled people the problems of how to live successfully, and then he discovered that almost every problem of every person could be permanently solved by following the divine injunctions given in the scriptures.

Suppose that for a period we read the problems discussed in the "trouble" columns of some newspaper, and think how many of them would immediately disappear if those concerned kept the Ten Commandments and lived the Sermon on the Mount. Or suppose that we were all strictly honest, and fair; or suppose that we loved our enemies; or suppose that we kept those two great commandments wherein we loved God with all our heart and our neighbors as ourselves. Dr. Link says that the best way to put order into life is to live by a set of sound principles, and the most sound principles ever given in the world are those making up the religion of Christ.

There would be no questions about our happiness and our success in every area of our lives, if we fully devoted ourselves to God's laws. All who are engaged in counseling those with marital problems soon discover that every problem arises because of the abuse of some religious principle. If we were all to practice those great laws of honesty, morality, sobriety, industry, the golden rule, and have proper regard for the rights and dignity of each other, then the vexing problems in our marital affairs would disappear as completely as did the dread physical diseases of a few years ago. Righteousness would also put an end to our business scandals, to malpractice and malfeasance in our professions. Simple righteousness would soon bring success in government, and the gangsterism in labor unions would also disappear. A full return to religion could stop the hot and cold wars, and bring about the "Peace on earth, good will toward men" dream for which the angels sang on the hills of Judea nineteen hundred years ago.

Almost all of our problems arise because we close the great scriptures and turn our backs on religion. When we are confronted with the wrong in our lives, we sometimes say that how we live is our own business; and anyway what does it matter inasmuch as God is dead and revelation from him has ceased. But regardless of whether or not God is dead, a policy of "each man for himself" can wreck our civilization and bring misery and failure upon each individual in it.

Most education is about ourselves. We study medicine to learn how to keep ourselves well physically. Psychology, psychiatry, and the other studies of the mind are devoted to how to keep ourselves well mentally. Agriculture is how we feed ourselves; sociology is how we live together agreeably; law is how we keep our lives orderly; and business is how we deal profitably with each other. And then we have this great science of religion that tells us how to keep ourselves well spiritually. It is our weakness and sin in this particular area that brings about our most serious blunders and our worst failures. It is only recently that we have learned very much about agriculture; medicine was in its comparative dark ages until just a few years ago. We are eagerly seeking new inventions that will give us more of life's comforts and more idleness, but we ignore those basic practices of religion that have been known since the world began, and on

which all of our success is predicated. We do what is even worse
when we actually fight religion. The Communist nations seem to
take great delight in placing a ban on religion, as though it were
an evil plague; whereas if it were followed, it would give any
nation an unheard of amount of prosperity and power, with a
maximum of mental and social health. The practice of genuine
religion will also make any individual successful and happy.

I know of a man who seems to do nearly everything wrong.
He is extremely egotistical and self-centered. He is immoral and
causes problems for everyone around him. He has adequate
financial resources for his needs, but his immaturity and godless-
ness makes him an object of pity by those close enough to
know him. Every good thing that he touches is blighted and
infested with decay, and what he needs more than anything else
is a good philosophy of religion to lift him above his own selfish
interests. He needs something to believe in. He needs a cause to
fight for that is bigger and more important than himself.

Recently a man reported that he was bitterly opposed to
the Church. Someone engaged in Church work had offended him,
and in his immaturity he seemed to think that it would help
him in some way if he turned against the Church itself, and
everyone in it. He therefore put on a campaign to tell everyone
how thoroughly he disbelieved in those great principles which
Deity himself had given as a standard to go by. He seemed to
think that to pull everyone else down would lift him up, or that
if he criticized the Church, it would prove him to be right. To
complete his logic, he began criticizing his wife and children for
their participation in Church activities. There are many people
who are not content in merely being evil. They seem to feel that
it helps them to satanize others. It is a natural principle that
"misery loves company" and the claim that "everybody's doing
it" seems to make it right. Some who claim not to believe in
God seem to get a kind of satisfaction in criticizing those who
do. It is easy to put all Church members together and call them
by unsavory names. However, it only means additional problems
when we downgrade those who disagree with us, including God.
The greatest kind of wisdom is to find out what God thinks on
every point, and then put ourselves in harmony and follow him
to the limit.

Thomas Carlyle once said that a man's religion is the most important thing about him. That is what he believes in, and thinks about, and works at, and fights for, and lives by. Actually, religion is the most effective process by which we reach any success and happiness, as well as making our lives worthwhile. We sometimes make some unwarranted distinctions between religion and practical things and then we cross off our list those things that have a religious label. However, religion is important in every part of our lives.

Of the three most important religious commandments ever given, the first has to do with our relations with God; the second has to do with our relations with other people; and then for third place, try to think of something more important than that one in which God said, "In the sweat of thy face shalt thou eat bread." (Gen. 3:19.) Incidently that is not a command of punishment. That is a command of opportunity. This is not just the way we get our bread, it is also the way we overcome our problems, develop our personality, build our character, strengthen our courage, and carry on our part of the work of the world with the most effectiveness. This is also the way that we do almost every other worthwhile thing in the world.

Certainly we cannot exclude God from any part of life. Jesus said, "This is life eternal, that they might know thee the only true God, and Jesus Christ, whom thou hast sent." (John 17:3.) But it is also an important part of every daily success not only to know God, but to follow him.

In our sin weakened efforts to try to understand God we sometimes spiritualize him out of existence, or we convert him into some mere figure of speech, or we half believe that he is dead, and we therefore treat the great Christian doctrines as unworthy of our devotion. A great minister recently indicated one method by which we destroy reality when he said, "Certainly I believe in the devil." He said: "I believe in many devils. I believe in the devil of hate, the devil of fear, the devil of war and the devil of booze." This man has no belief at all in the devil that Jesus talked about. He also believes in God in about the same way that he believes in the devil. He believes that God has lost interest in his creations and in the ability to reveal himself. In spite of our world conditions, some people feel that

we can now take care of ourselves; and that we don't need God
anyway, inasmuch as he has lost the power to exalt or to
condemn. We have deprived God of his body and made him an
"it" instead of a "thou." Because our judgment is no better than
our information, we make a great many mistakes in our relations
with God, merely because we fail to understand him. God is our
eternal Heavenly Father, in whose image we were created. He has
a body and a set of feelings, faculties and senses.

Christ is the head of the Church. He is the author of
religion. He established and sponsors the principle of useful
labor. He is the author of the idea of fairness and good will in
our dealings with each other. He was the greatest teacher who
ever lived. He was the greatest minister of religion and the
greatest example in living his own doctrine.

Jesus taught us what our relationships with God should be.
And he indicates that our divine destiny hinges on our obedience
to his commands. The first principles of the gospel are faith in
the Lord Jesus Christ, repentance, baptism, and the gift of the
Holy Ghost. We need to be faithful to God and valiant in our
righteousness to the end of our lives. Therefore we come back to
the conviction of Carlyle that a man's religion is the most
important thing about him, and we ought to work with that idea
in mind. Certainly our lives do not consist only in the abundance of the things that they possess, nor are they limited to
these few years allotted to our mortal probation.

If our lives are as successful as the Creator intended they
should be, we must get a good supply of real religion into them
at the earliest possible date. May God bless us in this important
enterprise.

The Resurrection

The greatest of all of our human concepts has to do with the immortality of the personality and the eternal glory of the human soul. God, who is the author of life, is also the author of a divine program for our eternal progress and happiness. And the program only falls short of its possibility when we fail to do our part in bringing it about. The fact that we do not understand all of the details should not prevent us from being faithful and obedient; as no one really knows very much about anything. We don't understand our own birth, or life, or death. Some have said that they would not believe anything that they did not understand, but this philosophy places such a severe limit upon our list of beliefs that any substantial success becomes impossible.

One of the most profound pronouncements of Jesus was that declaration in which he said, "All things are possible to him that believeth." (Mark 9:23.) If an individual believes in the laws of health and nutrition he may bring great blessings upon himself, even though he may not understand all of the processes involved. One may have the benefits of light, power, and heat without understanding very much about electricity.

We honor Sir Isaac Newton for discovering the law of gravity, and yet gravity itself has not yet been discovered. We have merely discovered some of the things that gravity does. No one can really understand electricity, or sunshine, or how the grass grows. We don't understand how our minds work or how our body cells reproduce themselves. We didn't even discover the circulation of our own blood until Harvey's time a little over three hundred years ago. Even now the wisest scientist working in the best-equipped laboratory has never yet come close to creating a red corpuscle or making an acorn that will grow. No one can either create life or indefinitely prevent death. The most precious commodity in existence is life, and one of the most important events in life is death.

Death is the gateway to immortality. Certainly death is not an accident or a mistake. It is a part of the program of God that the spirit and the body be temporarily separated as a prelude to the final cleansing and education of the spirit, before the resurrection of the body and the exaltation of the soul. Because we think of death and some of the things associated with it as unpleasant, we frequently refuse to give them the proper attention. But only when we adequately think about death can we effectively prepare for it. Death does not cease to exist merely because it is ignored. We can bring great benefits upon ourselves by having an effective belief in all of the laws of God, including the literal resurrection of the body. And certainly we cannot withhold belief in the resurrection until all of the processes involved are fully understood. The most effective instrument of all of our success is to have faith in God, our eternal Heavenly Father.

There can be no question about the fact that most of us seriously underestimate God. Many people disbelieve in him, and others *almost* disbelieve in him, as they imagine him to be some mysterious, incomprehensible, impersonal influence that they cannot conceive. Just think how it would help us if we thought of God as the scriptures describe him. The scriptures acclaim God as an all-wise, all-knowing, all-powerful person in whose image we were created. He is the literal Father of our spirits, and Jesus Christ was actually begotten by him in the flesh. God is the Creator of innumerable worlds with all of their laws, wonders, order, and beauty, and we have his definite word that many of them are inhabited. God is not only the Father of our spirits, but he has our best interests at heart. In making his eternal program for us he did not limit our benefits to those few things that we, as dull and often disobedient mortals, could understand and live up to.

With all of our boasted knowledge, we probably do not know a millionth part of what God knows, nor do we understand even a small part of the blessings that he has in store for us. Paul said, "Eye hath not seen, nor ear heard, neither have entered into the heart of man, the things which God hath prepared for them that love him." (1 Cor. 2:9.) With all of our infirmities and weaknesses, why should we question God? Or why should we disbelieve or ignore him? God does not do things that are harmful or whimsical or temporary. The scripture points out that "whatsoever God doeth, it shall be forever." (Eccles. 3:14.) Yet in spite of his word, and in spite of our own reason, we sometimes imagine that a short trouble-filled mortality is all there is to life. Consequently we live accordingly and do very little to promote the program that our magnificent Eternal Father has devised for the children he loves.

Some people just don't think about eternal life one way or the other. Some imagine that we will live forever and be deprived of these tremendous creations that we call our bodies, our personalities, our emotions, and our memories. Others think that we will become like a lot of little raindrops that are all merged in a common ocean where all individual identity will be lost. Someone has asked: "What kind of a business do we think God is in anyway? How could we think that he would bring human souls into being, give them minds to think with, hearts to love with, and hands to work with, and then let time wash them all away as if they had no value at all?" Such an idea is incredible and is completely unworthy of such a tremendous being as our eternal Heavenly Father.

We expect our small children, who are without experience or understanding, to accept counsel from their wiser and more experienced parents. If a five-year-old insists on going on his own, we would expect him to have trouble. Or if he absented himself from school, or insisted on disobeying the laws of health, we might predict an unprofitable future for him. Suppose that with a full trust in God we attempt to find out as much as we can about that tremendously stimulating idea of a personal literal bodily resurrection. We may attain all of God's blessings if we develop sufficient faith to live for them.

To begin with, there are several kinds of resurrection. There is the resurrection of the just and there is the resurrection of the unjust, and there are a great many degrees in between. On this point Jesus said: "The hour is coming, in the which all that are in the graves shall hear his voice, and shall come forth; they that have done good, unto the resurrection of life; and they that have done evil, unto the resurrection of damnation." (John 5:28-29.) Everyone both good and bad will be resurrected. "For as in Adam all die, even so in Christ shall all be made alive," (1 Cor.

15:22), but if we go about it in the right way we can improve
the quality of our individual resurrection. In writing to the
Hebrews, the Apostle Paul mentioned some who were doing
certain things in order that "they might have a better resurrection"; and in a discourse made to the Corinthians, he indicated that some would be resurrected to the glory of the sun,
some to the glory of the moon, and some to the glory of the
stars. Then he said: ". . . for one star differeth from another star
in glory. So also is the resurrection of the dead." (1 Cor.
15:41-42.)

In modern-day revelation we are informed that if we fully
live the law of the gospel, we may become celestial spirits with
the power to resurrect celestial bodies. We may think that the
body is pretty wonderful just as it is, but Paul says: "It is sown
in corruption; it is raised in incorruption: It is sown in dishonor;
it is raised in glory: It is sown in weakness; it is raised in
power: It is sown a natural body; it is raised a spiritual body."
(1 Cor. 15:42-44.) If we cannot understand just how this is
possible, just try to understand how God could so effectively put
this great masterpiece of flesh and blood, bone and tissue,
intelligence and reason, vision and personality together in the
first place. When even weak mortal man can do such wonderful
things as we see about us every day, why should we place any
limits on God's ability to do as he has promised?

We have before us the example of the resurrection of Jesus
with multitudes of mortal witnesses. But following the resurrection of Jesus many others were also resurrected. The scripture
says, "And the graves were opened; and many bodies of the
saints which slept arose, and came out of their graves after his
resurrection, and went into the holy city, and appeared unto
many." (Matt. 27:52.) The first resurrection began over nineteen
hundred years ago and will end when Christ comes in his glory
to reign upon the earth during the millennial era of a thousand
years. When he comes, those who have lived godly lives will be
caught up to meet him. (See 1 Thess. 4:17.) And John says:
"They lived and reigned with Christ a thousand years. But the
rest of the dead lived not again until the thousand years were
finished. This is the first resurrection. Blessed and holy is he that
hath part in the first resurrection: On such the second death
hath no power, but they shall be priests of God and of Christ,

and shall reign with him a thousand years." (Rev. 20:4-6.) Those who do not qualify for the resurrection of the just will have to wait for the resurrection of the unjust that will take place after the millennium.

One of our biggest problems in believing in the resurrection probably comes about because we don't understand the importance of our bodies in the first place. In spite of the fact that the human body is God's greatest miracle, there are some people who have been taught that their bodies were given to them as some kind of punishment. They think that they were intended as a prison, and that the death of the body is a welcome release for the spirit. However, if a mortal body were not necessary, it never would have have been created in the first place. If it were not necessary for eternity, the resurrection would never have been instituted. If a body of flesh and bones were not necessary for God the Father, then God the Son would never have been resurrected. The resurrection of Jesus was not merely to satisfy some temporary convenience. Jesus did not lose his body after his resurrection. It did not evaporate, nor did it expand in some mysterious way to fill the immensity of space. God is not an incomprehensible mass without body, personality, feelings, or shape. Modern revelation reaffirms the Bible teaching that God is our Heavenly Father and that we, his children, resemble the parent in whose image we were created. The Father and the Son have both reappeared upon the earth in this latter-day dispensation, and we know that each is a separate, individual, glorified, personal being. A verse of modern scripture says: "The Father has a body of flesh and bones as tangible as man's; the Son also; but the Holy Ghost has not a body of flesh and bones, but is a personage of spirit." (D&C 130:22.)

In spite of the incompleteness of the spirit by itself, there are some who insist upon depriving God himself of his body. Some would reduce our Heavenly Father to a spirit or make him a mere influence. Someone has described him as an eternal principle. How would you like to lose your body or any part of it or become a mere influence or an eternal principle? Certainly God is as great as we are. Some reject the word of the Lord by pleading ignorance, but even then we involve ourselves in some very serious problems. It doesn't seem to bother us too much that we don't understand vitamins, or electricity, or sunshine, and we are still anxious to do what is necessary to obtain their benefits. And surely if God can create us in the first place, we may be certain that he has the ability to keep his promises in getting us resurrected.

Dr. Henry Eyring was once asked to comment on the conflict between science and religion. He said he didn't think there was a conflict in God's mind. The resurrection may seem difficult to us, but we may be sure there is no problem so far as God is concerned.

Some time ago Dr. Wernher Von Braun said: "Many people seem to feel that science has somehow made religious ideas untimely or old-fashioned. But," said he, "I think science has a real surprise for the skeptic. Science for instance, tells us that nothing in nature, not even the tiniest particle, can disappear without a trace. Nature doesn't know extinction, all it knows is transformation. Now if God applies this fundamental principle to the most minute and insignificant parts of his universe, doesn't it make sense to assume that he applies it also to the human soul? I think it does. And everything science has taught me, and continues to teach me, strengthens my belief in the continuity of our spiritual existence after death. For nothing ever disappears without a trace."

Some day each of us will arrive at that time and place when this great event will become a reality and a personal experience for us. How grateful we will be then, if we have qualified for the highest blessings in the resurrection of the just. William James once said that "the best argument favoring eternal life is the existence of a man who deserves one." Our most important responsibility is to deserve a celestial resurrection, and if we obey God's laws he will take care of all the rest. After our resurrection pure spirit will flow in our veins. We will be like God our Eternal Father and will live forever with him in his kingdom.

The Seventh Commandment

One of the most important events in the history of our world took place some 3400 years ago when in a cloud of fire God descended upon the top of Mount Sinai and gave us the Ten Commandments. Moses tried to describe this tremendous event by saying: "And Mount Sinai was altogether on a smoke, because the Lord descended upon it in fire: and the smoke thereof ascended as the smoke of a furnace, and the whole mount quaked greatly." (Exod. 19:18.) Then to the accompaniment of lightnings and thunders the Lord gave us those important basic rules to govern our lives.

In the seventh of these all-important laws the Lord said, "Thou shalt not commit adultery."

Many people have tried to rate these commands in the order of their importance. That may not be entirely feasible because our good and evil inclinations vary so radically that a comparison may not always be meaningful. I suppose, however, that the first commandment given would also be the first in order of importance. In it God says, "Thou shalt have no other gods before me." If we really kept this commandment, we would keep all of the others more or less automatically. Next in order most people would probably place murder. Our lives are about all that any of us have.

Under the law of Moses if one stole an ox the judgment was that he should make restitution by handing over to the injured one five other oxen as damages. But how could a murderer make a similar restitution? A murderer not only destroys an irreplaceable life, but he also destroys the opportunities, pleasure, hopes and ambitions of many possible descendants as well. Under the law of Moses the penalty for murder was the death of the murderer. Yet even death cannot pay for the harm done. But in our day we don't seem to think that murder is very serious. To us, other people's lives are sometimes pretty cheap. And almost every newspaper tells of the many murders that are being committed on the slightest provocation. Some people kill for money, some kill out of hate, some kill for pleasure, and some for spite. We also have some thrill killers. They are like vandals who have pleasure in destruction, or wanton hunters who delight in unnecessary slaughter. Denying God is sin number one. Sin number two is to murder those formed in his image. Then in third place most people would list adultery. There are several evidences that God also feels this way. One is that he prescribed the same penalty for adultery that he did for murder; except that for adultery, he specified that most miserable form of execution—death by stoning.

However, in our day the sins of denying God, committing murder, and being immoral have been reduced in seriousness by many people. We take up popularity polls among students and even ask the adulterers themselves how they think we should regard this sin. However, to properly govern our relations between the sexes, we had better know how God thinks on this subject. One of the unpleasant consequences of this evil is the crop of new lives that are brought into the world each year by weak, irresponsible, ignorant people with no means of providing homes or parents for their offspring. Instead of giving these children the chance for happiness that they are entitled to, they are started out with many handicaps. Immorality is motivated by a thoughtless, selfish, sinful recklessness, where one's own distorted sense of pleasure is the primary consideration. A man recently came to talk about the problems that some of his evil exploits were causing him. He seemed to think that anything that pleased him must be right. He was not at all restrained by any feeling of responsibility for the havoc he was causing in the lives of those he was seducing. Nor did he seem to feel that what he did was anybody's business, including God's. If he broke his wife's heart and caused her a lifetime of shame, humiliation, and torture, he didn't see how that should concern anyone else but him. Through his unspeakable example, he was destroying the faith of his children and their belief in human honor. The conflicts caused by his sins were cutting him off from Church attendance and the association of other good people. It also made it seem out of place for him to kneel with his family in prayer, or talk to them about love and God and righteousness and eternal life.

It is amazing how little and stupid we human beings can sometimes become in order to satisfy our own selfishness. If we want an expert opinion we should listen to the way God voted on this subject, when his voice thundered forth from the top of Mount Sinai: "Thou shalt not commit adultery." Some time ago a minister of religion declared that in his opinion the Ten Commandments no longer served as an effective basis for religious teaching. He said that they were negative in attitude, dictatorial in spirit, and gave people the idea that the church was some kind of a wet blanket to take the joy out of life. He felt that the harsh "Thou shalt not's" were not in good taste in our day. This minister said, "I never refer to the Ten Commandments in my church." He didn't say whether he believed that the great laws of chastity, honesty, worship, and respect for human life should be done away with; but he did think that these important commands of God were now outmoded and no longer useful.

Another religious leader said that the stern "Thou shalt not's" were much too harsh for our present-day sensitivities. He suggested that the spirit of the Ten Commandments should be toned down by substituting some softer words such as "advise," "suggest" or "recommend." We make a very serious mistake when we make ourselves so vulnerable and so touchy in being corrected that we cannot even bear to hear God's truths without first applying a few layers of sugar coating. Sometimes we become antagonistic to everything that disagrees with our ideas or calls our attention to our own weaknesses.

It might strengthen us to feel the intensity of God's reaction to this sin in the case of David, King of Israel. David involved himself with the wife of one of his soldiers by the name of Uriah. The Lord was very displeased and sent Nathan the prophet to advise David of the judgment that he had thus brought upon himself. Because a stronger language, not a softer one, is sometimes needed to get important ideas over to people, the ancient prophets often used the more picturesque language of parables. Through a comparison a situation can sometimes be presented for consideration solely on its merits without the individual becoming so personally involved as to destroy his judgment. Therefore, Nathan gave David the following parable. He said:

"There were two men in one city; the one rich, and the other poor. The rich man had exceeding many flocks and herds: but the poor man had nothing, save one little ewe lamb, which he had brought and nourished up; and it grew up together with him, and with his children; it did eat of his own meat, and drank of his own cup, and lay in his bosom, and was unto him as a daughter. And there came a traveler unto the rich man, and he spared to take of his own flock and of his own herd, to dress for the wayfaring man that was come unto him; but took the poor man's lamb, and dressed it for the man that was come to him." The scripture then says: "And David's anger was greatly kindled against the man; and he said to Nathan, As the Lord liveth, the man that hath done this thing shall surely die: and he shall restore the lamb fourfold, because he did this thing and because he had no pity. And Nathan said to David, Thou art the man. Thus saith the Lord God of Israel, I anointed thee king over Israel, and I delivered thee out of the hand of Saul; and I gave thee thy master's house, and thy master's wives unto thy bosom, and gave thee the house of Israel and of Judah; and if that had been too little, I would have given unto thee such and such things. Wherefore, hast thou despised the commandment of the Lord, to do evil in his sight? thou hast killed Uriah the Hittite with the sword, and hast taken his wife to be thy wife."

The Lord said: "Now therefore, the sword shall never depart from thine house; ... I will raise up evil against thee out of thine own house.... And David said unto Nathan, I have sinned against the Lord.... And Nathan said unto David, Because by this deed thou hast given great occasion to the enemies of the Lord to blaspheme, the child also that is born unto thee shall surely die." (2 Sam. 12:1-14.)

To us in these days, loaded as we are with immorality, this particular parable should have great meaning. Certainly this sin is not less offensive in the sight of God now than it was then. When David was given a chance to appraise the situation before he knew that he was the offender, he was very angry and followed the Israelitish law in pronouncing sentence upon the offender—who happened to be himself. The law said that if a man took a sheep that did not belong to him he should make restitution by giving back four sheep as damages. If this law were followed today, most of us would be in bankruptcy. Most people don't want to pay for their sins even once, let alone four times.

Some people may think it difficult enough to stay in the sheep business under the most favorable conditions. But if we tried to stay in the sheep business by stealing sheep, we would go in the hole four thousand sheep a year for each thousand that were stolen. When we are tempted to do the wrong things, we might well keep in mind that it was the Lord himself who set this penalty at four sheep for one. The penalty for stealing an ox was five for one, and it may be much higher than that in the more serious things. The scriptures say that God is unchangeable, and we might keep in mind that he has always taken a pretty dim view of all kinds of sin. Certainly it is very unprofitable to have to pay for sins at four, or five, or a hundred for one.

David had two other charges against him. He had committed adultery and then, in an attempt to cover up, he had had Uriah sent to the battle front, and there Uriah was killed. Under the law of Moses the penalty for each of these sins was death. David might have been able to pay for many stolen lambs at four for one but how could he pay two death penalties at four for one? God does not want to inflict penalties upon us. We are his children. He had once called David a man after God's own heart. But God's house is a house of order, and he will not tolerate us doing evil and just taking what we want in sinful ways. And he has made it plain that each individual must suffer for his own sins. David's punishments were many and very severe. He was specifically prohibited from building the temple which was one of the great desires of his heart. The child died that was born as a result of his sin. David's son, Absalom, became a traitor and drew away a large part of David's army, and led a civil war against his father in an attempt to unseat him from the throne of Israel. Another son, Adonijah, also came out in open rebellion against his father. David's sin was followed by a long series of misfortunes which embittered the entire twenty-year balance of his life. He suffered many other disastrous consequences during this life, but his trouble continued even after his death when several members of his family met violent deaths at the hands of Bathsheba's second son, Solomon.

In addition to all of this, David would also be required to

spend a long period of time suffering the torments of hell. This
was in spite of the fact that David also had many things on the
credit side of the ledger; and after great suffering, much humiliation and a sincere repentance, David received a promise from
God which David quoted, saying, "For thou wilt not leave my
soul in hell." (Ps. 16:10.) However, over a thousand years later,
Peter said, "For David is not ascended into the heavens." (Acts
2:34.) And David is still paying the heavy price of his sins. We
should keep in mind that the seventh commandment still stands
in full force as far as we ourselves are concerned. Some groups
or individuals may become a law unto themselves, and may take
their own vote about whether or not this law should be obeyed.
This command may not suit the purposes of some hippie or
other organizations, but the seventh commandment was not made
by hippies or those evil men and women who foster its violation.
It was given by God and he is the one to whom we must all
answer. And as in the days of David, God is still prescribing the
penalties. God cannot be intimidated by rebellions or the votes
of those favoring some "new morality." It may not be very
much consolation to anyone on judgment day to know that
there were many other offenders. Even to say that "everyone's
doing it" may not help us very much then. Sometimes we hope
to be excused on the grounds that times have changed. But that
is probably what they were thinking in Noah's day when the
flood came and took their lives. In addition to being drowned,
they were also required to pay for their sins in eternity. And it
was on a much higher ratio than four for one. The Apostle Peter
tells us that twenty-five hundred years later they were still in the
eternal prison house, suffering for their sins. Then while the
body of Jesus lay in the tomb his spirit went and preached the
gospel to those who had denied God's teachings twenty-five
hundred years earlier. (See 1 Pet. 3:18-20.) If the times have
changed it might be interesting to remember who has changed
them. God has never been impressed when a group of irresponsible, lustful, selfish, sinful, thoughtless people have tried to
change his laws.

From any point of view the greatest opportunity of our
lives is to obey these great laws of God made for our good.
They have been given to make us into the kind of people that
we ought to be. And may God help us to hear as we listen
again to that great command from the top of Mount Sinai
saying, "Thou shalt not commit adultery." That is still the law.

Sir Launfal

Among the prized volumes on my library shelves are some books of poems. It has been said that each human soul has a poetic instinct that quickens his responses when great ideas are presented dressed in their best clothes. The poets stand next to the prophets in their ability to arouse our spirits and develop in us a whole-souled idealism. Poetry is also able to stimulate our divine discontent and help us to see beyond the fraction that we presently are to the perfection that we may sometime become. Some of the great poems should be memorized, read aloud, and lived with. And when the greatest ideas are dressed in language that has been metered, measured, charged with motivation and set to word music, they carry with them a more intense spirit and have more power to awaken the best in our souls.

One of the great poems that we should try to get the spirit of is James Russell Lowell's "Vision of Sir Launfal." This poem was composed at almost a single sitting under a spell of poetic ecstasy. The haste was not because of any desire to finish it in a certain time, but a divine impatience always springs up in our souls when we become completely involved with some great idea. This restlessness in Mr. Lowell's mind would not allow him to relax his attention until his poem had been given its life by expression.

It tells the story of one of King Arthur's knights who made a vow to go in search for the Holy Grail. This was the cup out of which Jesus drank at the last supper. As Sir Launfal contemplated this undertaking, he prayed for a vision to guide him. His prayer was granted in a dream. A vision came into his soul that lasted for an entire lifetime though it was received during a single night. We might go with Sir Launfal as he rides away in the beautiful morning of that pleasant early summertime. The young knight himself had the exuberance and hope of youth. It was not only Nature's summertime but there was a joyous

summer in Sir Launfal's soul. The prelude to the first part sets
the stage and prepares us for the first half of the story. It also
gives us the spirit in which the projected accomplishment was
undertaken. We can feel the mood that the poem is to exemplify, as well as the lesson that it will teach. The prospect for
this great experience is compared to an organist, sitting idly
before the keys, scarcely aware of what he is playing. As he
ponders over the keys, the vision begins to form and the subject
of his quest stands out clearly before him. Our lives themselves
frequently assume their meaning in this manner. We also have
some preludes that bridge over the gulf between the dreaming
period of life and the reality of the actual accomplishment. The
prelude picks us up in whatever mood may possess us and leads
us a step at a time into the vision of our life's accomplishment.

Mr. Lowell says:

Over his keys the musing organist,
Beginning doubtfully and far away,
First lets his fingers wander as they list,
And builds a bridge from Dreamland for his lay.

Then, as the touch of his loved instrument
Gives hope and fervor, nearer draws his theme,
First guessed by faint, auroral flushes sent
Along the wavering vista of his dream.

Mr. Lowell contradicts Wordsworth's thesis that heaven lies
about us only in our infancy. Moses was an adult when he
climbed Mount Sinai, and except for the inferiority and smallness
of our daily thoughts, we might also climb to those heights
where we could see God face to face. Heaven protects and
inspires the worthy to the very end of their lives. Mr. Lowell
says:

Not only in our infancy
Doth heaven with all its splendors lie;
Daily, with souls that cringe and plot,
We Sinais climb and know it not.
Over our manhood bend the skies;
Against our fallen and traitor lives
The great winds utter prophecies;

Characteristically we spend too much of our lives in working for the wrong things. The author says:

Earth gets its price for what earth gives us;
The beggar is taxed for a corner to die in,
The priest hath his fee who comes and shrives us.
We bargain for the graves we lie in;
At the Devil's booth are all things sold,
Each ounce of dross costs its ounce of gold;

For a cap and bell our lives we pay,
Bubbles we buy with a whole soul's tasking.
'Tis heaven alone that is given away,
'Tis only God may be had for the asking;

What a thrilling idea that the greatest blessings, including the love of God, are given to us free of charge, and yet how tragic that we pay the most exorbitant prices for the very things that hurt us most! Lowell says:

No price is set on the lavish summer;
June may be had by the poorest comer.

In the first part of Sir Launfal's vision we have what is probably the greatest passage in our literature describing the early part of an American summer. Lowell was familiar with the ebbs and flows of the ocean and he refers to this early period in June as the "high-tide" of the year. This productive spirit of early summer is also symbolic of our own lives as our visions of high attainment start us on our ways. Mr. Lowell says:

And what is so rare as a day in June?
Then, if ever, come perfect days;
Then Heaven tries earth if it be in tune,
And over it softly her warm ear lays;

Whether we look, or whether we listen,
We hear life murmur, or see it glisten;
Every clod feels a stir of might,
An instinct within it that reaches and towers,
And groping blindly above it for light,
Climbs to a soul in grass and flowers.

The flush of life may well be seen
Thrilling back over hills and valleys;
The cowslip startles in meadows green,
The buttercup catches the sun in its chalice,
And there's never a leaf or a blade too mean
To be some happy creature's palace;
The little bird sits at his door in the sun,
Atilt like a blossom among the leaves,
And lets his illumined being o'errun
With a deluge of summer it receives;
His mate feels the eggs beneath her wings,
And the heart in her dumb breast flutters and sings;
He sings to the wide world, and she to her nest—
In the nice ear of nature which song is the best?
Now is the high-tide of the year,
And whatever of life hath ebbed away
Comes flooding back with a ripply cheer
Into every bare inlet and creek and bay.
Now the heart is so full that a drop overfills it;
We are happy now because God wills it;
No matter how barren the past may have been
'Tis enough for us now that the leaves are green.
We sit in the warm shade and feel right well
How the sap creeps up and the blossoms swell;
We may shut our eyes, but we cannot help knowing
That skies are clear and grass is growing.
The breeze comes whispering in our ear
That dandelions are blossoming near,
That maize has sprouted, that streams are flowing,
That the river is bluer than the sky,
That the robin is plastering his house hard by;
And if the breeze kept the good news back,
For other couriers we should not lack;
We could guess it all by yon heifer's lowing—
And hark! How clear bold chanticleer,
Warmed with the new wine of the year,
Tells all in his lusty crowing!

Joy comes, grief goes, we know not how;
Everything is happy now,
Everything is upward striving,
'Tis as easy now for the heart to be true

As for grass to be green, or skies to be blue,
'Tis the natural way of living.
Who knows whither the clouds have fled?
In the unscarred heaven they leave no wake;
And the eyes forget the tears they have shed,
And the heart forgets its sorrow and ache;

The soul partakes of the season's youth,
And the sulphurous rifts of passion and woe
Lie deep 'neath a silence pure and smooth,
Like burnt-out craters healed with snow.
What wonder if Sir Launfal now
Remembered the keeping of his vow?

In this spirit Sir Launfal begins his search for the Holy
Grail. As he leaves the gate of his own castle, a leper holds out
his hand for alms. In scorn the young knight tosses him a piece
of gold. But because of the spirit in which it is offered, the
leper lets the gold lie. Then for a long lifetime in many lands,
Sir Launfal seeks for the Holy Grail. And only after many years
do we see him again, under changed circumstances as he returns
to the area that had once been his home. Now his wealth and
youth have been exchanged for poverty and old age. It is now
the dead of winter and it is also the winter of Sir Launfal's life.
The castle no longer belongs to him. An attendant serving the
new owner shouts him away from the gate. Therefore he sits
alone, attempting to protect himself from the cold and snow by
remembering some scenes from the light and warmth of long
ago. At this point the leper once again appears and asks for
alms. Now Sir Launfal has no gold to give him. The knight's
entire possessions now consist of a single crust of stale brown
bread, but this he gladly shares with the beggar. He also gives
him a drink of water from his wooden bowl. This gift is not as
valuable as the first one but it is more readily accepted because
of the improved spirit in which it is given. The author says:

'Twas a moldy crust of coarse brown bread,
'Twas water out of a wooden bowl—
Yet with fine wheaten bread was the leper fed,
And 'twas red wine he drank with his thirsty soul.

Then the beggar casts off his disguise and reveals himself as

the Christ. Sir Launfal sought to find the chalice out of which
the Savior drank but instead he found the Savior himself. He
tells Sir Launfal that his service, which shows the true spirit of
charity, has been accepted. It will also help us if we get into our
hearts those great lines, saying:

Not what we *give* but what we *share*,
For the gift without the giver is bare;
Who gives himself with his alms feeds three—
Himself, his hungering neighbor, and Me.

This is the message that Christ has been trying to teach
since the world itself began. Jesus said: "Inasmuch as ye have
done it unto one of the least of these my brethren, ye have
done it unto me." (Matt. 25:40.) Again he said: "He that
receiveth my servants receiveth me; and he that receiveth me
receiveth my Father. And he that receiveth my Father receiveth
my Father's kingdom; therefore all that my Father hath shall be
given unto him." (D&C 84:36-38.)

We may not be conducting a search for the Holy Grail as
such. But we must find the purpose of life and how we
ourselves may make the most acceptable contribution.

Sometimes we use the high tide of our lives for selfishness
and sin, and after the dead of winter has arrived we discover
that all that we have left is the unsatisfactory possibility of some
kind of a deathbed repentance. Like Sir Launfal, we need to
launch a search to find the Savior of our souls. Anyone can have
a lifetime of experience if we use up a lifetime to have it in.
But then there is an inadequate amount of time left in which to
practice the lessons that we have learned. Then we often wish
that we could live our lives over again. There are no rehearsals in
life. We can't rehearse birth, or death, or success. We must be
right the first time. And what a thrilling advantage it gives us
when, like Sir Launfal, we can get a lifetime of benefit from the
determinations of a single night. Then while our lives are at their
high tide, we still have many years left to put the lessons into
operation.

Sir Launfal prayed for his life to be directed, and the vision
came as the answer to his desire. God will also give us a vision.

Sir Launfal finished his quest without his armor and the other accouterments in which the days of his pride had dressed him. But a lifetime had taught him that anyone should be dressed in a stronger mail who would seek and find the Holy Grail.

We may not have in our possession the cup from which the Lord drank at the Last Supper; however, all of the blessings for which the divine sacrifice was made are available to us. And through the sacramental ordinance, which he anciently instituted, we may partake of the emblems of his death. Christian people everywhere know that with his disciples, Jesus partook of these meaningful emblems in remembrance of his sacrifice. The Church was restored to the earth for this final dispensation on April 6, 1830, and the Lord has given us a sacramental prayer that includes the sacred covenant that he desires each of us to take. We say: "O God, the Eternal Father, we ask thee in the name of thy Son, Jesus Christ, to bless and sanctify this bread to the souls of all those who partake of it, that they may eat in remembrance of the body of thy Son, and witness unto thee, O God, the Eternal Father, that they are willing to take upon them the name of thy Son, and always remember him and keep his commandments which he has given them; that they may always have his Spirit to be with them, Amen." (D&C 20:77.)

The Thinker

There is an interesting little statue that we see around occasionally called *The Thinker*. It shows a man in a sitting position with his elbow on his knee and his chin resting on his hand. His attitude and expression indicate that he is absorbed in deep meditation. This little image is usually displayed in homes or offices as an ornament. But its more subtle purpose is to remind us of that interesting mental process where various kinds of good ideas, programs, and images are formed in the mind to bring about some useful accomplishment. The original of this statue was carved by the French sculptor Rene Rodin, who died in 1917. He was a noted realist, and some of his other sculptured creations were "The Hand of God," "The Prayer," and "Adam and Eve." Mr. Rodin became famous for his visual portrayal of great ideas.

It has been said that a thing's importance is not always found in the object itself, but it may have an even greater value for what it stands for, or is a sign of, or serves as a symbol for. And what greater idea could anyone cultivate than the one symbolized by Mr. Rodin's image? We have one of our greatest human experiences when we get an active idea working in our minds. There is nothing more exciting or worthwhile than that which a good mind can do with an idea.

From the brain of Thomas A. Edison came electric lights, refrigerators, washing machines, phonographs, and television sets that have transformed our world with light, filled it with music and understanding, and lifted the burden of toil and drudgery from the backs of men and women. But all wonders have not yet been performed. Every individual is the custodian of some wonders in their mental, spiritual, social and financial forms. These ideas are presently moving around in our own minds struggling to be born. And we might agitate Mr. Rodin's idea about "thinking" in order to bring some of these important live births about.

It has been said that if you want to hatch out something, just set your mind on it. And when we set our minds on our own great possibilities, we not only hatch out a lot of wonderful things but we also increase the power of the mind itself. Most of the satisfactions we have in life come from the way that we ourselves think. This is even true of happiness itself. Abraham Lincoln once said, "We are only as happy as we make up our minds to be."

Someone has stimulated us with the question, "How would you like to create your own mind?" but isn't that exactly what we all do? William James said, "The mind is made up by what it feeds upon." The mind, like the dyer's hand, is colored by what it holds. If I hold in my hand a sponge full of purple dye, my hand becomes purple, and if I hold in my mind and heart the great ideas of faith, love, ambition, and devotion to God, my whole personality is colored accordingly. Even our souls themselves are fashioned by what and how we think. A great human being is the finest creation of God, and the mind was created to be its presiding officer. It is by thinking that we produce the great wonders of reason, creativeness, character, faith, and the ability to direct our lives to their highest potential.

The mind that crowns God's magnificent masterpiece was given the highest position in our stature, with the assignment to so direct our love, faith, and industry that we might make the best and the most of our own lives.

However, this great resource has some reverse possibilities. When we think negative thoughts we develop negative minds. Some people have morose minds. Some have created depraved minds that produce a poison fruit in the form of depraved, degrading thoughts. The scriptures point out that some people will be damned. And we might try to imagine what it would be like to have a damned mind and forever feed on the evil, darkness, and depression of damned thoughts.

On the other hand think of this godly privilege: we may now engage in that tremendous process of developing celestial minds that will think only celestial, constructive, happy thoughts. These are the kind of thoughts that God thinks. We should get as much mileage as possible from the fact that our future success will be determined by what we presently think. Physically we become what we eat, but mentally, spiritually, socially, and morally we become what we think. And we may think as big and as straight and as high as we like.

Napoleon Hill once wrote a great book entitled, *Think and Grow Rich.* But this does not exhaust our possibilities. We can also think and grow wise. We can think and grow faithful, and we can think and grow godly. To be a great thinker does not require us to think only original thoughts. All of the greatest thoughts about love, beauty, faith, kindness, and success have already been thought again and again. But as we rerun them through our own minds they produce an increasing rate of return for us.

At birth almost everything, including ideas, is small and poorly formed. But thoughts can grow and become more perfect as they are rethought, and with the tremendous expansion of our literature we now have a far wider selection of ideas from which to choose than we have ever had before. And we may select for our own rethinking those ideas that are in their most perfect form. Every thought that passes through the mind makes a characteristic mark or engram upon the brain. And if we run through our minds the same kind of thoughts that ran through the minds of Shakespeare, Emerson, Lincoln, or the Apostle Paul, our minds will eventually come to respond as did the minds of Shakespeare, Emerson, Lincoln and the Apostle Paul. According to its use the mind develops a set of markings about as characteristic as our fingerprints. And when a great idea is run through our minds enough times it may make an even greater improvement in us than it did in the man who thought it originally.

Thinking a great thought originally may not be nearly as important as applying one that has already been thought by someone else. Sometimes it takes a long time to think a thought through from birth to maturity. But we may take the greatest ideas that are now fully developed and available in their finest form, and use them to the limit of our ability in developing the most favorable characteristics in our own minds. We might even improve on Mr. Rodin's idea, and dedicate a statue to the *re*thinker. It is only natural that the rethinker can show the greatest profit because of his larger volume and his greater selection.

Over a century ago my great-grandmother walked across the plains to help make a home for me in the valleys of the Rocky Mountains. Her labor helped to redeem a wilderness and make a forbidding desert to "blossom as the rose." As a grown man, I moved into the city that she and thousands of others had built. The temple had been completed. The streets had been paved, the light lines were up, the sewers were in, and many other conveniences had been built and paid for. And for my entire lifetime I have had far more benefits from their enterprise than they did who built them. They toiled to produce what they never lived to enjoy. And we have the same situation in regard to our ideas. We have had the great scriptures handed down to us free of charge, which cost the lives of many of the prophets and apostles who wrote them. As Christians we not only have what the ancients had, but we have the judgment of time shining upon the life of Christ, and the voices of many additional witnesses bearing testimony of his divinity. Without effort on our part we have more of the word of the Lord than all previous generations combined. The scriptures also tell of the successes and failures of the lives that wrote them in a way that they themselves did not fully understood. We may have the profit that their lives produced without taking their risks or making their mistakes.

Jesus rethought the same ideas many times and then said, "Follow me." What a thrilling challenge that each of us can follow him in his thinking, and develop the courage and good works that make future good thoughts possible! The more we rethink the thoughts of Deity the deeper our grooves become, the broader are the marks left on our character, and the more readily we are able to mold ourselves into the image of his righteousness. How tragic when we comprehend some great Christian ideal and then say, "I never gave it another thought." If we rethink the Master's thoughts enough times and with enough intensity our lives will tend to respond as his did.

There are many interesting word combinations denoting our mental activities. We speak of "thinking," or of "thinking it through," or of "thinking it over." With our thoughts we make plans, organize philosophies, and direct the most important of all values, which is our own lives. And when we put on our thinking caps and keep them *on*, and keep them working, we may cause the most constructive elements in our lives to take on their most attractive appearance. Any mind becomes more productive as it develops the thinking attitudes, the ability to conceive, the power to visualize, and the ambition to build images, have dreams, and project the soul forward and upward.

John Milton said, "The mind in its own place and of itself can make a heaven of hell or a hell of heaven." The mind can also do almost any other thing that it sets up for itself. Of course this wonderful mental ability must be powerized and given direction. Someone has said that there is nothing more dangerous than an animated blind horse. Improperly directed thoughts can quickly mold us into something that we don't want to be.

During the long conflict between ancient Rome and Carthage, Cato, the old Roman Senator, ended every speech by saying, "Carthage must be destroyed." This technique for stamping an important idea into our mind by "rethinking" is related to Winston Churchill's "V" sign for victory which he always flashed around on everyone during the Second World War.

Recently a great sales corporation adopted another victory slogan which said, "Think five." They thought they could sell five billion dollars' worth of merchandise in one year. But they needed to get the goal firmly fixed in everyone's mind and have everyone feel a proper share of the responsibility. This idea to "think five" was lodged in everyone's mind with an importance great enough to give it special power. It became a kind of intercompany greeting that was on everyone's lips. As a means of implementing and reinforcing the objective, each member was asked to devise five specific ways of his own for bringing the company objective about.

Business and military organizations have accomplished many miracles by their own processes for broadening the engrams and deepening the mental pathways leading to some objective firmly fixed in the minds of those concerned. But every child of God has the greatest of all objectives in making the best and the most of his own life. This requires that we have the right kind of thoughts in the think-tank that supplies our minds. Each of us should have at least five good deep engrams leading to the goal. In the days of ancient Israel, the Lord instituted among the people the custom of wearing phylacteries. God knew that there were certain ideas that were indispensable to their contemplated success. The Lord had the people memorize these success ideas and write them down on pieces of parchment, enclose them in little leather tubes, and wear them around their necks, on their hands, and in other places on their persons where they would always be in sight.

The Lord said: "And these words, which I command thee this day, shall be in thine heart: and thou shalt teach them diligently unto thy children, and thou shalt talk of them when thou sittest in thine house, and when thou walkest by the way, and when thou liest down, and when thou risest up. And thou shalt bind them for a sign upon thine hand, and they shall be as frontlets between thine eyes." Some of the Israelites also wore these phylacteries upon their fingers like rings. On one of these phylacteries was inscribed these words, "Thou shalt love the Lord thy God with all thy heart, and with all thy soul, and with all thy might." (Deut. 6:5-8.)

The Lord prescribed this process of consolidation and joint action so that they could concentrate all of the elements of personal power into one determined effort. This formula containing one of the most important secrets of success involves a joint action of the heart, the mind, the soul, and the might. We can serve God with our minds, by our study, our thoughts, our understanding, and an uplifting mental attitude. We serve God with our hearts and souls, by our devotion, adoration, worship, and obedience. We serve God with our might, by the exercise of a firm determination, an unobstructed will power, and a vigorous physical activity. This kind of coordination places the greatest accomplishments within our easy reach.

Suppose that we adopted a strong philosophy of thinking, and suppose that we were going to "think five." What would our strongest thoughts be? Daniel Webster said, "The greatest thought that has ever entered my mind is the consciousness of my individual responsibility to God." Jesus said, "This is life eternal, that they might know thee the only true God, and Jesus Christ, whom thou hast sent." (John 17:3.) Just suppose that we could actually get these thoughts firmly established in our minds.

William James said, "The greatest discovery of my generation is that you can change your circumstances by changing your attitudes of mind." Everyone wants to change his circumstances, but only a few are willing to change themselves. Leonardo da Vinci showed himself a thinker when he said, "Thou, Oh God, doth sell us all good things at the price of labor." And Jesus said, "All things are possible to him that believeth." With this kind of faith operating in our minds our lives will be outstandingly successful. May God help us to rethink his thoughts effectively.

Thou Shalt Not Kill

Dr. Henry C. Link once said that nothing puts so much order into human life as to live by a set of sound principles. God tried to put order into our world by giving it the finest set of the best principles. To live most successfully and pleasantly we need to be in full harmony with the laws of gravity, electricity, light, heat, etc. When we violate any natural law the other considerations involved always go wrong. If the farmer plants his corn in the chill of a December blizzard, he cannot hope to get the kind of crop that might come if he planted his seeds in the warmth of the May sunshine. We have also been given a set of sound religious laws by which we can get the most from our personal behavior. God himself came down onto the top of Mount Sinai and gave ten great commandments which are the fundamental laws upon which all human success is based.

One of the most important of these laws is only four words long. It is commandment number six which says, "Thou shalt not kill." Life is the most important commodity in the universe, and God has always seemed particularly jealous about keeping its control in his own hands. He doesn't want us tampering with the sources of life, nor trying to bring about its untimely termination. With all of the wisdom produced by our modern knowledge explosion, plus all of the skill of our greatest men of science, we have never yet discovered God's secrets of life. And no combination of scientists has ever yet been able to produce one kernel of corn that would grow. Nor have they ever been able to bring into being one live red corpuscle. In rating the enormity of the sins, God has placed the destruction of life very near the top of the list. And he has decreed comparable penalties for its violation. However, in the midst of the human ignorance and disobedience so prominent in our day, murder has become a very common everyday event.

Cain started our first crime wave by killing his brother

Abel. And as punishment, the Lord set a mark upon him and made him an eternal fugitive and vagabond. But since that time, we have popularized many different kinds of killing. We have instituted devastating wars among nations. Although we understand the suffering, pain, disease, poverty and sin which always come as a natural result, wars have reached their worst destructiveness during our greatest age of science, education, and civilization. In my short lifetime we have had two full-scale world wars in which millions have been killed in battle, and other millions have died from starvation and disease.

We shoot each other with bullets, we drop bombs on cities, train thousands of gangsters, and threaten to destroy each other with germs and poison gas. Hitler killed six million Jews, most of whom were his own countrymen. And Joseph Stalin put millions of his own subjects to death.

In addition to tribal, national, and global wars, we also have some destructive family feuds and wasteful individual conflicts. In the United States last year over 20,000 people killed themselves. Of course, there are different degrees of crime involved in killing. Some kill in cold blood, some kill in self-defense, some are killed as a result of drunkenness, and others are destroyed in some kind of accident.

The penalty for taking human life has always been very high. Under the Law of Moses, the penalty for murder was death. And most present-day governments also impose the death sentence for a wilful murder. But even if a killer forfeits his own life, that still does not pay off the bill. He can never bring the dead man back to life, or restore the blessings in the lives of his dependents. It appears that many people, including Cain, will suffer forever for their sins. Even before Cain took Abel's life, he had already made himself into a kind of murderer. Cain took his first steps toward murder when he allowed selfishness to get hold of him. He took another step when he offered an unacceptable offering to the Lord, and he got a little nearer still when, because he was corrected, he became angry and made a covenant with Satan. Each of these preliminaries might well be considered as a part of his final deed, for if he hadn't taken those first steps he never would have taken the last one. Jesus reminded us of these preliminaries when he said: "Ye have heard that it was

said by them of old time, thou shalt not kill . . . but I say unto
you that whosoever is angry with his brother without a cause
shall be in danger of the judgment." (Matt. 5:21-22.)

When Cain became angry and developed a sullen, moody,
evil spirit, he was well on his way to becoming a murderer. The
scripture says that his countenance fell. That in itself is pretty
serious. Cain became jealous and he coveted his brother's flocks.
Then in trying to cover up his sin, he lied to the Lord. Cain led
himself up to murder by committing those forerunner sins that
preceded the final act. If we want to avoid murder, we should
avoid it in all of its parts. Murder is never committed with the
muscles of the arm until we have first developed the evil
emotions, formed the bad attitudes, and practiced the other
forms of disobedience to God of which murder is made up.
Actually there are several kinds of murder.

Jesus said, "Fear not them which kill the body, but are not
able to kill the soul; but rather fear him which is able to
destroy both soul and body in hell." (Matt. 10:28.) Sometimes
we can bring about a destruction of our souls by an accumula-
tion of smaller sins. When we kill someone's faith, or destroy his
honor, or neutralize his ambition, we are guilty of a serious
degree of murder. This may be only a part of the death, but no
whole would be complete without its parts.

Some time ago Mildred N. Hoyer published an interesting
article entitled "A Thief in Church." It told of a woman who
came to church with a serious problem on her mind. She hoped
that in the quiet of her worship she could get the help necessary
to solve her difficulties. At least, she hoped to acquire enough
courage and faith to sustain her during her crisis. But in the pew
behind her sat a thief. He did not snatch her purse or take her
jewels, but he talked and whispered and shuffled his feet during
the worship service. He so disturbed those sitting near him that
much of the devotional benefit was lost. He robbed his fellow
churchgoers of their sense of peace and their awareness of God's
presence, which could have been one of their most priceless
possessions. He even robbed them of a spirit of reverence toward
their Heavenly Father which they came there to get. Such a
thief may be shocked to hear himself so accused. It may never
have even occurred to him that reverence had such a great value,
or that one could steal anything so intangible.

If the penalty of this great command "Thou shalt not steal" should be applied as in Victor Hugo's *Les Miserables*, to a person stealing a loaf of bread to appease the hunger of his family, then certainly it should also apply to someone who steals one's love of truth, or his desire to be fair. Some people rob their children of their sense of security and their determination to honor God. If a convict should be sent to jail for stealing some trivial material thing, what should be the sentence of a husband who steals his wife's peace of mind and destroys her confidence in human nature?

Shakespeare says, "He who steals my purse, steals trash . . . but he who filches from me my good name, robs me of that which not enriches him and makes me poor indeed." (Othello.) As there are different grades of stealing, so there are different kinds of murder. There are many ways to kill one's spirituality. Sometimes we become murderers by being responsible for some important fraction of one's death. What is one's situation when he kills the opportunities, or the ambitions, or the faith of someone else? We are told that adultery is next to murder in God's catalogue of crime. But most adulterers are killers as well.

I know of a man whose wife worked his way through school enabling him to get a good job. She married him in good faith based on his promise to honor the principles of righteousness, but by his deceitful sins and widespread immorality he has betrayed his wife and broken her heart. He has killed her respect for him and her confidence in human beings generally. She cannot get him out of her life because of the cries of her children and the financial restraints that he has imposed upon her. But she has gone dead inside, and she is suffering the living death of a continual humiliation and constant shame. The children once thought of their father as the greatest man in the world. But his evil caused his attitude toward them to deteriorate, even before they began hearing the rumors of his evil activities. As his deception, unfairness, and immorality continues, and as the children feel the degradation that is being forced upon their mother, a terrible bitterness builds up in their hearts, creating a lot of dead scar tissue that is incapable of performing the normal functions. Instead of admiration and love they now think of him as something evil and dirty, and as much as possible they try to prevent people from learning that he is their father. When they think of the times when he used to take them to church and pray with them at home, it makes even the idea of religion seem evil, because of its association with him in their minds.

What a terrible thing it can be to lose confidence in one's own father and feel that his life is not worthwhile! The children see the blight of death caused by his sins, and their relationship causes them to breathe the foul stench of his immorality. A good horticulturist keeps the dead branches pruned out of his trees, and when our own evil begins to cause some fraction of death in us we should prune it out before the poisonous cells spread to other parts. Yet what can anyone do for trees or men when they go rotten inside? To those who don't know the guilt of this father he still looks all right on the outside, but his own family sees the weakness and decay inside that foretells the fall of many whose lives he will touch. His own family members are also his victims, as they are a part of him. And many of the half-deaths and terrible miseries of those that he has seduced might have been avoided and those people might have made something fine of their lives, if it had not been for him.

Just think about how much of people can be killed by the influence and bad example of others. This idea that "everybody's doing it" may not be logical, but its influence can be like a poisonous gas that may kill some people no less effectively than a bullet wound or a sword thrust. The power of example has enough impact to change the lives of almost everyone. If all of our friends go to college, we are likely to want to go to college. If all of our friends have a certain kind of hairdo, we have a tendency to want to fall in line. If the hemline goes up an inch or two, some young female hearts may be almost broken if they are not allowed to go along. Even if someone becomes a hippie and wears strange dress, dirty clothes, and has a smelly, unkempt person, someone is likely to think that it is a smart idea and want to join him. It is thought that everyone must be judged not only for what he does, but also for the influence that he exerts over others. And when a moral leper is at large, he scatters his evil, destructive attitudes all over the community.

It has been said that even "one man can, if he will, change the morale of the whole community." And this statement applies whether the direction taken is up or down. One pied piper playing on his pipes can lead many people to their doom. A number of years ago a popular minister of religion wrote a best-selling book filled with his own ideas of theology. After over 200,000 copies had been sold, he said that he now disbelieved almost everything that he had written in his book. But even if publication is immediately stopped, people will go on reading their own copies, and the false doctrines will continue to kill the faith and destroy the correct beliefs of many people. But this minister of religion is still following this destructive pattern. He has merely stopped teaching those things that he has already changed his mind about. But later he will probably decide that many of the things that he is presently teaching are wrong. We have no more right to *teach* the things that are wrong than we have to *do* the things that are wrong. And ignorance of the law is no excuse.

The Apostle Peter said: "No prophecy of the scripture is of any private interpretation, for prophecy came not in old time by the will of man: but holy men of God spake as they were moved by the Holy Ghost." (2 Pet. 1:20-21.) In our theology we should remember to stick to the word of the Lord. Peter also pointed out that in our day many false teachers would arise who privily would bring in damnable heresies, even denying the Lord that brought them. (See 2 Pet. 2:1.) We are seeing the fulfillment of this prophecy, as many men are teaching their own ideas and representing it as authorized Christianity. And these false doctrines are killing faith, destroying the sense of right, and weakening the ambition of many people to serve God. It is an awful thing to destroy a human life, but it is also an awful thing to destroy the belief in a divine principle, or a godly ambition, or an uplifting idea. No one can falsely influence others without bringing a comparable condemnation upon himself. Jesus said, "Whoso shall offend one of these little ones that believe in me, it were better for him that a millstone were hanged about his neck, and he were drowned in the depth of the sea." (Matt. 18:6.) How unpleasant it would be for one to come to stand before God, only to see around him the wasteful destruction that his bad example, his evil influence, and his unauthorized teachings had caused in the lives of others!

And so in our imagination we might again go and stand at

the foot of Mount Sinai and listen to that great command saying, "Thou shalt not kill." If we follow the law in all of its aspects, then we will increase the volume of life rather than the volume of death.

Tracking

There is an important test that must be passed by all Boy Scouts in order to qualify them for second class rank. It is called tracking or stalking. This is a part of the Scout program designed to teach a boy to be observant. And before he can get above a tenderfoot classification, he must demonstrate his ability to stick to a trail or to stalk an animal, or to follow the tracks of someone who has gone before him. There is another part of this particular test which requires a boy to be examined as to how many things he can remember after looking into a store window or some other place containing many objects. This interesting Scout requirement calls our attention to one of the very important success factors, not only in scouting but also in the bigger business of life itself. We need to be proficient in seeing, understanding, and remembering.

It was probably our inability in these fields that prompted Jesus to remind us that so many people have eyes that don't see, and ears that don't hear, and hearts that fail to understand. In Boy Scout language he was saying that we need to keep ourselves more mentally alert. At least in a preliminary way, the Boy Scout organization is trying to develop in people this important attitude of paying attention and remembering important things. There are so many of the great values available in our lives that we needlessly miss; and many of our greatest blessings depend upon how observant we are, and how effectively we can put into force in our lives the great lessons that we learn. We should also be aware of how well we can follow an ambition, or track an idea, or stalk an ideal.

One of the things that made Thomas A. Edison so successful was his ability to follow the trail of a useful thought to its lair where he could discover all of its secrets. While Mr. Edison was at the headquarters of the trailed idea he also got acquainted with all of its brothers and sisters. That is, ideas usually don't come singly, they usually arrange themselves in clusters, or chains, or family groups. And we need to be able to follow them so that we can discover their family relationships as well as their meanings.

For us merely to strike out in the general direction of success is like lashing the steering wheel fast and expecting our automobile to stay on the road and finally arrive at some predesignated destination. It takes constant steering to keep an automobile or a man going in a straight line.

Certainly the one who plans to track down success effectively must pay constant attention and be an expert in remembering, otherwise he runs the risk of missing the trail and having the quarry elude him. And while all people have different goals in life, everyone is tracking someone or something.

The Magi from the east were successful in following the star to Bethlehem. If an aviator can stay on the beam, he is able to bring his cargo of lives to any designated destination even on the darkest night. The mariner steers his ship by the compass, and the businessman is true to his convictions and steers by the North Star of his ambition. But in the more important business of life itself, too many people ignore those proven principles and use their own lives as guinea pigs. We proceed as though we felt that we, ourselves, must redo all of the past experimentation in living successfully. We seem to feel that we must rerun all of the trial-and-error tests and remake all of the mistakes personally. When we follow such a course we waste so much time and get bogged down in so many mistakes, that we frequently never survive our own experiences and never arrive at our planned destination.

Jesus did not come to the earth seeking some great brain who could devise a plan for our eternal salvation. That had already been done in the council of heaven. What Jesus came seeking for was someone who could follow a plan that had already been made. Of his own success he said, "Father, not my will but thine be done." Because of this thrilling characteristic of following his Father's directions, the Master did not need to make a single mistake or commit a single sin in order to find out that it was wrong. He said, "My meat is to do the will of Him that sent me." And his great success came about by fully utilizing the wisdom of his Father and following those important success principles that had already been made available to him.

Many years ago, James Allen wrote an inspiring little *tracking* book entitled, *As a Man Thinketh* in which he talks about the importance of following ideas. He also has an interesting chapter under the title of "Visions and Ideals," and he points out that those who follow great ideals and develop that sure, certain vision of always being alert to great values become the saviors of the world. He says that our visible world is supported by a great invisible world, and men are nourished and strengthened by the great dreams that they hold in their hearts. If even momentarily we close our eyes to truth, or forget our ambitions, or allow our ideals to fade, then the greatest objective can easily be lost. A dream is of no value unless it is followed to its reality. No one should be disturbed about following a proven, known highway, for no one can break very many new trails or do very much exploring and yet reach their success destination on time. No one ever invents the entire program for his own accomplishment and all of those who stay on the freeway of success have a tremendous advantage. All great men build on the accomplishment of others. There are enough ideas of proven excellence and known value to make every life outstandingly successful without running any risks. Of course, that does not mean that we should not have individual ambitions but they should be founded on the proven principles of righteousness. And this idea of following a great ambition is one of the most profitable of all of our possibilities.

Mr. Allen says that he who cherishes a beautiful vision or follows a lofty ideal in his heart can be perfectly certain that one day he will attain it. Columbus enshrined in his mind the vision of another world, and he discovered it. Copernicus fostered the vision of a greater universe, and he was soon able to reveal it to others. Washington and Lincoln were close followers of their ideals and dreams.

Mr. Allen says: "Cherish your visions, cherish your ideals; cherish the music that stirs in your heart, the beauty that forms in your mind, the loveliness that drapes your purest thoughts, for out of them will grow all delightful conditions, and all heavenly environment; of these, if you but remain true to them, your world will at last be built."

He continues: "Dream lofty dreams, and as you dream, so shall you become. Your Vision is the promise of what you shall one day be; your ideal is the prophecy of what you shall at last unveil.

"The greatest achievement was at first and for a time only a dream. The oak sleeps in the acorn; the bird waits in the egg; and in the highest vision of the soul a waking angel stirs. Dreams are the seedlings of realities.

"Your circumstances may be uncongenial, but they shall not long remain so if you but perceive an ideal and strive to reach it. You cannot travel *within* and stand still *without*.

"Into your hands will be placed the exact results of your own thoughts; you will receive that which you earn; no more, no less . . ."

Henry J. Kaiser once said: "What a man can conceive in his mind, he can accomplish . . . Faith in our own ability to attain releases the power that enables us to accomplish whatever we set out to do. If we are concerned about being held back or kept from the things we want, we should realize that the only person standing between us and what we seek is ourselves."

Our biggest problems come when we have no definite ideals to follow. In our early years we sometimes fail to decide what we want to be when we grow up, then a natural indecision takes over our lives and serves us as an excuse for not trying. We say, "Why should I study this or that subject when I am not sure that is the course I will follow?" When we are older we say, "Why should I live by the holy scriptures when I am not sure that they are true, or it may even be that God has died or lost interest in us."

These doubts should give us no concern; for everyone knows that it is right to be honest, that it is right to be godly, thoughtful, and industrious. If we follow what we are certain of, all of the other necessary knowledge will soon be forthcoming. Jesus said, "If any man will do [God's] will, he shall know of the doctrine." Emerson said, "Do the thing and you shall have the power." We can achieve any kind of a life that we are willing to live. This great truth has been written a thousand times by the prophets, the philosophers, and our own experience. We fail only because we do not have the follow-through, or the tracking ability, to make reality out of our dreams and to put our ambitions into actual operation.

LuVain Bue challenges our accomplishment along these lines with this idea: "In your mind's eye, imagine four chairs in front of you. In the first chair is a man who is blind; in the second chair is a man with a serious speech defect; in the third chair is a man who is deaf; and in the fourth chair is a man who was so badly broken up in an automobile accident that the doctors told him he would never walk again. These men all had real handicaps, but they also had an imagination and they knew how to follow their dreams through to their reality.

"The blind man was John Milton, who achieved immortality by writing *Paradise Lost*. The man who was tongue-tied at birth was Demosthenes. He became the greatest orator in ancient Greece. The man who was deaf was Beethoven, the great composer of symphonies. The man in the fourth chair who would never walk again was Ben Hogan, who became a four-time winner of the National Open Golf Championship. There is just no stopping a great human being who knows where he wants to go and is willing to follow the rules and stay on the track."

Milton said, "The mind in its own place, and of itself, can make a heaven of hell or a hell of heaven." It can also overcome our deficiencies, and take us any place that we want to go, either here or hereafter. If we have handicaps, most of them are only in our minds, not in our potential. Just find out what you want and then go after it! If you will follow the trail long enough, the prize will sooner or later fall into your hands.

A strange sight is occasionally seen at sea where the wind and the surface ice will be going in one direction, while moving majestically in the opposite direction will be a great iceberg. The explanation is that only about one-ninth of the iceberg is above the surface. Deep down in the bosom of the ocean, the bulk of the iceberg is in the arms of the ocean's powerful subcurrents.

Life is also like that. And when we live on the surface of

life, we are influenced by the shallow, superficial movements of surface conditions. But some people have character in depth. This provides us with the power to keep our lives always going in the right direction, in spite of the fact that passing breezes and surface ice may have a contrary point of view. More than anything else we need the religion of Jesus to give greater depth and direction to our lives. And then if we ever feel that we aren't going any place, it will be because we haven't decided where we want to go, or we are failing in our tracking tests.

Two thousand years ago the great Intelligence of heaven was sent into the world with a message saying, "Follow me." And every human life must finally be judged by how well it carries out that single direction. A straight and narrow path has been laid out leading to the most worthwhile destination. It has been perfectly marked, and brilliantly lighted so that no one needs to lose the path except by his own choice. And yet our biggest problems arise because we don't stick to the trail. Cain got off the track. In his disloyalty Judas Iscariot couldn't follow. Benedict Arnold failed because his life was not based deep enough in the virtues of truth and patriotism. Too frequently we forsake the straight and narrow way and follow the detours. We are driven before the surface ice of sin as we develop and too freely indulge our cravings for evil. When we are also following the trail of ignorance and evil, we get so far off the track of success that we lose the scent of right living, and consequently we forfeit the blessings. We should remember that we must remain a tenderfoot eternally unless we learn to pass the test in the tracking examination of life.

Life itself is always giving us some tests in following the trail of righteousness. Edwin Markham wrote a poem on this subject entitled "The Testing":

When in the dim beginning of the years,
God mixed in man the raptures and the tears,
And scattered through his brain the starry stuff,
He said: "Behold! Yet this is not enough;
For I must test his spirit to make sure
That he can dare the vision and endure.

"I will withdraw my face,

Vail me in shadow for a certain space,
Leaving behind me only a broken clue—
A crevice where the glory glimmers through,
Some whisper from the sky,
Some footprint in the road to track me by.

"I will leave man to make the fateful guess,
Will leave him torn between the *no* and *yes*,
Leave him unresting till he rests in me,
Drawn upward by the choice that makes him free—
Leave him in tragic loneliness to choose,
With all in life to win or all to lose."

Certainly we should never confuse the road to our God-given destiny with that broad road leading to death. This broad road is easily identified, as it is strewn with many failures, and marked with the footprints of Satan himself. However, if we are not deeply based in righteousness, we may be blown about by the surface winds of evil and wrong; and if we have not effectively done our planning, we may find ourselves headed in the wrong direction.

On the other hand, what a thrilling idea it is to have our soul based solidly in the truth, as we follow the footprints of him who was sent here to be our guide! We sing a sacred song that says, "I walked today where Jesus walked." And what a thrilling experience it would be to stand on that very spot of ground where Jesus stood, while we tried to absorb the spirit of his life! Or suppose that we go on into Gethsemane and kneel on that spot where, under the burden of our sins, he sweat great drops of blood at every pore. And while it may not be very practical to walk today where Jesus walked, yet there is something that is practical and has a great deal more value, and that is that we can think today what Jesus thought. We can feel as he felt, we can live as he lived, and we can become what he expected us to become. We can also fulfill to the letter that great command to follow him. We can follow him in his philosophy. We can follow him in his faith. We can follow him in his industry. We can follow him in his worship. And we can follow him in his glory.

Trees

One of the interesting things about our world is the great variety of trees that cover the earth. They are made important to us by both their beauty and their utility. They furnish our earth with one of its chief sources of landscaping, and they also help to provide our food and shelter. In the third day of creation, God said, "Let the earth bring forth grass, the herb yielding seed, and the fruit tree yielding fruit after his kind, . . . and it was so." A lover of trees might well imagine the Creator's pride expressed in the scripture that says, "And God saw that it was good, and the evening and the morning were the third day." (Gen. 1:11, 13.)

It is interesting to know that the trees were yielding fruit on the third day whereas man did not appear upon the scene until the sixth day. And what a great day it must have been when God invented trees in all of their variety, beauty, utility, magic, and color! Trees were assigned to provide us with shade, lumber, turpentine, paper, sugar, food, nuts, and flowers. God made the pine, spruce, birch, sycamore, maple, elm, hemlock, cedar, dogwood, and many kinds of nut and fruit trees. And then he threw in a few giant redwoods for good measure. Joyce Kilmer once wrote an inspiring poem about trees:

> I think that I shall never see
> A poem lovely as a tree,
> A tree whose hungry mouth is press'd
> Against the earth's sweet flowing breast;
> A tree that looks at God all day,
> And lifts her leafy arms to pray;
>
> A tree that may in summer wear
> A nest of robins in her hair;
> Upon whose bosom snow has lain;
> Who intimately lives with rain.
> Poems are made by fools like me,
> But only God can make a tree.

God provided one of our greatest natural resources when he covered our earth with forests. Trees provide the material for many of our homes and the furniture that goes into them. Some of our trees are made into logs and burned in the fireplace. A tree serves as a reservoir in which is stored up the sun's heat of a hundred summers, to be released to us in times of cold. On the side, the leaves of trees serve as wonderful little manufacturing plants that furnish us with the oxygen that human beings must breathe in order to live.

But trees also serve us in many other useful ways. Bryant said: "The groves were God's first temples, ... and in the cool and silence of the darkling wood [man] knelt down and offered to the mightiest, his solemn thanks and supplication." So far as I know, trees are among the greatest wonders of creation. Through them God provides us with red apples, black cherries, blue plums, and yellow peaches. Some of these tree wonders were assigned to produce pears, some oranges, some grapefruit, some lemons, and some bananas.

Fruit trees not only produce in abundance but their fruit is loaded with the most delicious and helpful kinds of tastes, calories, and vitamins. In these products an all-wise Creator stores away this natural food in a limitless supply to provide us with health, energy, vision, understanding and life itself. There is a saying that "an apple a day keeps the doctor away." Good fruit not only keeps the doctor away but it also builds up our strength, enthusiasm, personality, and spirit. One of the most important qualities of fruit is that it is such a lot of fun to eat. It is an inspiration to me merely to think about these wonderful creations with their flavors, colors, nourishment, and juices all given to us direct from God.

Of course there are a lot of things that we don't know about trees. What does a tree's life consist of? How does a tree know whether to produce figs or apricots? And where did all trees get the identical recipe? And how does it know when it is time to send its sap down in the fall and bring it back up in the spring? Where does the tree get the know-how and skill to manufacture its finished products of wood, foliage, blossoms, fragrance, and fruit? Trees differ from human beings, and yet they have life the same as we do. They also have a spirit; they were also created by God, and they began in heaven the same as we did. The scriptures tell us of two creations for both trees and men. In describing the spiritual creation the Lord said, "And every plant of the field before it was in the earth, and every herb of the field before it grew: for the Lord God had not caused it to rain upon the earth, and there was not a man to till the ground." (Gen. 2:5.)

In a modern revelation the Lord confirms and supplements this idea by saying, "For I, the Lord God created all things, of which I have spoken, spiritually, before they were naturally upon the face of the earth." (Moses 3:5.) In preparing a place for man to live, the Lord planted the Garden of Eden. This must have been a wonder, as this garden was created before the fall of man had brought its curse upon the earth. We think the earth is a pretty wonderful place just as it is, but it is now in its fallen or telestial state, whereas before the fall, the earth was in its paradisiacal or terrestrial state. Adam and Eve were placed in this Garden of Paradise not only to dress and keep it, but also to enjoy its benefits. Speaking of this wonder of creation the Lord said, "And out of the ground made I, the Lord God, to grow every tree naturally, that is pleasant to the sight of man; . . . and it became also a living soul. For it was spiritual in the day that I created it." (Moses 3:9.)

The Lord pointed out that all of these wonderful creations had been prepared for the benefit and use of man. But the Lord did some other wonderful things. He planted some other trees that we presently do not know very much about. He said, "And I the Lord God planted a tree of life in the midst of the garden, and also the tree of knowledge of good and evil." (Moses 3:9.) The fruit of these trees had some extraordinary powers. Among other things, the fruit from the tree of knowledge of good and evil had the ability to make people wise. (See Moses 4:12.) It also had the power to bring the condition of mortality on our race.

Then God said to Adam: "Of every tree of the garden thou mayest freely eat, but of the tree of the knowledge of good and evil, thou shalt not eat of it, nevertheless, thou mayest choose for thyself, for it is given unto thee; but remember that I forbid it, for in the day thou eatest thereof thou shalt surely die."

(Moses 3:16-17.) After Adam and Eve had eaten of the tree of
knowledge of good and evil they became mortal and their eyes
were opened. Then the Lord God said, "Behold, the man is now
become as one of us, to know good and evil." (Gen. 3:22.)
(And I would like to point out in passing that the right kind of
knowledge still tends to have that effect upon people. It still
tends to make men and women become as God.) And lest they
should reach out and partake of the tree of life and live forever
in their sins, cherubim and the flaming sword were placed there
to guard the tree of life, until the time when man could be
redeemed. (See Moses 4:31.)

This blessing of eating from the tree of life is one that
apparently is not now in our own best interests. However, it is
being held in reserve for us until we are prepared to make the
most of it. Through John the Revelator the Lord said, "To him
that overcometh will I give to eat of the tree of life which is in
the midst of the paradise of God." (Rev. 2:7.) When we have
overcome all of our problems we will be permitted to eat of the
fruit from the tree of life. That will be something! But in the
meantime we may eat of some kinds of knowledge to our heart's
content. The Lord has said that "whatever principle of intelligence we attain unto in this life, it will rise with us in the
resurrection. And if a person gains more knowledge and intelligence in this life through his diligence and obedience than
another, he will have so much the advantage in the world to
come." (D&C 130:18-19.)

In the early spring of each year we set aside a special day
called Arbor Day. This is a legal holiday devoted to the planting
of trees. The poets and philosophers have always regarded a tree
as a symbol of human life. And Lucy Larcom says that "he who
plants a tree plants hope and joy and peace and youth and
love."

And we can make these traits grow on some of the
wonderful trees that we plant in our own lives on our spiritual
Arbor Days. The Psalmist said: "And he shall be like a tree
planted by rivers of water, that bringeth forth fruit in his
season: his leaf also shall not wither; and whatsoever he doeth
shall prosper." (Ps. 1:3.) Jesus also compared people to trees and
said, "By their fruits ye shall know them." To fulfill a man's

highest destiny he must develop the right kind of ideas and bring forth some of those fruits of kindness, helpfulness, righteousness and love recommended by the Lord. Isaiah calls good men and women the "trees of righteousness." (Isa. 61:3.)

When one plants a tree he is not planting something that will die after yielding only one harvest. A tree is a creation that will keep on giving shade and shelter, flowers, fragrance, and fruit for many years. I recently saw a peach orchard that had gotten a little bit overenthusiastic about its job of production. Its crop was so heavy that the owner of the orchard had to go around and prop up the branches to keep them from being broken off by the heavy load of fruit. But God did not put his most productive gifts into trees, he put them into his own children, and he requires that we produce good fruit. He cursed the barren fig tree because it did not yield effectively. And he expects that his children will also be productive, and that they will yield something much more valuable than a crop of peaches or apples or grapefruit. He expects us to produce faith, righteousness, and all kinds of good works. If our fruits are good enough they will help us to qualify for eternal life. The trees of our lives should be kept pruned, sprayed, fertilized, and irrigated. Certainly our lives should not be less productive, less fruitful, or less beautiful than the creations to which God has compared us. There are many different kinds of service.

George P. Morris wrote a poem entitled, "Woodman, Spare That Tree." It was written about a tree that had played an important part in Mr. Morris' development during his childhood. And when the land on which it stood passed into the hands of others, Mr. Morris paid the new owner money in return for his promise that they would never destroy this sturdy old oak that meant so much to him. It is our job to see to it that our trees of righteousness are cultivated and that they grow in us to bring forth a hundredfold. What a thrill to go into a blossoming apple orchard in the spring and see its beauty and think of the great potential that is involved. It is a mass of color and it fills the air with fragrance. When vitalized and fed, these millions of blossoms will follow the pattern set by the Creator and become fruit. The poet has said:

Heaven and earth helps him who plants a tree,
And his work its own reward shall be.

A nation's growth from sea to sea
Stirs in his heart who plants a tree.

It should inspire us that when one plants a tree he is planting a harvest of many things. All trees originally came from heaven, and certainly there are many trees that are still growing in heaven. We know that there will be trees growing and producing during the millennium. Isaiah says, "And they shall build houses, and inhabit them; and they shall plant vineyards, and eat the fruit of them." (Isa. 65:21.) During the millennium the earth will be returned to a paradisiacal state and its trees also will be in their paradisiacal condition. There will be trees growing upon our earth after the millennium when our earth and our trees will be celestialized. God has said, "Blessed are they that do his commandments, that they may have the right to the tree of life, and may enter in through the gates into the city." (Rev. 22:14.) John the Revelator saw a vision of that Holy City, the New Jerusalem that is to come down from God out of heaven after the millennium. This vision shows us many of the conditions as they will be when all things shall have reached this perfect state. John said: "And the city had no need of the sun, neither of the moon, to shine in it; for the glory of God did lighten it, and the Lamb is the light thereof. And the nations of them which are saved shall walk in the light of it: and the kings of the earth do bring their glory and honor into it. And the gates of it shall not be shut at all by day: for there shall be no night there. And they shall bring the glory and honor of the nations into it. And there shall in no wise enter into it anything that defileth, neither whatsoever worketh abomination, or maketh a lie: but they which are written in the Lamb's book of life." (Rev. 21:23-27.)

John further recorded: "And he shewed me a pure river of the water of life, clear as crystal, proceeding out of the throne of God and of the Lamb. In the midst of the street of it, and on either side of the river, there was the tree of life; which bare twelve manner of fruits and yielded her fruit every month; and the leaves of the tree were for the healing of the nations. And there shall be no more curse: but the throne of God and of the Lamb shall be in it; and his servants shall serve him. And they shall see his face; and his name shall be in their foreheads." (Rev. 22:1-4.)

We could not live very long here without the oxygen coming from trees. Then what will the leaves of these celestial trees be like, that are for the healing of the nations? May God bless our lives that we may take advantage of all of these wonderful creations that he has provided for our use, particularly those greater benefits that he has planted in our own lives.

An Understanding Heart

About a thousand years before Christ a son—who was named Solomon—was born to King David in Jerusalem. Solomon became his father's successor and ascended the throne of Israel while he was still a teenager. Knowing the serious problems that his young son would face, David gave him a charge hoping to make him a better king. The Old Testament says: "Now the days of David drew nigh that he should die; and he charged Solomon, his son, saying . . . I go the way of all the earth: be thou strong therefore, and show thyself a man; and keep the charge of the Lord thy God, to walk in his ways, to keep his statutes, and his commandments, and his judgments, and his testimonies, as it is written in the law of Moses, that thou mayest prosper in all that thou doest, and whithersoever thou turnest thyself: that the Lord may continue his word which he spake concerning me, saying, If thy children take heed to their way, to walk before me in truth with all their heart and with all their soul, there shall not fail thee (said he) a man on the throne of Israel." (1 Kings 2:1-4.)

This would be a great charge for anyone to live by, and Solomon was an outstanding young man who seemed to do everything right. The record says that he loved the Lord and he walked in the statutes of his father David, who had been an outstanding king. In those days in Jerusalem, the people had certain areas with extra religious significance called "high places." These were special locations on some hilltop where people sometimes went to more fully devote themselves to God. One of the most famous of these high places was located at Gibeon, and it was here that Solomon went soon after becoming king.

There upon the altar he offered a thousand offerings unto the Lord. Then by night the Lord appeared to Solomon in a dream and gave him the privilege of selecting his own blessings. Without any apparent reservation or limitation the Lord said to Solomon: ". . . . Ask what I shall give thee. And Solomon said:

Thou has shewed unto thy servant David my father great mercy, according as he walked before thee in truth, and in righteousness, and in uprightness of heart with thee; and thou hast ... given him a son to sit on his throne. And now, oh Lord, my God, thou hast made thy servant king instead of David my father: and I am but a little child: I know not how to go out or come in. And thy ... people ... cannot be ... counted for multitude. Give therefore thy servant an understanding heart to judge thy people, that I may discern between good and bad." The records say that it pleased the Lord that Solomon had asked what he did, and God said unto him: "Because thou hast asked this thing, and has not asked for thyself long life; neither hast asked riches for thyself, nor hast asked the life of thine enemies; but has asked for thyself understanding to discern judgment; behold, I have done according to thy words: lo, I have given thee a wise and an understanding heart; so that there was none like thee ... And I have also given thee that for which thou hast not asked, both riches, and honour: so that there shall not be any among the kings like unto thee all thy days. And if thou wilt walk in my ways, to keep my statutes and my commandments, as thy father David did walk, then I will lengthen thy days." (1 Kings 3:5-14.)

The record says that God also gave Solomon "largeness of heart." Under the advantages of these blessings Solomon did many wonderful things including building the great temple at Jerusalem to the name of Jehovah. After Solomon had dedicated the temple, the Lord again appeared to him and said: "I have heard thy prayer and the supplication, that thou has made before me: I have hallowed this house, which thou hast built, to put my name there forever; and mine eyes and my heart shall be there perpetually. And if thou wilt walk before me, as David thy father walked, in integrity of heart, and in uprightness, to do according to all that I have commanded thee, and will keep my statutes and my judgments: then I will establish the throne of thy kingdom upon Israel forever, as I promised to David thy father ... but if ye shall turn from following me, ye or your children, and will not keep my commandments and my statutes which I have set before you, but go and serve other gods, and worship them: then will I cut off Israel out of the land which I have given them: and this house, which I have hallowed for my name, will I cast out of my sight; and Israel shall be a proverb and a byword among all people." (1 Kings 9:1-7.)

In other words the Lord also gave Solomon some responsibility with his wisdom by placing a choice before him. As long as Solomon loved the Lord and had an understanding heart, he was successful, prosperous, and happy, and all of his expectations were fulfilled. But eventually Solomon began having a little trouble with his heart. The scripture says that King Solomon loved the daughter of Pharaoh and many strange women of idolatrous nations. The Lord had already specifically forbidden the Israelites to intermarry with these idolatrous people. He said, "For surely they will turn away your hearts after their gods." But Solomon's heart trouble caused him to disobey the Lord and, as the Lord had foretold, these idol-worshipping women turned his heart to worship idols. The record says: "His heart was not perfect with the Lord his God, as was the heart of David his father . . . And Solomon did evil in the sight of the Lord . . . and the Lord was angry with Solomon because his heart was turned from the Lord God of Israel, which had appeared unto him twice. . . . wherefore the Lord said unto Solomon, Forasmuch as this is done of thee, and thou hast not kept my covenant and my statutes, which I have commanded thee, I will surely rend the kingdom from thee and will give it to thy servant. Notwithstanding in thy days I will not do it for David thy father's sake: but I will rend it out of the hand of thy son." (1 Kings 11:1-12.)

Therefore Solomon not only lost his own benefits that God had so freely granted, but he also lost much of the national strength and many of the religious blessings that had already been built up for his people by David his father. It is interesting that the wisest man who had ever lived led his own nation into idolatry, against the Lord's instructions. He broke up the Lord's kingdom and caused the Lord's chosen people to be carried away to serve in foreign bondage.

This is a famous example of the great truth that the Lord usually puts his blessings in *our* hands on a kind of lend-lease basis. We are usually permitted to keep only those blessings that we use effectively and where we fulfill the conditions under which they are given. Probably the wisest thing that Solomon ever did was to pray for "an understanding heart" and the most foolish thing that he ever did was not to follow God's directions. As long as Solomon obeyed God and followed the good example of his father he was outstandingly successful. But when his merit dwindled, the blessings also began to disappear. Many of our blessings can come only from God. But where possible we must answer some of our own prayers. That is, Solomon's prayer for wisdom could be answered only by Solomon himself doing wise things. When he did unwise, disobedient things the blessings were revoked. The result was that Solomon died an idolator very much out of favor with God. Even the matchless blessings of an understanding heart were taken away when he refused to understand. This universal law also applies to us. God has made it plain that we may have any blessing where we are willing to keep the law on which that blessing is predicated. But we are not permitted any blessing when we disobey its governing law. Those blessings that come within our power to earn, all seem to be on a do-it-yourself basis. For example, there is no particular point in asking God to give us big arm muscles without obeying God's laws of diet and exercise. But even after we have the muscles developed, we must continue to exercise them if they are to be retained. It would be superfluous to ask God to forgive our enemies, as we can do that better than he can. In the first place he isn't mad at them and in the second place we made them ourselves, and we are the only ones who can properly restore what has been done. Or suppose that we want to change ourselves into more faithful, righteous, fair-minded men and women. There are certain kinds of wonderful action-oriented prayers that God will answer with absolute certainty in a minimum amount of time.

It is probable that the thing that most of *us* should desire most, is the thing that teenager Solomon prayed for as he ascended the throne. He said, "Give thy servant an understanding heart." It is interesting to wonder about what he had in mind specifically. In his prayer Solomon gave us a number of the details. He said he wanted an understanding of people, that he might judge them effectively. He also wanted to be able to discern between good and bad. He also wanted to understand righteousness and government and leadership, so that he could be as successful a king as his father David had been.

Then the Lord told Solomon that he would grant all of these and in addition, if Solomon would do certain things which the Lord and his father spelled out for him, then Solomon would also receive riches, honor, and a long life. But most other people can also get these same benefits if they follow the same set of rules. The Lord said that Solomon could have all of these "If thou wilt walk in my ways and keep my statutes and my commandments as did thy father David." However, when Solomon began overlooking these important do-it-yourself provisions the promises were cancelled.

In thinking about the great men and women of the scriptures and elsewhere who have received substantial blessings from God, we may sometimes think that they received them as free gifts. However, we often overlook the fact that most of these same blessings are also available to us if we do not overlook this divine qualification clause. God is no respecter of persons and under the rules, all of us are like Solomon in that we are eligible to select our own blessings. We know that General Motors wants people to pay for their automobiles. That is only fair. We know also that General Motors repossesses those automobiles on which the payments are not made as agreed. So does God. Think of the millions of wonderful blessings that life repossesses where, like Solomon, we fail to keep up our end of the bargain. Through Isaiah, the Lord told ancient Israel why some people lose their wisdom. He said: "Forasmuch as this people draw near me with their mouth, and with their lips do honor me, but have removed their heart far from me . . . therefore . . . the wisdom of their wise men shall perish, and the understanding of their prudent men shall be hid." (Isa. 29:13-14.) If our hearts are not right, our benefits are in serious danger of being lost. Therefore the Lord's great grant of wisdom to Solomon was cancelled because Solomon didn't keep up his payments.

Some time ago I listened to the man who in my opinion is the greatest salesman in the world. In undertaking any sale he always makes a careful preparation. He finds out a great deal about the problems, needs, wants, and abilities of the prospect. He always makes sure what he proposes is in his client's best interests. Of course, a part of his unusual sales ability comes from his skill as a planner. But that is also true of every success in life. It has been pointed out that "planning is the place where man shows himself most like God." The planner is the thinker, the doer, the organizer; he is the one who develops his reason and builds the roadway upon which his future success can travel.

Notice how well Solomon had planned what he wanted in the way of blessings. He also knew in advance the conditions on which they would be granted. Now just suppose that we were going to go to some "high place" of our own to ask the Lord for this great blessing of an understanding heart. I am absolutely certain in my own mind that if we do the right things, the Lord will answer our prayers and he will make them permanent if we keep the payments up to date. The scripture says that the Lord was greatly pleased when Solomon wanted an understanding heart. He would probably be just as pleased if we wanted the same blessing. That is probably what he would rather have us want than any other thing.

All great fathers want their sons to excel in wisdom and righteousness, and so does God. The most important thing we all need is an understanding heart. If we get that, most of the other things the Lord promised Solomon will also come to us, more or less automatically. Solomon outlined to God the particular areas where he needed understanding, and when he went to Gibeon he prayed a wonderful and important prayer. It will always help us to remember that we have been created in God's image and that he has already endowed us with a set of his own attributes and potentialities. We can be sure that he does not want that image marred with any serious sins, petty prayers, little deeds, aimless ambitions, or inferiority complexes. Suppose therefore that we get ready with a good prayer for an understanding heart. As a kind of subheading, our hearts need to understand God. Many people, including Solomon, fail because they ignore God, and don't understand the benefits of obeying his success laws. Because righteousness has so many natural rewards, Solomon also wanted to be able to discern between good and bad. Only by eliminating evil can any big prayer ever be fully answered. Even when Solomon was a teenager, he knew the difference between good and evil; but as he grew older he began shutting his eyes to evil, and then the prayers' answers began to be withdrawn.

Solomon prayed for a heart that could understand his people. But he then went directly against his own prayer by laying unbearable taxes upon them to promote his own wealth and magnificence. Finally when the people reached the breaking point he lost the kingdom. But at least, at one time, Solomon had "largeness of heart." And I know of many people who also have this same need. The scripture says that people should be "born again." If we desire, we may be reborn a hundred times, and each time we can be born better with a bigger heart. The heart is the seat of life and strength. The Bible tells of God granting people new minds, new attitudes, new ways of life, and more understanding. But the Lord has gone much further and has actually put much of this power into our own hands. Through Ezekiel he said, "Cast away from you all your transgressions ... and make you a new heart and a new spirit: for why will ye die, oh house of Israel?" (Ezek. 18:31.) And may God bless our prayers for wisdom and an understanding heart.

The Unpardonable Sin

In our world of contrasts we have many extremes of good and bad. The greatest value there is in the world is life, and the greatest opportunity for increased value is growth. By some power that no one understands, acorns can become oak trees, caterpillars can become butterflies, helpless babies can become strong, responsible adults, and the offspring of God can sometime hope to become like their eternal parents. Doubt can be changed into faith, courage can grow out of fear, and responsibility can develop where once there was only irresponsibility. One of the most important parts of any success is a firm conviction that foreheads can get broader, hearts can get bigger, interest can become more intense, muscles can get stronger, faith can get greater, enthusiasm can be expanded, and industry can become more powerful. But we must remember that this forward-moving, upward-looking possibility also has a reverse gear. Greatness can sometimes degenerate, strength can become weakness, love can turn to hate, and righteousness can be replaced by sin. The opposites of growth are deterioration, stagnation, decay, and death.

On the extreme end of the worsening processes of life is an offense that has been called "the unpardonable sin." There are some wrongs against life that are so serious that they are designated by that terrible label as being "unforgivable." The unpardonable sin is an extreme sin against great knowledge, great righteousness, and God. This offense was described by the Apostle Paul, when, in writing to the Hebrews, he said: "For it is impossible for those who were once enlightened, and have tasted of the heavenly gift, and were made partakers of the Holy Ghost, and have tasted of the good word of God, and the powers of the world to come, if they shall fall away, to renew them again unto repentance; seeing they crucify to themselves the Son of God afresh, and put him to an open shame." (Heb. 6:4-6.)

Before the war in heaven, Satan was a personage of great intelligence and power. In a position of outstanding talent and great responsibility, he stood very close to God himself. And because of his superior understanding and authority he was called Lucifer, the Light Bearer, the brilliant son of the morning. Yet in the face of all of these advantages, he rebelled against God. And inasmuch as God cannot look upon sin with the least degree of allowance, Satan was cast out of heaven. In the minds of most people a little sin is frequently tolerated, and often it is even looked upon as a desirable way to break the monotony of righteousness. But once a sin is permitted to get a foothold, who knows what the end will be? Because sin is also eligible to be increased through growth, it can soon impose upon us the most destructive, as well as the most dangerous of all conditions. Partly for this reason there can be no peaceful coexistence with sin so far as God is concerned, and no sin is ever permitted in God's presence. Because of the seriousness of Satan's sin, the heavens wept over him and he was called Perdition. (See D&C 76:26.)

The dictionary says that perdition indicates an entire loss. It carries the meaning of an utter destruction, or an eternal death. Those who followed Lucifer as he walked out of heaven were called the sons of Satan, or the sons of perdition. That is also the title given to those who most ardently follow Satan in this life. The seriousness of perdition is accounted for by the old law to the effect that "Where much is given, much is expected." Even if we were permitted to excuse the little sins of ignorance and weakness, where would we stop? Try to think of something that would be more terrible than for God to tolerate any measure of sin in himself. If God were a violator of the law, the security and happiness of the entire universe would be placed in jeopardy. Because Satan was high in the councils of God, his *power* was greater and his *sin* was greater also. Because of his tremendous influence, one-third of heaven itself was made empty by his evil.

This offensiveness of sinning against great knowledge is also emphasized by Peter, the chief apostle of Jesus, who said: "For if after they have escaped the pollutions of the world through the knowledge of the Lord and Saviour Jesus Christ, they are again entangled therein, and overcome, the latter end is worse with them than the beginning. For it had been better for them not to have known the way of righteousness, than, after they have known it, to turn from the holy commandment delivered unto them." (2 Pet. 2:20-21.) We have the authority of Jesus himself confirming the terribleness of this offense. He spoke of it both in the meridian of time, and also in our own day.

In Jerusalem he said: "Wherefore I say unto you, all manner of sin and blasphemy shall be forgiven unto men . . . but whosoever speaketh against the Holy Ghost, it shall not be forgiven him, neither in this world, neither in the world to come." (Matt. 12:31-32.) And in our own day the Lord again discussed this sin, as well as its consequences, in even greater detail. He said:

"Thus saith the Lord concerning all those who know my power, and have been made partakers thereof, and suffered themselves through the power of the devil to be overcome, and to deny the truth and to defy my power—They are they who are the sons of perdition, of whom I say that it had been better for them never to have been born. For they are vessels of wrath, doomed to suffer the wrath of God, with the devil and his angels in eternity; concerning whom I have said there is no forgiveness in this world nor in the world to come—having denied the Holy Spirit after having received it, and having denied the Only Begotten Son of the Father, having crucified him unto themselves and put him to an open shame. These are they who shall go away into the lake of fire and brimstone, with the devil and his angels—and the only ones on whom the second death shall have any power; yea, verily the only ones who shall not be redeemed in the due time of the Lord, after the sufferings of his wrath. For all the rest shall be brought forth by the resurrection of the dead . . . For he saves all the works of his hands, except those sons of perdition who deny the Son after the Father has revealed him. Wherefore, . . . they shall go away into everlasting punishment, which is endless punishment, which is eternal punishment, to reign with the devil and his angels in eternity, where their worm dieth not, and their fire is not quenched, which is their torment. And the end thereof, neither the place thereof, nor their torment, no man knows; neither was it revealed, neither is, neither will be revealed unto man, except to them who are made partakers thereof. Nevertheless, I, the Lord, show it by vision unto many, but straightway shut it up again; wherefore, the end, the width, the height, the depth, and the misery thereof, they understand not, neither any man except those who are ordained unto this condemnation." (D&C 76:31-48.) It is small wonder that John calls this unpardonable sin a sin unto death. (See 1 John 5:16.)

It is difficult to imagine more terrible words than "unpardonable" and "unforgivable." There are a lot of words that represent unpleasant ideas. Just think of the disaster in meaning that may lie behind such words as *unprofitable, unreasonable, unmerciful,* and *unspeakable.* But none of them compare in permanence, intensity or undesirability to the words "unpardonable" and "unforgivable."

The dictionary says that *unpardonable* means *inexcusable.* It indicates one who is unworthy of forgiveness, and ineligible for any release from its punishment. Some people take the attitude that inasmuch as we will probably never reach the degree of intelligence once possessed by Lucifer, we do not need to worry about the idea of the total loss contained in the word "perdition." But no wrong thing is unimportant. In fact it may be that we should fear the small wrongs even more than the great wrongs, for big evils always grow from little evils. If we prevent the little evils from being born, there will be no seed from which the fruit of big evils can grow. And with no little sins to begin with, there can then be no sons of perdition.

Jesus gave some great ideas to a group of people who were calling themselves the children of Abraham. He said to them, "If ye were Abraham's children, ye would do the works of Abraham." Then he said, "Ye are of your father the devil, and the lusts of your father ye will do." (John 8:39, 44.) These folks had let themselves go too long without taking their bearings. Occasionally we too should check up and find out how many of the things that we are presently doing are authored by Satan. For to the extent that we follow Satan, we are also the sons of Satan. And from some points of view, there may even be some comparatively small sins that in at least one way may be unforgivable.

There is an old fable that tells of a horse that once ran

away from his master. Finally the horse repented and returned to his master and said, "I have come back." The master said, "Yes, you have come back, but the field is unplowed." How does one go about repenting of unplowed ground or lessons not learned or virtues not acquired or services not performed? How does one repent of ignorance or sloth or indecision or indifference, or any of the sins of a misspent life? How does one replace past neglect, or repent of damage that has already been done? How does one repent of wasted opportunities? It is a challenging idea that the things that may be forgiven in one, may be unforgivable in one with a different attitude. Many sins may remain unforgiven forever, merely because there has been no effort made toward repentance or restitution. There are some very good ways to get a lot of sins forgiven.

An interesting provision in the law of Moses says that if a man had stolen a sheep, he could be forgiven if he repented and returned four sheep to the injured man as damages for the one he had stolen. In the opinions of some, damages of four-for-one may be too much. It may be that two for one would be more fair. But if one were really sorry for what he had done, and if he really wanted to have the offense completely wiped out, he might be willing to repay eight sheep for one or even a hundred sheep for one in order to have the record cleared. The circumstances themselves may also alter the situation. It may be that the offender got the sheep by some mistake or act of carelessness with no intentional fraud in mind. Under these circumstances the injured party may be fully satisfied if he merely got his one sheep back. However, if the offender were defiant and vindictive, and was merely trying to make the best possible deal to serve his own selfish interests, then even a thousand sheep might not clear the slate so far as the injured one was concerned. Even a thousand sheep may not make you feel very friendly toward him that has wronged you, nor give you enough confidence in him that you would want to trust him in the future.

There is one very good way to get forgiveness, and it works with either God or man; and that is a six-stage process called repentance. The six steps are confrontation, confession, restitution, forgiveness, reconciliation, and a complete turning away from evil so as to always assure a successful performance in the future. If we give each one of these six steps sufficient quality and quantity, we can be sure of pleasing God and everyone else concerned. If we can recognize our wrong and confess it, that helps. If we make restitution by doing four good deeds to counteract the effects of the one we did wrong, then God is also likely to be pleased. But if we want to make certain, it might not be a bad idea to pay God back a hundred for one. Enough good deeds will not only help us turn away from evil, but they will assure a sufficient reconciliation with God that he will want to grant us forgiveness. If we become experts in repentance a lot of otherwise unforgivable sins may be forgiven. Even God may be pleased in getting back a hundred for one.

It is thought that we seriously hurt ourselves when we lose faith in our chances to be forgiven. We should remember that a discouraged man is always a weak man. One man recently indicated that he felt that there was no hope for him to be forgiven, and that he might just as well go on in his sins. This was an idea expressed by Shakespeare's Macbeth. In his wars Macbeth had killed a lot of men, and therefore he said, "I am in blood stepped in so far, that should I wade no more, returning were as tedious as to go o'er. . . ." In various stages of transgression people tend to feel as though they have already passed the point of no return. Some say, "I am lost anyway, why should I bother to turn around or worry about making restitution?" Macbeth may have felt that after he killed his first man he had reached his maximum of guilt, so that what he did thereafter made little difference as far as he was concerned. But that is never true. It is never as bad to kill one man, as it is to kill two men. It is never as bad to kill a thousand men, as it is to kill two thousand. It is never as bad to kill a million men, as to kill two million. And even killing has different degrees of guilt and of consequences.

A soldier who kills while fighting for his country or protecting his home, is not in the same category as the one who kills deliberately in cold blood. I suppose that it is possible to go so far that we lose all power over ourselves. Certainly it would be pretty difficult to repent if we had lost all desire to repent. But one of the greatest ideas there is in our world is the idea of piling up assets on the credit side of the ledger, and then, insofar as it is possible, to keep our debit marks at zero.

May the Lord help us to keep ourselves forgivable with a big credit on the right side of the book of our lives.

The Uphill Heart

For as long as anyone can remember, the human heart has been regarded as the seat of life, the center of understanding and the source of several kinds of strength. Many years ago, the wise man Solomon said, "As he thinketh in his heart, so is he." (Prov. 23:7.) And so it has always been. The Bible concordance has over eight hundred scriptural references to the heart. It speaks of people who have faint hearts, pure hearts, willing hearts, wise hearts, understanding hearts, cheerful hearts, deceitful hearts and courageous hearts. As the greatest blessing that he could conceive of, Solomon asked God for an understanding heart. The scriptures speak of the heart as a synonym for the mind, the soul, the spirit, and one's entire emotional nature. The heart also regulates his spiritual and mental ability. The heart is the most determining factor in the quality of our total lives. The Bible says that men judge other men by looking upon their outward appearance, whereas God judges people by looking upon their hearts. The dictionary defines the heart as a hollow muscular organ which by rhythmically contracting keeps up the circulation of the blood. The dictionary explains that "in human adults this little organ is about five inches long and three and one-half inches broad, of conical form. It is placed obliquely in the chest with the base or broad end upward and to the right."

We sometimes compliment someone by saying that his heart is in the right place. And certainly the Creator was helping our symbolism when he gave the heart rhythm and placed its base "upward" and "to the right." The great secret of our success is to always keep it functioning in its "upward" position.

The world's most urgent need is to have good men with righteous hearts, ambitious hearts, cheerful hearts and courageous hearts. A roadside billboard for an oil company says, "A clean engine produces power," and so does a clean heart. But recently I saw a very interesting statement about another kind of a heart.

Someone said that the only ones who really make the grade in life are those who have "an uphill heart." Then I tried to discover what some of the advantages would be to having a really great heart. Paul Spiecher says that a fighting edge that one has when he is not afraid is a greater asset than intellect, experience, ability or foresight. A great heart also gets joy out of accomplishment and receives pleasure from challenge. In 1605 Cervantes wrote a challenging book about life when it is lived as a conquest of difficult problems. His story has inspired greatness and an uphill heart in many others.

It was a similar spirit that made Patrick Henry say: "The battle is not to the strong alone. It is to the vigilant, the active, the brave." Great-heart qualities are frequently very contagious. As Oscar Hammerstein said, "A heart can inspire other hearts with its fire."

Louis Kossuth once said that since the writing of human history began, Joan of Arc has been the only person of either sex who ever held supreme command of the military forces of a great nation at age seventeen. It was her mission to save France in its greatest crisis. And as she led her armies to battle she rode a white horse and carried in her hand the sacred sword of Fierbois. Her sword was the symbol of her unusual authority and the strict righteousness which she always maintained. She understood that every success in or out of battle is more easily attainable when the quest is carried out according to the principles of right and justice. Joan said to her generals that even the rude business of war could be better conducted without profanity or any other of the brutalities of speech or behavior. It was on this basis that the Maid of Orleans became the savior of France. Some people could not understand why Joan continued to be alert, vigorous and confident, while her strongest men became exhausted by the long marches and severe exposure which victory required. But usually it is our hearts that get tired, and an uphill heart pointed toward a great purpose can make a weak body strong and it makes its possessor able to bear the most exhausting fatigue.

Once with an almost impossible objective ahead, Joan said to her advisers, "I will lead the men over the wall." One of her generals said, "Not a man will follow you." Joan said, "I will not look back to see whether anyone is following or not." Then she held her sword high above her head and with an authoritative command to charge she flashed her sword toward the enemy. And to a man, the soldiers of France followed. With her sacred sword, her consecrated banner, her belief in her mission, and her uphill heart she swept everything before her. She sent a thrill of courage and enthusiasm through the French army such as neither King nor general could produce. She broke the siege of Orleans, drove the enemy out of France, and crowned the Dauphin King at Rheims. And for over five hundred years since that time her spirit has inspired men and women everywhere to more effectively meet the great challenges of life.

Under God each of us has also been given a share of the responsibility for carrying forward the work of the world. And we need to bear it with spirit, good will, and enthusiasm. What a tragedy that so frequently we become bored with life! In the great business of living we frequently falter and fail under the weight of those few simple duties that life has given us to do. Then with a weary, discouraged, hopeless heart we feel that life is too difficult, and we say that it is so hard for one to live his religion. Then it often seems like a great sacrifice to obey God and it becomes enervating and unpleasant to walk along that straight and narrow path that leads to eternal life. Some people have so many difficult temptations to be overcome, and often the only temptations that they are aware of are the temptations downward.

Some time ago I looked up in the dictionary the meaning of this interesting word "temptation." It says that "to tempt is to arouse a desire for." But our desires may lead us either up or down. The direction is determined by which kind of heart we are developing. And far too many people are being attracted by the temptations down. These are the temptations of sin, the temptations of booze, the temptations of sloth, and the temptations of idleness. William James, the great Harvard psychologist, once said that "only that which holds our attention determines our action." No one has ever yet fallen into a mud puddle who didn't first get too close to it. And weak hearts, wicked hearts and discouraged hearts are set-ups for the "temptations downward." At least so far as our figure of speech is concerned their hearts have their big ends downward and they are pointed toward the left.

Recently a mission president reported that in his mission there were three hundred people who wanted to be baptized but they were prevented from doing what God had commanded because they were not strong enough to overcome the temptations of tobacco. For some people there seems to be a very strong temptation to fill their lungs with nicotine, saturate their tissues with booze, and load up their flesh with venereal disease. Some can arouse uncontrollable desires to keep their mouths filled with profanity, their minds filled with bitterness, and their hearts inclined toward disobedience to God. The beast goes down on all fours, which tends to throw his vision upon the ground, but man was created upright in the image of his Maker that he might look up to God.

John Bunyan's *Pilgrim's Progress* tells the story of a man with a muckrake who could look in no direction but down. His interests were all centered on the earth's material things and he spent his time raking to himself the chaff and muck of the earth. There was an angel standing over his head with a celestial crown in his hand offering to exchange the crown for the muckrake. But this man had never learned to look in any direction but down and he therefore disregarded the offer of the angel as he continued to rake unto himself the muck and dirt of the earth. But there is also an angel standing over our heads offering us a celestial crown if we can just look up. If we can just look up to God and courage, righteousness and faith! A good uphill heart can make us eligible for some of the most thrilling, exciting temptations upward. These are the temptations of culture, the temptations of spirituality, the temptations of honor, the temptations to become like God. We need the temptations of a few impossible dreams, and the ability to live those pleasant lines which say:

> Look up my soul, be not cast down;
> Keep not thine eyes upon the ground.
> Break off the shackles of the earth,
> Receive my soul the Spirit's birth.

It is important to understand that life was not intended to be merely an effortless ride on a roller coaster. Usually success is not found in the swamp, it is at the top of the mountain. Because life is an uphill job, we need an uphill heart. Then getting there can be an interesting, exciting, and pleasant experience. Jack Dempsey once indicated a helpful success trait when he said that of the two primary requirements for success in the fight ring, the first was the ability to give a big punch and the second was the ability to take a big punch. Some prizefighters might qualify as the greatest punchers, and still be counted out in the first round because they can't take it. Many people lose the battle of life because they can't take the little bumps that are a part of everyday living.

Jesus said: "Blessed are ye, when men shall revile you, and persecute you, and shall say all manner of evil against you falsely, for my sake. Rejoice, and be exceeding glad: for great is your reward in heaven: for so persecuted they the prophets which were before you." (Matt. 5:11-12.) The kind of people that Jesus was talking about could not only take it but they could rejoice while taking it. Paul said to the Hebrews, "For ye ... took joyfully the spoiling of your goods, knowing in yourselves that ye have in heaven a better and an enduring substance." (Heb. 10:34.) Picture these pleasant people who have fun in their hardships and compare them to those tired, bored individuals who always have such a difficult time enduring the short period they spend in church and feel that every little righteousness puts their ability under strain. It was a great human being with an uphill heart who wrote the old ballad "Carry On." He said:

> Things may not look well,
> But then you never can tell,
> So carry on, old man, carry on.
> Be proud of your mission,
> Greet life with a cheer,
> Give it all that you've got,
> That's why you are here.
>
> Fight the good fight
> And be true to the end.
> And at last, when you die,
> Let this be your cry—
> Carry on my soul! Carry on!

Many times I have been thrilled by the tremendous power and speed of our modern automobiles. They seem to go uphill almost as easily as they do downhill. This provides a striking contrast with the automobile that my father owned in 1909. I remember that we had to get up full speed in order to make it over the small grade of the railroad crossing near our home. And at other times we had to get out and push or the car couldn't make the hill. Recently a modern but disappointed car owner said to his salesman, "While you were making the sale you swore up and down that this was a good car." The salesman said: "I did not. I swore on the level that this was a good car." It is only the game fish that like to swim upstream and it is the game people that can take the uphills just as well as the downhills. With an uphill heart it is possible for one to have that wonderful sense of feeling stronger than anything that can happen to him. Abraham Lincoln had an uphill heart. Lincoln fought disaster, melancholia, despair, and failure all of his life but he never lost his great sense of humor and he never quit fighting. Winston Churchill had an uphill heart, and Jesus of Nazareth had the greatest uphill heart. He said, "He that endureth to the end shall be saved." A common kind of heart failure makes us want to quit the battle before the victory is won. We must guard against the kind of heart disease that kills our challenge and prevents us from being doers of the word. A downhill heart usually ends up as a hopeless heart or a broken heart. One of the greatest values in life comes from developing an uphill heart, one that thrives on challenge and sustained righteousness. Then we can develop stronger affinities for those thrilling temptations upward.

> I raised my eyes to yonder heights,
> And longed for lifting wings
> To bear me to their sunlit crests,
> As on my spirit sings.
>
> And though my feet must keep the path
> That winds along the valley's floor,
> Yet, after every upward glance,
> I'm stronger than before.

Upon This Rock

In looking forward to the last days, Jesus foretold a time when great hate, uncertainty, and fear would ravish the earth, and all things would be in commotion. He told of the wars and rumors of wars by which the earth would be desolated in the last days. He said: "For nation shall rise against nation, and kingdom against kingdom: and there shall be famines, and pestilences, and earthquakes, in divers places . . . Then shall many be offended, and shall betray one another, and shall hate one another." (Matt. 24:7, 10.) He said, "Because iniquity shall abound, the love of many shall wax cold." (Matt. 24:12.) He indicated the extreme to which these circumstances would go when he said: "For then shall be great tribulation, such as was not since the beginning of the world to this time, no, nor ever shall be. And except those days should be shortened, there should no flesh be saved." (Matt. 24:21-22.)

In establishing a kind of timetable for his glorious second coming, Jesus said: "Now learn the parable of the fig tree; when his branch is yet tender, and putteth forth leaves, ye may know that summer is nigh: so likewise ye, when ye shall see all these things, know that it is near, even at the doors." (Mark 24:32-33.) Certainly as we read the signs of the times we know that some momentous events, including great desolation, are about to take place as the prelude to Christ's coming to reign upon the earth as King of kings and Lord of lords. We don't need to go beyond the newspapers to know that the world is in commotion, and men's hearts are failing them for fear. The great nations are spending a large part of their available funds for armaments in the impossible task of protecting themselves against each other. We now have sufficient means to wipe out the civilization of the entire earth; but the crime, arson, and violence in our own city streets also threaten our society with death.

Our wickedness has conjured up a genie of hate and violence that threatens our existence unless we can be successful in the awesome task of putting the genie back into the bottle. But there are, as yet, no signs of any letup. And so far as wickedness is concerned we see almost nothing but excess and increases.

However, in the midst of all of this trouble there is one bright spot shining beyond the darkness, which offers us a hope of relief, and that is—the Lord is preparing to take over the administration of our troubled world. Over nineteen hundred years ago the Savior himself looked down to our day with our last chance to repent and live according to gospel principles. He foretold the apostasy from God, and the long dark ages that would come upon the world following his death. The twelve apostles whom he authorized to carry on his work, with the exception of John the Revelator, all met a violent death. John was banished to Patmos, that rocky little island in the Aegean Sea. During the long spiritual night since that time, God's laws were broken, many of his ordinances were changed, and the Church that he established under divine leadership degenerated to become a mere human institution. Later, those who protested against the errors of the mother church broke away and were splintered into hundreds of segments, and none of the branches had any more authority than the tree from which they were broken. It was decreed that before the winding-up scene a final chance should be given for men and women to accept and live by the original principles and authority of the gospel of Christ. Jesus himself foretold the restoration of his original Church when he said, "And this gospel of the kingdom shall be preached in all the world as a witness unto all nations; and then shall the end come." (Matt. 24:14.) In his lonely exile on Patmos, John the Revelator was also permitted to see the restoration of the gospel in the latter days. In recording this vision, he said: "And I saw another angel fly in the midst of heaven, having the everlasting gospel to preach unto them that dwell on the earth, and to every nation, and kindred, and tongue, and people, saying with a loud voice, Fear God, and give glory to him; for the hour of his judgment is come." (Rev. 14:6-7.)

God created the world and all things therein. He placed men and women here upon this earth to learn to walk a little way by faith. God is the author of righteousness and the sponsor of truth and peace. It is God's desire that his earth be governed by law, order, and his gospel principles. But divine law has always been resisted in favor of atheism and sin. On many occasions during the history of our earth, God has made attempts to establish his order upon the earth; but by and large men and women have chosen to go their own disobedient ways.

In the beginning Adam and Eve partook of the forbidden fruit and brought about the fall of man. Cain started the first crime wave by slaying his brother. It wasn't long before things got so bad that God sent a flood to cleanse the earth. The earth had not been dry for very long when another set of troubles brought about the scattering of man from the confusion center at Babel. There have been many individual civilizations like Babylon, Persia, Sodom and Gomorrah, Rome, and the peoples of ancient America, who have been punished with destruction. The Lord had tried to build up a special civilization among the posterity of Abraham, but even the chosen race insisted on going contrary to his commands.

In spite of the problems continuing from the beginning of time until now, it has been the divine decree that in the last days another chance should be given to the people to accept his gospel. In fulfillment of this promise God the Father, and his Son, Jesus Christ, again appeared upon the earth in the early spring of 1820 in upper New York state, to reestablish among men a belief in the God of Genesis, the God of Calvary, and the God of the latter days. God's promised angel has come and the Church of Jesus Christ has again been organized upon the earth with the same offices that he established in the primitive Church. The Church of Jesus Christ is again led by apostles and prophets. Divine revelation between the heavens and the earth has been reestablished, and people are again being given the privilege of making an official covenant that they will live by God's laws.

Because the people of the past and present have apostatized and turned away from God, many have claimed that the heavens have been permanently closed and that there will never be any more revelations to men. But revelation is the basis on which God has always carried on his work. Matthew recorded a fundamental principle when he said: "When Jesus came into the coasts of Caesarea Philippi, he asked his disciples saying, Whom do men say that I the Son of man am, and they said, some say that thou art John the Baptist: and some Elias; and others, Jeremias, or one of the prophets. He saith unto them, But whom say ye that I am? And Simon Peter answered and said, Thou art the Christ, the Son of the living God. And Jesus answered and said unto him, Blessed art thou Simon Barjona: for flesh and blood hath not revealed it unto thee, but my Father which is in heaven. And I say also unto thee that thou art Peter, and upon this rock I will build my church; and the gates of hell shall not prevail against it. And I will give unto thee the keys of the kingdom of heaven: and whatsoever thou shalt bind on earth shall be bound in heaven: and whatsoever thou shalt loose on earth shall be loosed in heaven." (Matt. 16:13-19.)

Peter was given a very important assignment, and he was given all of the necessary authority to carry on the work of Christ's Church. But certainly it was not intended that in any way Peter should take the place of Christ as Head of the Church. Christ was the foundation on which the Church was established, and no one can ever take his place.

There are some who have made the mistake in thinking that the Church of Christ was founded upon Peter, but this could not possibly have been so. As quoted above, when Peter made his fervent declaration of faith, proclaiming that he knew that Jesus was the Christ, Jesus said to him, ". . . Flesh and blood hath not *revealed* it unto thee, but my Father which is in heaven. And I say also unto thee, that thou art Peter, and upon this rock I will build my church. . . ." (Matt. 16:17-18.) Upon which rock? Certainly it was not upon the rock of Peter. It could not have been upon the rock of any man. It was upon the rock of God, the rock of revelation by which he has always directed his Church. It was built upon the same power that made known to Peter that Jesus was divine.

It is one of the most serious errors to assume that Christ would build his Church upon any human being. The arm of flesh is weak. All men are subject to frailties and evil. When Jesus was taken to be crucified, all of his followers ran away, and Jesus himself quoted an ancient prophecy saying, "I will smite the shepherd and the sheep will be scattered."

Peter, James and John, who, under Christ, were the pre-

siding officers in the Church, could not stay awake to watch
with him during his agony in Gethsemane. Neither Peter nor any
other man has ever been considered to be an infallible repository
of truth. The very night before Jesus was crucified, Peter denied
the Lord three times. But besides this it would surely not be the
Church of Jesus Christ if it were founded upon flesh and blood.
It is one of our present-day problems that we have placed too
much trust in men, and we have been disappointed too many
times.

The thing that has always confused us is that we have too
many man-made doctrines and too many man-made interpreta-
tions of *divine* doctrines. There are too many splinters in what
was once his Church. Some have thought that if Christ built his
Church upon a man why shouldn't they do the same thing. As a
consequence, many hundreds of so-called Christian churches have
been organized by men, built upon men, and given men's names
with man-made doctrines and ordinances differing widely from
those announced by Christ.

We honor Peter as a servant of the Lord, but it was not
Peter's church then, and it is not Peter's church now. Peter only
lived a comparatively short time, whereas the Church was intended to go on forever. The Church of Jesus Christ was not
built upon Peter, either while he was alive or after he was dead.
It was built on the Godhead of Christ which Peter had declared
by a divine revelation. And Paul reminds us that there is "one
Lord, one faith, one baptism, one God and Father of all." (Eph.
4:5-6.) He also said, "Though we, or an angel from heaven,
preach any other gospel unto you than that which we have
preached unto you, let him be accursed." (Gal. 1:8.)

Paul did not preach the gospel of Peter. He said, "We
preach not ourselves, but Jesus Christ the Lord." (2 Cor. 4:5.)
Again he said: "But I certify you, brethren, that the gospel
which was preached of me is not after man ... neither was I
taught it, but by the revelation of Jesus Christ." (Gal. 1:11-12.)
Paul indicated the humanness of Peter when he said, "But when
Peter was come to Antioch, I withstood him to his face, because
he was to be blamed." (Gal. 2:11.) Peter and many others had
great powers while they had the spirit of the Master, but the
Church must always be the Church of Jesus Christ. He gives it

its doctrines, and directs its course by revealing his will to those who are officially called as was Peter to be officers in his Church.

After his ascension into heaven, the resurrected Jesus appeared to the people upon the western hemisphere, and organized his Church among them. Among other things, the people said to him: "Lord, we will that thou wouldst tell us the name whereby we shall call this church; for there are disputations among the people concerning this matter. And the Lord said unto them: Verily, verily, I say unto you, why is it that the people should murmur and dispute because of this thing? Have they not read the scriptures, which say ye must take upon you the name of Christ, which is my name? For by this name shall ye be called at the last day; and whoso taketh upon him my name and endureth to the end, the same shall be saved at the last day. Therefore, whatsoever ye shall do, ye shall do it in my name; therefore ye shall call the church in my name; and ye shall call upon the Father in my name that he will bless the church for my sake. And how be it my church save it be called in my name? For if a church be called in Moses' name then it be Moses' church; or if it be called in the name of a man then it be the church of a man? but if it be called in my name then it is my church, if it so be that they are built upon my gospel." (3 Nephi 27:3-8.) And in a modern revelation the Lord has said, "For thus shall my church be called in the last days, even The Church of Jesus Christ of Latter-day Saints." (D&C 115:4.)

The Church has been restored to the earth. And all of its principles have been fully reestablished. The world now has three great volumes of new scripture outlining in every detail the simple principles of the doctrines of Christ. And to every doctrine there is an authoritative declaration saying, "Thus saith the Lord."

May the Lord help us to make the most of this tremendous situation.

The Vision of Sir Launfal

In 1848 James Russell Lowell published a poem entitled "The Vision of Sir Launfal." The poem has to do with the search made for the Holy Grail by one of the knights of King Arthur's court. Sir Launfal was one of the noblemen of the realm who had large possessions and great power. He lived in a magnificent castle and entertained many of the famous lords and ladies of England.

According to an ancient legend, the Holy Grail was the cup out of which Jesus drank during the Last Supper when he met with his disciples in the upper room. The story has it that after his resurrection this cup was taken to England by Joseph of Arimathea. There it remained for many years in the custody of Joseph's descendants, where it became the object of many pilgrimages and much adoration.

However, it was incumbent upon the custodians of the Holy Grail to keep themselves chaste in thought, word, and deed, and always live above any possible reproach. And because one of the keepers failed in this important requirement, the Holy Grail disappeared. Then many of the greatest knights of King Arthur's round table went in search of it in order to bring its blessings back to the people. Inasmuch as it could not be retained by anyone with an impure life, it naturally followed that it would be the greatest personal honor to the one who was able to recover it.

Finally the great Sir Launfal himself decided to take up the search. And he made a vow that he would never again sleep in a bed or allow the comforts of a pillow under his head until he should begin to keep his vow. Nor would he ever stop searching for the Holy Grail until it was found. Then as he lay on a bed of rushes prior to beginning his quest he had a dream in which he spent his entire lifetime in this important undertaking. In his dream he lived through all of the wanderings, privations, and sufferings that would naturally be connected with such a search. But because of the devotion and service given by this proud knight, his character and personality were changed and rebuilt in such a way that he was fitted to effectively reflect the spirit of the lowly Nazarene himself. When Sir Launfal awoke the next morning he was a different man with different aims in life, and he now resolved to spend the rest of his days living the lessons that he had learned in the experiences of his God-given vision.

There are also a great many lessons that we can transfer to ourselves from this delightful poem. Frequently one may feel a thing so strongly and deeply that mere prose may make its expression inadequate. Words can sometimes be made stronger by adding the music of metre, the harmony of rhyme, and the power of a more forceful expression. On these occasions we may leave the lower regions of communication and rise to that more elegant form of speech that has been measured, weighed, powerized, and set to music. This kind of poem cannot be skimmed over as one might do in reading a newspaper story. Poetry must be read slowly with alert attention given to the pictures that are presented in every line.

The ideas of this great poem are so constructed that they dissolve in one's mind. Each paragraph gives up its own particular thought to the reader. But every human being has a kind of poetic instinct. Each of us has been touched with a hunger for beauty and a craving for music in our speech. And everyone with this genuine poetic instinct loves the rhythm of the verse no less than the thought it contains. It is good for one's soul occasionally to climb to some mountain top of thought and reverently spend a few hours in this magic land of poetic beauty. We can get ideas from prose, but poetry gives us the spirit in which the ideas are dressed. The poem also sets the mood that the ideas exemplify. It prepares a seedbed in the heart and creates a climate in which the ideas may grow most effectively. Poetry is like a lecture that has enough visual aids and sound effects to dissolve the great ideals and make them available to the bloodstream.

This poem begins by giving us a picture of the landscape which embodies the emotional spirit of the poem, before the story itself is set before us. Lowell draws us a technicolor

picture of that great doctrine of Jesus which says, "Inasmuch as
ye have done it unto one of the least of these my brethren, ye
have done it unto me." (Matt. 25:40.) But poetry not only gives
us its teaching, it also brings on an awakening in us. It furnishes
the arousement that gives the ideas their power. The warm,
stirring, religious impulses in this poem incite our spirits by
translating theological truths into their more noble action form.

In a great poem our own imagination can learn to fly with
a freer wing, develop a greater enthusiasm, and experience a
more genuine enjoyment. We now go with Sir Launfal on the
divine mission embodied in his own life, as he leaves the security
and abundance of his own great castle in search of the Holy
Grail. As the vision begins to dawn we hear him say:

My golden spurs now bring to me,
And bring to me my richest mail,
For tomorrow I go over land and sea
In search of the Holy Grail. . . .

The drawbridge dropped with a surly clang,
And through the dark arch a charger sprang,
Bearing Sir Launfal, the maiden knight,
In his gilded mail, that flamed so bright
It seemed the dark castle had gathered all
Those shafts that the fierce sun had shot over its wall
In his siege of three hundred summers long,
And, binding them all in one blazing sheaf,
Had cast them forth, so young and strong,
And lightsome as a locust-leaf.
Sir Launfal flashed forth in his unscarred mail,
To seek in all climes for the Holy Grail.

It was morning in the sky and it was morning in the young
knight's life as his quest began. As he cleared the drawbridge

He was 'ware of a leper, crouched by the gate,
Who begged with his hand and moaned as he sate;
And a loathing over Sir Launfal came.
The sunshine went out of his soul with a thrill,
The flesh 'neath his armor did shrink and crawl,
And midway in its leap, his heart stood still

Like a frozen waterfall;
For this man, so foul and bent of stature,
Rasped harshly against his dainty nature,
And seemed the one blot on the summer morn—
So he tossed him a piece of gold in scorn.

But the leper raised not the gold from the dust:
"Better to me the poor man's crust,
Better the blessing of the poor,
Though I turn me empty from his door,
That is no true alms which the hand can hold;
He gives only the worthless gold
Who gives from a sense of duty;
But he who gives but a slender mite,
And gives of that which is out of sight,
That thread of the all-sustaining Beauty
Which runs through all and doth all unite—
The hand cannot clasp the whole of his alms,
The heart outstretches its eager palms,
For a God goes with it and makes it store
To the soul that was starving in darkness before."

Then for all of the long life which was spent in his dream,
Sir Launfal searched for his treasure without success, and only
after many years he returned armorless, horseless, penniless, and
old, to the castle that had once been his home. It is now the
opposite time of year from the season when his quest began. It
is also the opposite time of his life. The air is filled with cold
and ice. It is the middle of winter, and it is the Christmas time.
Sir Launfal's hair is now thin and grey, his clothing is worn and
comfortless. Mr. Lowell says:

But the wind without was eager and sharp;
Of Sir Launfal's gray hair it makes a harp,
And rattles and wrings the icy strings,
Singing in dreary monotone,
A Christmas carol of its own,
Whose burden still, as he might guess,
Was "Shelterless, shelterless, shelterless!"

The voice of the seneschal flared like a torch
As he shouted the wanderer away from the porch,

And he sat in the gateway and saw all night
The great hall-fire so cheery and bold
Through the window-slits of the castle old.
Built out of its piers of ruddy light
Against the drift of the cold.

There was never a leaf on bush or tree,
The bare boughs rattled shudderingly;
The river was dumb and could not speak,
For the weaver Winter its shroud had spun;
A single crow in the treetop bleak
From his shining feathers shed off the cold sun;
Again it was morning, but shrunk and cold
As if her veins were sapless and old,
And she rose up decrepitly
For a last dim look at the earth and sea.

Sir Launfal turned from his own hard gate,
For another heir in his earldom sate;
An old, bent man, worn out and frail,
He came back from seeking the Holy Grail.
Little he recked of his earldom's loss;
No more on his surcoat was blazoned the cross;
But deep in his soul the sign he wore,
The badge of the suffering and the poor.

Sir Launfal's raiment thin and spare
Was idle mail 'gainst the barbed air,
For it was just at the Christmas time,
So he mused, as he sat, of a sunnier clime,
And sought for some shelter from cold and snow
In the light and warmth of long ago;

Then Sir Launfal was again made aware of the pitiful beggar
at his side, suffering from hunger, disease and cold. The beggar's
flesh was white with leprosy, and he said to Sir Launfal, "For
Christ's sweet sake, I beg an alms." But Sir Launfal saw this
gruesome human being with a different emotion than that which
had been excited in him on this very spot so many years before.
In the gruesome sight Sir Launfal saw:

The leper, lank as the rain-blanched bone,
That cowers beside him, a thing as lone

And white as the ice-isles of Northern seas
In the desolate horror of his disease.

And Sir Launfal said, "I behold in thee
An image of Him who died on the tree.
Thou also hast had thy crown of thorns;
Thou also hast had the world's buffets and scorns;
And to thy life were not denied
The wounds in the hands and feet and side.
Mild Mary's Son, acknowledge me;
Behold through him, I give to thee."
Then the soul of the leper stood up in his eyes
And looked at Sir Launfal, and straightway he
Remembered in what a haughtier guise
He had flung an alms to leprosie,
When he girt his young life up in gilded mail
And set forth in search of the Holy Grail.

The heart within him was ashes and dust;
He parted in twain his single crust,
He broke the ice on the streamlet's brink,
And gave the leper to eat and drink;

'Twas a mouldy crust of coarse brown bread,
'Twas water out of a wooden bowl—
Yet with fine wheaten bread was the leper fed,
And 'twas red wine he drank with his thirsty soul.

As Sir Launfal mused with a downcast face,
A light shone round about the place;
The leper no longer crouched at his side,
But stood before him glorified,
Shining and tall and fair and straight
As the pillar that stood by the Beautiful Gate—
Himself was the Gate whereby men can
Enter the temple of God in man.

His words were shed softer than leaves from the pine,
And they fell on Sir Launfal as snows on the brine,
That mingle their softness and quiet in one
With a shaggy unrest they float down upon;
And a voice that was softer than silence said,
"Lo it is I, be not afraid!

"In many climes, without avail,
Thou hast spent thy life for the Holy Grail;
Behold it is here—this cup which thou
Didst fill at the streamlet for Me but now;
This crust is my body broken for thee,
This water His blood who died on the tree;

"The Holy Supper is kept, indeed,
In whatso we share with another's need;
Not what we give, but what we share—
For the gift without the giver is bare;
Who gives himself with his alms feeds three—
Himself, his hungering neighbor, and Me."

Sir Launfal woke as from a swound:
"The Grail in my castle here is found!
Hang my idle armor up on the wall;
Let it be the spider's banquet hall.
He must be fenced with stronger mail
Who would seek and find the Holy Grail."

The castle gate stands open now,
And the wanderer is as welcome to the hall
As the hangbird is to the elm-tree bough.
No longer scowl the turrets tall;
The summer's long siege at last is o'er.
When the first poor outcast went in at the door,
She entered with him in disguise,
And mastered the fortress by surprise.
There is no spot she loves so well on ground;
She lingers and smiles there the whole year round;

The meanest serf on Sir Launfal's land
Has hall and bower at his command;
And there's no poor man in the North Countree
But is Lord of the earldom as much as he.

We may not have all of the things for which Sir Launfal
sought, but we have the same great privileges of making the
search; and it is written that only he who fails to seek, fails to
find.

We Are Seven

S ome of the most uplifting influences in our lives are those associations that we have with great human beings. I have always been very grateful for the life of Abraham Lincoln. And I like to think about him as he went out of his way to be scrupulously honest and try to make others happy. One day he dismounted his horse to give assistance to a baby bird that had fallen out of its nest. It is a very productive enterprise to identify with Lincoln and feed on such philosophy as that found in his second inaugural address in which he said: "With malice toward none; with charity for all; with firmness in the right, as God gives us to see the right." Lincoln's faith and good works can be transplanted into us so that they will motivate our own ambitions, and fill our lives with excellence.

In organizing our human society in our own interests, God perfected a great and special institution called the family. This is a small, intimate unit where he gave the members an especial feeling of love for each other, and an ability to help each other upward and onward. One of the strongest of our human emotions is that one which parents feel for their children. And under the right circumstances the love of children for their parents can sometimes almost grow into an attitude of adoration. From many points of view my own mother and father made a rather humble approach to life. But I am very grateful that I was born where I was with the particular father and mother who became my parents. I am also very grateful to be able to identify with the brothers and sisters, living and dead, who make up the family of my parents. I am very thankful for another group of souls composed of the wife, children, in-laws, and grandchildren that make up my own family. And God provided that the family unit should be eternal. Including my parents, seven of the twelve members of my father's family have already passed to the other side. Two of my sisters died when they were very young. I never knew my older sister, Mary, who died just before I was born, yet I love her with a great devotion and I look forward to a pleasant association with her after I have also graduated from this life. She died in the purity of her infancy, and according to the law of God she has qualified for celestial glory. What a thrill I think it will be for me to embrace and rejoice with my celestial sisters!

My sister, Laura, died when she was seven years old, and I was about fourteen. I remember what good times she and I used to have together. It seemed to me that we were really kindred spirits. She used to like to ride on my shoulders as she went with me to do the farm chores. And it was particularly pleasant to sing and laugh with her. I know that in my advanced age of fourteen years I was something of a hero to my little sister, and in turn I was very proud of her. Then one day she developed the burning fever of diphtheria, and for the next few hours I stood close by as my wonderful little sister passed away. Each Memorial Day I take some blossoms and lay upon her grave, and as I meditate upon our family relationship and welfare I can almost hear her laugh as she mispronounced my name. I remember how nice she looked in the modest little dress in which she had her picture taken. And I like to imagine the radiance that will be in her face and the beauty of her dress when I see her again. I suppose that there will then be more appropriate things for her to do than to ride upon my shoulder but I will look forward to hearing her laugh and to having a good talk with her about the good old days.

It can also be a great delight to associate here and now with that larger and greater family of God. What a joy it can be each Sabbath day to meet in our Heavenly Father's house with our fellow human beings who are all dressed up in their best clothes and have on their smiling faces! Then we can take our good friends by the hand and call them "brother" and "sister" and feel the thrill of this exciting relationship of being children of God as we sing and pray and worship together. Then we also identify with our heavenly parents and our brothers and sisters.

To me one of the most interesting expressions of one of our human relationships was given in William Wordsworth's poem entitled "We Are Seven." In 1793 Mr. Wordsworth met a little eight-year-old girl in the area of Goodrich Castle, as he was going up to Bristol. This little girl and her mother lived alone in a humble cottage near the churchyard cemetery. Mr. Wordsworth received the inspiration for his poem as he talked with this fine young spirit about her family. Children of any age are always very important people. For a very long period they lived and developed themselves in the company of God in heaven. The great human creations of mind, body, spirit, and personality could never have been brought about in eight years if we began here at zero.

In expressing the relationship between this life and our antemortal existence, Mr. Wordsworth said:

> Our birth is but a sleep and a forgetting:
> The soul that rises with us, our life's Star,
> Hath had elsewhere its setting,
> And cometh from afar:
> Not in entire forgetfulness,
> And not in utter nakedness,
> But trailing clouds of glory do we come
> From God who is our home.

The Bible observation that a little child shall lead them has a great deal of meaning written behind it, as well as in between the lines. Mr. Wordsworth never learned the name of the little girl who served as the heroine of his poem. Therefore I have supplied his heroine with an image and a name, as in my mind *my* little sister exactly fits into this role. The gentle, kindly little eight-year-old girl pictured by Mr. Wordsworth is very wise in the way she loves her brothers and sisters. Children sometimes manifest a love of God and a belief in his eternal purposes that may be characteristic of the adulthood of their antemortal years. We are thrilled by the expression of the divine love felt for her family that this wholesome little country girl brought with her from God. She seemed to have an instinctive feeling about immortality and the family unity which she believed in, even though she lived alone with her mother and the other two members of the family who rested in the churchyard nearby. Mr. Wordsworth said of her:

> A simple child
> That lightly draws its breath,
> And feels its life in every limb,
> What should it know of death?

I met this little cottage Girl:
She was eight years old, she said;
Her hair was thick with many a curl
That clustered round her head.

She had a rustic, woodland air,
And she was wildly clad:
Her eyes were bright and very fair;
—Her beauty made me glad.

"Sisters and brothers, little Maid,
How many may you be?"
"How many? Seven in all," she said,
And wondering looked at me.

"And where are they? I pray you tell."
She answered "Seven are we;
And two of us at Conway dwell,
And two are gone to sea.

"Two of us in the Church-yard lie,
My sister and my brother;
And in the Church-yard cottage, I
Dwell near them with my mother."

"You say that two at Conway dwell
And two are gone to sea,
Yet ye are seven! I pray you tell,
Sweet Maid, how this may be."

Then did the little Maid reply,
"Seven boys and girls are we;
Two of us in the Church-yard lie,
Beneath the Church-yard tree."

"But you run about, my little Maid,
Your limbs they are alive;
If two are in the Church-yard laid,
Then ye are only five."

"Their graves are green, they may be seen,"
The little maid replied,

"Twelve steps or more from my mother's door,
And they are side by side.

"My stockings there I often knit,
My kerchief there I hem:
And there upon the ground I sit,
And sing a song to them.

"And often after sunset, sir,
When it is light and fair,
I take my little porringer,
And eat my supper there.

"The first that died was sister Jane;
In bed she moaning lay,
Till God released her from her pain;
And then she went away.

"So in the Church-yard she was laid;
And, when the grass was dry,
Together round her grave we played,
My brother John and I.

"And when the ground was white with snow,
And I could run and slide,
My brother John was forced to go,
And he lies by her side."

"How many are you, then," said I,
"If they two are in heaven?"
Quick was the little maid's reply,
"O Master! We are seven."

"But they are dead; those two are dead!
Their spirits are in heaven!"
'Twas throwing words away, for still
The little maid would have her will,
And said, "Nay, we are seven!"

This little girl would not desert any member of her family either in her mind or in her heart. And I am sure that this attitude would please the great Father of us all who ordained the family to be his basic unit throughout eternity.

In expressing this same kind of immortalized love, Elizabeth Barrett Browning told her husband of the many avenues that her love for him had taken. And then in summary she said, "I love thee with the breaths, smiles, hopes and tears, of all my life!—and if God wills, I shall but love thee better after death." And so it will be for all of those who are faithful to God the Father, and to the family relationship that he has ordained.

The Apostle Paul looks forward to this reunion time and says: "For now we see through a glass darkly; but then face to face: now I know in part; but when that which is perfect is come, then that which is in part shall be done away." (See 1 Cor. 13:9-12.) Then our love and joy will receive a fullness that it has never known before. Certainly Jesus did not love his Heavenly Father less after his own death than he did before. His association was probably much more satisfying then than it had previously been. And Jesus had many other family members in heaven that he also loved.

The heroine of Mr. Wordsworth's poem did not think of her brothers and sisters who lived at Conway as being any more real than those who lived with God, where all of us had our beginning. Because of our inability to understand, even God sometimes becomes indefinite and unreal to us. Certainly we ought to develop some of the ability of our little sister to draw closer to God and the other members of our family who have preceded us across the borders of this life.

Jesus takes us behind the scenes in the 16th chapter of Luke, and tells us of the feelings of the departed for their families left behind after their earth life had been finished. I am sure that my father and mother and sisters and brothers still have an extreme interest in us who are left. And one of the greatest motivations of my life is the desire not to disappoint them. One of our most serious tragedies is that God and eternity and our personal identities and associations beyond the grave, sometimes become misty and unreal in our minds. It is much easier to make mistakes and to rebel against God when we believe that he is dead. We are more likely to be untrue to our brothers and sisters and parents when we believe that we are five instead of seven. Even in this life, we become selfish and rebellious when we live only for ourselves and for today. And it is probable that the most abused of all of our institutions, even though it is the most important, is the family. Our society now fosters some giant birth-control industries whose self-assumed mission in life is in trying to prevent children from being born, even though this is in direct violation of the word of the Lord. In a recent divorce proceeding a mother of four said that each of her children had been unwanted by their two fathers. Their lives had all been conceived by accident, and they had been treated accordingly after their births. But we further abuse our families by setting them a bad example. Our families will only be safe when we all "live by every word that proceedeth forth from the mouth of God." What a world we would have if each of us were completely and honestly true to each other, and to our father and mother in heaven! What fun life would be if we had a full measure of family love, faith, and unity! May God help us to keep these great family laws, and fully honor each other, as we learn to feelingly sing with Mr. Wordsworth's heroine, "We Are Seven."

What Will Ye Give Me

There are some interesting details given in the scriptures concerning the events leading up to the death of Jesus. There was a very strong desire among some of the leaders of the people to get rid of him. This desire increased sharply as the end of his ministry drew near. A group of the chief priests, scribes, and elders had already held a conference at the palace of Caiaphas, the high priest, to determine how they might best get him into their custody. The Passover was at hand and a large number of visitors were in Jerusalem. His enemies felt that it might be dangerous to arrest him on the feast day for fear of causing an uproar among the people. However, events took a turn in their favor when Judas came over to their side. The record says: "Then one of the twelve called Judas Iscariot, went unto the chief priests and said unto them, What will ye give me, and I will deliver him unto you? And they covenanted with him for thirty pieces of silver. And from that time Judas sought opportunity to betray him." (Matt. 26:14-16.)

The opportunity was not long in coming. Jesus was keeping the Passover feast with the twelve in an upper room in what has come to be known as the Last Supper. Judas knew approximately where Jesus would be for the next few hours. Therefore, after the supper was over and darkness had settled over them, Judas left the upper room and went about the grim business of earning the betrayal money for which he had bargained the life of the Savior of the world. In the meantime Jesus and the eleven left the upper room and went out into the Mount of Olives, where Jesus talked to them about his approaching death. When they came to the Garden of Gethsemane, Jesus excused himself from their immediate company to engage in a series of prayers to God. Because the hour was late and his followers were tired, they slept through much of this period. When the Master's heavenly communications had been finished, he said to his followers, "Rise, let us be going: behold, he is at hand that doth betray me. And while he yet spake, lo, Judas ... came with a great multitude . . . from the chief priests and elders of the people." Judas had already given them the betrayal sign saying: "Whomsoever I shall kiss, that same is he: hold him fast. And forthwith he came to Jesus, and said, Hail, master; and kissed him." Then his antagonists with their swords and staves laid hold on Jesus and took him to Caiaphas the high priest, where the scribes and elders were already assembled and waiting. (See Matt. 26:46-49.)

It is a little bit difficult to understand why anyone would do as Judas did for any price. Thirty pieces of silver was only the equivalent of a few dollars. However, if we look around us in our own day, and if we think about the idea a little bit, we may find that a lot of people are doing wrong things for a small amount of money or other consideration. I suppose that if we understood what causes people to make such serious mistakes, we might be better able to safeguard our own interests.

The Apostle Paul describes the qualifications of a bishop by saying that he should be vigilant, sober, of good behavior, given to hospitality, apt to teach; not given to wine, no striker, not greedy of filthy lucre, but patient, not a brawler, not covetous, one that ruleth well his own house, and having his children in subjection with all gravity. (1 Tim. 3:2-4.) But these qualities should be characteristic of all good people. We should be aware of the negative traits listed, in order to avoid them and the problems that they cause.

In the science of crime solution, a detective always looks for the motive first. If the motive can be discovered, the criminal can usually be identified. And many of our present-day problems with crime, riots, and sins are motivated by an unhealthy love of money. On several occasions the Apostle Paul refers to money as filthy lucre. Of course, money by itself is neither good nor bad. It is like industry or love or courage: it is good or evil according to how we use it. To "love" liquor or immorality or dishonesty also makes that kind of love filthy. And to "work" for evil causes, makes that kind of industry unworthy. Likewise, money can be made dirty depending on how we get it and what we do with it afterward. An unhealthy love of money is the villain that motivates the bank robbers, pushes the purse snatchers, and urges the auto thieves and looters to do their evil. The love of money is also the motive behind the labor strikes, the school teacher walk-outs, and many of the other present evils that are bothering us in every field. The powerful crime syndicates are organized for the purpose of getting money, regardless of who they hurt. And there are human beings whose life's work is to kill other people for a price. But there are many supposedly good people who are also betraying their friends, their ideals, the Church, the government, and their own better selves for money.

Back in prohibition days some people made themselves wealthy as bootleggers and rum-runners. Each year men sell millions of dollars of fraudulent investments and inferior goods in order to make a few dollars profit. If you want to eradicate coyotes or mountain lions, just offer a bounty for each one killed, or if you want to increase liquor consumption, dope addiction, or prostitution, just make it more profitable.

Some governments have greatly increased the number of illegitimate children being born by raising the amount of the allowance given to unwed mothers. When salesmen misrepresent their product, and when employees steal their company's money, and when shoplifters take merchandise without paying for it, they are activated by an unclean money motive. And in many of our dealings with others we are actually repeating the question of Judas. We say, "What's in it for me?" or "What will ye give me and I will deliver him unto you?"

Filthy lucre is often the motivation for those who lie, steal, kill, covet, bear false witness, and violate the Sabbath day. A price placed upon one's head places his safety in jeopardy. Of course, all money is not dirty, and the use of money for motivating people can be very beneficial if used in the right way. The great industries, educational institutions, and professions usually arrange to have a money motive. Our American system of free enterprise is built upon a competitive system of profit and loss. One of the primary differences between America and some of the more backward nations is that we are largely a nation of salesmen. Almost nothing is accepted without being sold and everyone needs some kind of an incentive. Even the horseless carriage and the iceless refrigerator were not accepted at first. And it is entirely proper for workmen to be compensated as long as the customers are benefitted and society itself is made better.

Every day there are some five million outside paid salesmen sitting down in the homes, offices, and factories of America trying to train people in the use of improved goods and services. But we recognize these things as good for our society, and the keen competition among manufacturers, dealers, and salesmen usually keeps the price as low as possible. In fact, our great American sales abilities make our production lines possible, and tend to lower prices. Money is the medium that we exchange for something else. Everyone has something to sell on which he is entitled to make a profit, and everyone has something to buy. Jesus even talked about laying up for ourselves some treasures in heaven. However, every sale made and every service rendered which does not show a profit for all concerned, is in some degree immoral. Certainly it is immoral to allow members of our society to make money from riots, looting, murder, rum-running, and bootlegging. And we do everyone a great disservice when we allow dope pushers to use their persuasive powers to fasten their awful addiction upon ignorant and gullible young people. Prospective laws are now being talked about that would prevent tobacco companies from using the great abilities of our best advertising firms in glamorizing and popularizing a product that we know destroys the health and happiness of millions of people. Certainly that money is filthy that goes into the promotion of liquor and immorality. We allow money-hungry labor leaders to shut down our industries and throw millions of people out of work to satisfy their own selfish purposes. We don't help ourselves very much when we relax our laws so as to promote liquor sales and to make evil things legal and profitable, under the guise that it helps business.

Even our government has in its coffers a lot of filthy lucre collected as a tax on liquor and tobacco sales, and the other corruption that we bring upon ourselves. The curse of alcohol and tobacco has placed a great blight upon our society and hurts everyone who touches it. Yet we allow the interests of evil to promote as big a thirst as possible for alcohol, and an appetite for nicotine and pornography. In spite of its evil many people are trying still further to increase the number of our liquor outlets and the training of paid liquor sales representatives. It is bad enough when liquor is dispensed in state liquor stores by salaried clerks with no special incentive for making sales; but when we begin offering special inducements for increasing liquor sales, our problems are bound to increase. When liquor is advertised, promoted and romanced in the midst of so much glamor, beauty, and excitement, people are bound to be influenced. Most of us are unable to eliminate all of the bad out of the good. We remember the experiment with Pavlov's dog—when he was shown a piece of meat and heard the ringing of a bell at the same time. These two experiences became merged together in the dog's mind and both soon came to mean the same thing. When the two became associated in the dog's brain, soon he could be attracted to non-existent meat by the ringing of the bell. In a similar way our appetites can be increased even for a deadly evil by seeing it enough times in the presence of wealth, glamor, romance, and the other attractions produced by advertising. Soon some people can't tell the evil from the good.

A brokenhearted mother recently told of her fourteen-year-old daughter who had become addicted to hippies, dope, immorality, and rebellion through the friendly association and intimate solicitation of some of her friends. She had previously been the scholastic leader in her class. She had aspired to do fine things with her life. But she got in with the wrong crowd. She heard about the friendship, sex thrills, and imaginary trips into a land of make-believe. Soon she was all mixed up, and this fine girl whose life promised so many wonderful things is now in a mental hospital. She is hooked by dope, venereal disease, an unbalanced mind, and an inability to tell right from wrong, all by age fourteen. Her father is an invalid unable to work, so the parents have sold their home and are spending their meager life's savings trying to pay the doctors' bills and other costs of the special care necessary to keep their daughter out of the reform school. But this girl is still fighting for her hippie friends who have brought this terrible destruction upon her and her family. What an awful price is being paid in money, misery, dishonor, mental illness, and sin in order for dope and liquor sellers to make a little dirty profit!

One of the arguments for increased liquor and tobacco sales and other evils is that it is good for business. And from a distorted point of view this may be so. Even this fourteen-year-old mentally ill girl will furnish a lot of extra work for doctors, liquor companies, dope pushers, and reform school workers. She may also assist in generating more business in others by passing her venereal disease and her venereal attitudes on to them. And in our so-called "enlightened society" we still tolerate the existence of these poisonous evils with the most stupid arguments. It is as though we were providing rattlesnakes and scorpions as playthings for our children and a few atomic hand grenades for ourselves. No wonder that in foreseeing our day the Lord said that he would come with his mighty angels in flaming fire to cleanse the earth of its wickedness. When this takes place, the question of how much money we have made out of it may not seem so important. Above all other considerations we must learn to be responsible.

The Lord once said to the Prophet Samuel, "For I have told Eli that I will judge his house forever for the iniquity that he knoweth; because his sons made themselves vile, and he restraineth them not." (1 Sam. 3:13.) And it is no small thing for us to make ourselves vile, corrupt our friends, and allow our children to be seduced for money. Before Judas sold Jesus to the chief priests he sold himself to Satan. He became the devil's serf and did his master's bidding. Judas sold himself, but so does the prostitute, and so does the dope addict, and so do all of us who deal in or tolerate any kind of sin. While we are trying to discover why Judas did as he did, we ought to try to figure out why we do as we do. Then we ought to change our ways and do as we ought to do. Whether our sins are in the category of omission or commission, before we ask "What's in it for me?" we should ask "Who will it hurt? Is it wrong or right, will it please God, and will the general consequences be unfavorable?"

Jesus spoke of being about his Father's business. That is also *our* job. Charles Dickens says that "mankind is our business." And so it is! Life is also our business! God is our business! Righteousness is our business, and the eternal glory of all human beings is our business. And it is my prayer that God will help us in this sense to be good businessmen.

Index